AppleWorks® 6
For Dummies®

W9-BZA-231

Cheat Sheet

Default Button Bars

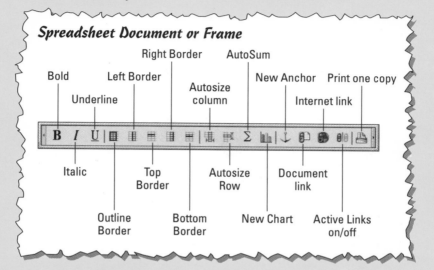

Spreadsheet Document or Frame

- Bold
- Underline
- Italic
- Left Border
- Right Border
- Outline Border
- Top Border
- Bottom Border
- Autosize column
- Autosize Row
- AutoSum
- New Chart
- New Anchor
- Document link
- Internet link
- Active Links on/off
- Print one copy

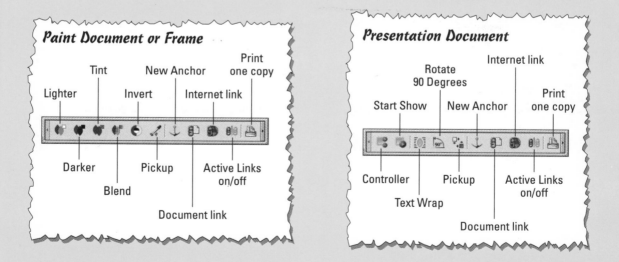

Paint Document or Frame

- Lighter
- Tint
- Darker
- Blend
- Invert
- Pickup
- New Anchor
- Internet link
- Document link
- Active Links on/off
- Print one copy

Presentation Document

- Start Show
- Controller
- Rotate 90 Degrees
- Text Wrap
- New Anchor
- Pickup
- Internet link
- Document link
- Active Links on/off
- Print one copy

For Dummies®: Bestselling Book Series for Beginners

TM

References for the Rest of Us!®

BESTSELLING BOOK SERIES

Are you intimidated and confused by computers? Do you find that traditional manuals are overloaded with technical details you'll never use? Do your friends and family always call you to fix simple problems on their PCs? Then the ...*For Dummies*® computer book series from IDG Books Worldwide is for you.

...*For Dummies* books are written for those frustrated computer users who know they aren't really dumb but find that PC hardware, software, and indeed the unique vocabulary of computing make them feel helpless. ...*For Dummies* books use a lighthearted approach, a down-to-earth style, and even cartoons and humorous icons to dispel computer novices' fears and build their confidence. Lighthearted but not lightweight, these books are a perfect survival guide for anyone forced to use a computer.

> *"I like my copy so much I told friends; now they bought copies."*
> — Irene C., Orwell, Ohio

> *"Quick, concise, nontechnical, and humorous."*
> — Jay A., Elburn, Illinois

> *"Thanks, I needed this book. Now I can sleep at night."*
> — Robin F., British Columbia, Canada

Already, millions of satisfied readers agree. They have made ...*For Dummies* books the #1 introductory level computer book series and have written asking for more. So, if you're looking for the most fun and easy way to learn about computers, look to ...*For Dummies* books to give you a helping hand.

IDG BOOKS WORLDWIDE®

1/99

AppleWorks® 6 FOR DUMMIES®

by **Bob LeVitus and Dennis Cohen**

IDG
BOOKS
WORLDWIDE

IDG Books Worldwide, Inc.
An International Data Group Company

Foster City, CA ◆ Chicago, IL ◆ Indianapolis, IN ◆ New York, NY

AppleWorks® 6 For Dummies®

Published by
IDG Books Worldwide, Inc.
An International Data Group Company
919 E. Hillsdale Blvd.
Suite 400
Foster City, CA 94404
www.idgbooks.com (IDG Books Worldwide Web site)
www.dummies.com (Dummies Press Web site)

Library of Congress Catalog Card No.: 99-67177

ISBN: 0-7645-0636-6

Printed in the United States of America

10 9 8 7 6 5 4 3 2 1

1B/SX/QU/QQ/IN

Distributed in the United States by IDG Books Worldwide, Inc.

Distributed by CDG Books Canada Inc. for Canada; by Transworld Publishers Limited in the United Kingdom; by IDG Norge Books for Norway; by IDG Sweden Books for Sweden; by IDG Books Australia Publishing Corporation Pty. Ltd. for Australia and New Zealand; by TransQuest Publishers Pte Ltd. for Singapore, Malaysia, Thailand, Indonesia, and Hong Kong; by Gotop Information Inc. for Taiwan; by ICG Muse, Inc. for Japan; by Intersoft for South Africa; by Eyrolles for France; by International Thomson Publishing for Germany, Austria and Switzerland; by Distribuidora Cuspide for Argentina; by LR International for Brazil; by Galileo Libros for Chile; by Ediciones ZETA S.C.R. Ltda. for Peru; by WS Computer Publishing Corporation, Inc., for the Philippines; by Contemporanea de Ediciones for Venezuela; by Express Computer Distributors for the Caribbean and West Indies; by Micronesia Media Distributor, Inc. for Micronesia; by Chips Computadoras S.A. de C.V. for Mexico; by Editorial Norma de Panama S.A. for Panama; by American Bookshops for Finland.

For general information on IDG Books Worldwide's books in the U.S., please call our Consumer Customer Service department at 800-762-2974. For reseller information, including discounts and premium sales, please call our Reseller Customer Service department at 800-434-3422.

For information on where to purchase IDG Books Worldwide's books outside the U.S., please contact our International Sales department at 317-596-5530 or fax 317-572-4002.

For consumer information on foreign language translations, please contact our Customer Service department at 1-800-434-3422, fax 317-572-4002, or e-mail rights@idgbooks.com.

For information on licensing foreign or domestic rights, please phone +1-650-653-7098.

For sales inquiries and special prices for bulk quantities, please contact our Order Services department at 800-434-3422 or write to the address above.

For information on using IDG Books Worldwide's books in the classroom or for ordering examination copies, please contact our Educational Sales department at 800-434-2086 or fax 317-572-4005.

For press review copies, author interviews, or other publicity information, please contact our Public Relations department at 650-653-7000 or fax 650-653-7500.

For authorization to photocopy items for corporate, personal, or educational use, please contact Copyright Clearance Center, 222 Rosewood Drive, Danvers, MA 01923, or fax 978-750-4470.

About the Authors

Bob LeVitus (pronounced Love-eye-tis) was the editor-in-chief of the wildly popular *MACazine* until its untimely demise in 1988. From 1989 to 1997, he was a contributing editor/columnist for *MacUser* magazine, writing the "Help Folder," "Beating the System," "Personal Best," and "Game Room" columns at one time or another.

In the meantime, he has written or co-written 34 mostly best-selling computer books, including *Mac OS 9 For Dummies* from IDG Books and *Mac Answers: Certified Tech Support,* 2nd Edition, from Osborne/McGraw-Hill.

Bob has spoken at more than 200 international seminars and conferences, having presented keynote addresses in several countries, and currently serves on the Macworld Expo Advisory Board. He is also a columnist for the *Houston Chronicle, Austin American-Statesman,* and *MacCentral.*

Most of all, Bob is known for his clear, understandable writing, his humorous style, and his ability to translate "techie" jargon into usable and fun advice for the rest of us.

LeVitus lives in Austin, Texas, with his wife, two children, and a small pack of Welsh Springer Spaniels.

Dennis Cohen isn't (just) a computer geek. He's been a vocal AppleWorks evangelist since its early days as ClarisWorks and worked on both the first U.S. and Japanese versions to run native on the PowerPC as a developer at Claris. Other products on which he worked during his time at Claris include FileMaker Pro, ClarisImpact for Japan, and Claris Resolve.

Dennis's first book for IDG Books was *Teach Yourself WebTV,* at least as an author; he has, however, been the technical editor for more than 50 titles, including all editions of the best-selling *Macworld Macintosh Secrets, Macworld Mac OS 7.6 Bible, Macworld Mac OS 8.5 Bible, Macworld Mac OS 9 Bible, Macworld ClarisWorks Office Bible, FileMaker Pro 4 Bible,* and *FileMaker Pro 5 Bible.*

When not editing or writing, Dennis is active in organized trapshooting, serving on the Board of Directors of the California Golden State Trap Association, reading, and playing with his Boston Terrier, Spenser.

ABOUT IDG BOOKS WORLDWIDE

Welcome to the world of IDG Books Worldwide.

IDG Books Worldwide, Inc., is a subsidiary of International Data Group, the world's largest publisher of computer-related information and the leading global provider of information services on information technology. IDG was founded more than 30 years ago by Patrick J. McGovern and now employs more than 9,000 people worldwide. IDG publishes more than 290 computer publications in over 75 countries. More than 90 million people read one or more IDG publications each month.

Launched in 1990, IDG Books Worldwide is today the #1 publisher of best-selling computer books in the United States. We are proud to have received eight awards from the Computer Press Association in recognition of editorial excellence and three from Computer Currents' First Annual Readers' Choice Awards. Our best-selling ...For Dummies® series has more than 50 million copies in print with translations in 31 languages. IDG Books Worldwide, through a joint venture with IDG's Hi-Tech Beijing, became the first U.S. publisher to publish a computer book in the People's Republic of China. In record time, IDG Books Worldwide has become the first choice for millions of readers around the world who want to learn how to better manage their businesses.

Our mission is simple: Every one of our books is designed to bring extra value and skill-building instructions to the reader. Our books are written by experts who understand and care about our readers. The knowledge base of our editorial staff comes from years of experience in publishing, education, and journalism — experience we use to produce books to carry us into the new millennium. In short, we care about books, so we attract the best people. We devote special attention to details such as audience, interior design, use of icons, and illustrations. And because we use an efficient process of authoring, editing, and desktop publishing our books electronically, we can spend more time ensuring superior content and less time on the technicalities of making books.

You can count on our commitment to deliver high-quality books at competitive prices on topics you want to read about. At IDG Books Worldwide, we continue in the IDG tradition of delivering quality for more than 30 years. You'll find no better book on a subject than one from IDG Books Worldwide.

John Kilcullen
Chairman and CEO
IDG Books Worldwide, Inc.

Eighth Annual
Computer Press
Awards ≥1992

Ninth Annual
Computer Press
Awards ≥1993

Tenth Annual
Computer Press
Awards ≥1994

Eleventh Annual
Computer Press
Awards ≥1995

Dedication

For my wife Lisa: L.Y.A.T.M.A.T.S.

— Bob LeVitus

To my family, friends, and Spenser, who make my life enjoyable.

— Dennis Cohen

Authors' Acknowledgments

Special thanks to our friends at Apple who were there for us every step of the way: Kate Wormington, the AppleWorks Product Manager; and Hala Shoukry, our voice on the AppleWorks Testing Team. Also, thanks to Jennifer Brabson, Alexei Folger, and the other members of the AppleWorks 6 team. Thank you all. We couldn't have done it without your help.

Thanks also to superagent Carole "Damnit, Stop Calling Me Swifty In Print" McClendon of Waterside Productions, for always connecting us to the projects we love.

And then there's IDG Books/Dummies Press . . . Extra special thanks to our acquisitions editor, Mike Roney, who's wise, fair, fun, and always up on things. Big-time thanks to Nicole Haims, our project editor, and Tim Borek, our copy editor. Thanks also to our technical editor Chris Breen.

Thanks to Mate Gross for getting Dennis to give an integrated product a chance back when ClarisWorks 1.0 was still called "Terminator."

Last, but not least, thanks to you for buying this book.

Publisher's Acknowledgments

We're proud of this book; please register your comments through our IDG Books Worldwide Online Registration Form located at http://my2cents.dummies.com.

Some of the people who helped bring this book to market include the following:

Acquisitions, Editorial, and Media Development

Project Editor: Nicole Haims

Acquisitions Editor: Michael Roney

Copy Editor: Timothy J. Borek

Proof Editor: Dwight Ramsey

Technical Editor: Christopher Breen

Editorial Manager: Rev Mengle

Editorial Assistant: Candace Nicholson

Production

Project Coordinator: Maridee Ennis

Layout and Graphics: Gabriele McCann, Tracy K. Oliver, Brent Savage, Jacque Schneider, Brian Torwelle

Proofreaders: Laura Albert, Corey Bowen, Vickie Broyles, John Greenough, Toni Settle

Indexer: Ty Koontz

Special Help
Amanda M. Foxworth, Kate Wormington, and Mike Rossetti, Apple Computer

---

General and Administrative

IDG Books Worldwide, Inc.: John Kilcullen, CEO

IDG Books Technology Publishing Group: Richard Swadley, Senior Vice President and Publisher; Walter R. Bruce III, Vice President and Publisher; Joseph Wikert, Vice President and Publisher; Mary Bednarek, Vice President and Director, Product Development; Andy Cummings, Publishing Director, General User Group; Mary C. Corder, Editorial Director; Barry Pruett, Publishing Director

IDG Books Consumer Publishing Group: Roland Elgey, Senior Vice President and Publisher; Kathleen A. Welton, Vice President and Publisher; Kevin Thornton, Acquisitions Manager; Kristin A. Cocks, Editorial Director

IDG Books Internet Publishing Group: Brenda McLaughlin, Senior Vice President and Publisher; Sofia Marchant, Online Marketing Manager

IDG Books Production for Branded Press: Debbie Stailey, Director of Production; Cindy L. Phipps, Manager of Project Coordination, Production Proofreading, and Indexing; Tony Augsburger, Manager of Prepress, Reprints, and Systems; Laura Carpenter, Production Control Manager; Shelley Lea, Supervisor of Graphics and Design; Debbie J. Gates, Production Systems Specialist; Robert Springer, Supervisor of Proofreading; Kathie Schutte, Production Supervisor

Packaging and Book Design: Patty Page, Manager, Promotions Marketing

◆

The publisher would like to give special thanks to Patrick J. McGovern, without whom this book would not have been possible.

◆

Contents at a Glance

Cartoons at a Glance

By Rich Tennant

Table of Contents

Introduction

● ●

*A*fter you invest in a computer, printer, and other hardware, the last thing you want to do is lay out more money for several boxes of software to help you create charts and graphs, newsletters, spreadsheets, databases, graphics, presentations, Web pages, and word-processing documents. Worse, you hate to get the software home and try to run it, only to discover that it takes up too much space on your hard drive.

You got your computer to make your life easier — not to spend the rest of your life figuring out heaps of complicated software.

Luckily for you, you're either looking at this book and checking out AppleWorks as a solution or, even luckier, you already own AppleWorks and have found *AppleWorks 6 For Dummies*. You found an excellent solution — a simple, powerful software program and a book that gives it to you straight and keeps it simple. Never mind all the hype about computers being hard to master. You found a team that defies that trend.

About This Book

If you have, or are considering using, AppleWorks 6, this book works for you.

AppleWorks 6 has so many features, chances are pretty good that you won't even use all of them . . . until that fateful day when you need to do something you've never done — and need to do it fast.

We wrote this book with that type of real-life need in mind. Take it out, get the lowdown on a feature, and then put it away again. Maybe you need to use just one function, such as word processing or spreadsheets. Just go over that chapter. Of course, you can read the book from cover to cover. We made it easy to use the book either way.

We set up each section so that you can find the answers you need without reading more than is absolutely necessary. You can find plenty of cross-references in case you need more information. Technical Stuff icons mark information and computer terms that you don't have to deal with. Tips are clearly marked so that you can just skim them. The idea is for you to get in, get the information you need to solve the problem at hand, and get back to work as quickly as possible.

Conventions Used in This Book

When we tell you how to do something, we tell you which menu to look in and which command to use. When a process involves several steps, we put them in a numbered list so they're easier to follow. When there's more than one way to get something done, we go over each approach, pointing out the fastest, easiest way.

By the way, AppleWorks really adheres to the "keep it simple" rule. Everything you need is clearly found in a menu, rather than buried somewhere, forcing you to memorize yucky key combinations to get something done.

We list menu commands like this:

Edit⇨Copy

This means that you pull down the Edit menu with your mouse and choose the Copy command.

Sometimes, you may be more comfortable using a keyboard shortcut rather than pulling down menus, so we point out the shortcuts to you. In the text, keyboard shortcuts are listed like this:

⌘-C

This keyboard shortcut requires you to press and hold the ⌘ key, press the letter C, and then release both keys at the same time. Notice that we use a hyphen between commands. The hyphens aren't part of the combination. Don't press them. AppleWorks almost always gives you command-key short-cuts for buttons in their dialog boxes. Unfortunately, you don't see them unless you hold down the command key. Occasionally, the screen shots we present will display those key equivalents. Just because you don't see them in the screen picture doesn't mean they aren't there — we just show them to you once in a while to remind you to look for them.

Another handy key to know is the Control key. When you hold it down and click in any AppleWorks window, you're presented with a *contextual menu*. Contextual menus usually just give you more immediate access to the menu items appropriate to the thing on which you clicked; however, every once in a while, you find options that don't exist in any of the other menus or buttons in the program. Contextual menus are your friends, explore what they have to offer.

What You're Not to Read

Scattered throughout this book are short notes, definitions, and discussions of a more technical nature. They're here only for the curious. Don't read them. Well, okay, you can read them if you really want to. We've been careful to mark these items with Technical Stuff icons. These tidbits are a great source of AppleWorks trivia. Repeating any technical stuff you read in this book is the quickest way we know of to kill a conversation at a dinner party.

Foolish Assumptions

The first thing that we assume about you is that you're no dummy. Otherwise, you wouldn't have bought this book. The term *Dummies* is a written form of a nod and a grin to let you know that we understand how daunting all this computer stuff can be sometimes. We've been there. It's that feeling you get when you sit in front of your computer, mouse in hand, knowing that somehow you can use all this technology to do something wonderful, but having no idea how to do so.

We realize that you may be new to computing, so we make using AppleWorks as easy as possible for you. We tell you when to use the mouse, when to hold down the mouse button, and when to release it. However, we expect that you have the basics down — getting around your screen, clicking, dragging, and selecting a command from a menu.

(For help mastering the general behavior of your computer's operation, we recommend that you check out Bob LeVitus's *Mac OS 8.5 For Dummies* or *Mac OS 9 For Dummies,* published by IDG Books Worldwide, Inc.)

We also assume that you are currently using AppleWorks 6. If you're not and your computer will support it, then run out and buy AppleWorks 6 right now; you'll be glad you did.

How This Book Is Organized

We divide this book into eight parts. Each covers a different area of AppleWorks. We divide each part into chapters, and then we break down the chapters into bite-sized bits. You can quickly wolf down the morsels of information you need without getting mental heartburn.

Here's what you can find in each part:

Part I: What AppleWorks Does

This part provides an overview of AppleWorks 6: its features, the methods and practices common to all areas of the application, and the on-screen help systems. This part points out the main environments or functions of AppleWorks, as well as what the other bundled software has to offer. You can find out about how to open and save documents, the parts of a window, the tools, the menus, and the buttons. This part is a good place to start if you're a beginner.

Part II: Working with Text: The Keys to Success

At some point, you'll need to work with text, whether to write a letter or to add captions to a spreadsheet or illustration. Text handling, whether in a word-processing document or in a text frame within another environment, is the focus here. This part is also where we introduce you to AppleWorks tables.

Part III: Working with Graphics and Graphics-Based Documents

You can create graphics by drawing or painting. We compare these methods here, followed by chapters focusing on each. When you want to create a company logo or add a diagram to your document, this is the place to go. It's also the place to find out about page layout — something that comes in handy because you can add text, spreadsheets, charts, and paintings to a draw document to do full-fledged page composition. We cover clip art and AppleWorks Internet search here, too. And then we get into presentations. Presentations are actually in a class by themselves 'cause they are one of the major new features of AppleWorks 6. We had to put them somewhere and most of the presentation tools are the graphics tools, so they're here.

Part IV: Working with Numbers: It All Adds Up!

Spreadsheets are the focus here, from formulas to formatting. Creating a chart (even one with custom icons) from your spreadsheet data is easy, so come here to find out how. Spreadsheets are also another kind of table, so if you want to use a spreadsheet for your table, come here for more details on formatting it.

Part V: Working with Files: Smoothing Out the Rough Edges

Databases are great places to keep customer or student records, or an inventory of your CDs, videotapes, or books. Discover how to create and use them here.

Part VI: Mastering AppleWorks Internet and Automation Features

AppleWorks offers Internet connectivity. We introduce all the basics here. AppleWorks also enables you to create Web pages. We cover that here, too. AppleWorks also lets you automate many tasks from both within and outside AppleWorks using AppleScript, and we get you started on that, also.

Part VII: The Part of Tens

In this part, we show you ten real-life uses for AppleWorks and solutions for ten problems you may encounter while using AppleWorks. In this case, two times ten equals a lot more than just the number 20. It equals lots of ideas and help.

Part VIII: Appendixes

If you want to make the most of the timesaving buttons in AppleWorks, Appendix A is for you. We show you how to add buttons to button bars, customize buttons, and create new buttons. For even more creative control, check out Appendix B. There, we tell you how to create your own patterns, gradients, and wallpaper textures to spice up your graphics.

Icons Used in This Book

Icons in this book form a kind of road map that you can use to navigate the text. Scan the margins for the following types of information:

Points out a useful hint, trick, or shortcut.

Reminds you to do something, or points out a concept to file in your memory bank.

Reminds you not to do something that you may regret later (or sooner!).

Points out geeky, technical stuff that you can feel free to skip.

Where to Go from Here

For your reading pleasure, may we suggest that . . .

- ✔ If you're totally new to AppleWorks, begin with Part I for the basics, and then jump to the part that covers what you need to do first.
- ✔ If you have a specific project in mind and already have the basics, turn directly to the part that covers what you need.
- ✔ If you don't have a specific project to work on, but just want this book to be handy when you need it, put it away and have some fun (of course, get back to work if you have to). We'll wait till you need us.

Part I
What AppleWorks Does

In this part . . .

AppleWorks isn't flashy and it isn't overkill. It's simple to use: It doesn't bury commands tons of levels deep. In fact, it doesn't bury them at all. It doesn't cost a bunch of money, but don't let that fool you. It doesn't come in a huge box with inches of manuals. Don't let that fool you, either.

Like we said, AppleWorks is powerful. Simple and powerful — simply powerful.

This part gives you an overview of what AppleWorks can do. It covers the basics that you need to start working with the application. If you're just beginning with AppleWorks, take a quick look here. There's even some good stuff in this part for old hats to discover.

Chapter 1

A Quick Overview of AppleWorks 6

. . . .

In This Chapter

▶ Understanding AppleWorks?

▶ Word processing

▶ Drawing

▶ Painting

▶ Using spreadsheets

▶ Adding information into databases

▶ Using communications functions

▶ Getting the scoop on helpful features

. . . .

AppleWorks springs from the days when "works" software packages were commonly combos of mini-programs that worked independently of one another. But AppleWorks (called *ClarisWorks* back then) is different. Not just a few unrelated applications thrown into the same box, AppleWorks programs all work together, melding their functions beautifully to give you more flexibility and lots of power. In this chapter, we tell you about the applications and a few extras that add even more value to the AppleWorks suite of programs.

Understanding Basic AppleWorks Functions

The first question that most people ask about AppleWorks is, "What is it? A word processor? A drawing program? A spreadsheet program? A presentation program?" The answer is "Yes." It's all that and more. AppleWorks is the software equivalent of a Swiss Army™ Knife — a whole tool chest rolled into one application.

Computer software tends to fall — or be placed by us — into categories. *Works* is a generic term for a program that provides the basics of most or all these types of programs. Originally, works programs gave you a mini-version of each supported software type. AppleWorks goes way beyond that, incorporating full-fledged versions of six software types, not just samplers. The *Works* in AppleWorks means that you get it all:

- Word processing
- Drawing
- Painting
- Spreadsheets
- Presentations
- Communications

But AppleWorks is more than just six separate applications integrated into one package. It's *seamlessly integrated,* as the Apple people say. If the suite were only six separate applications, you would have to do your typing, then your drawing, and *then* try to paste your illustration into your text. *Seamlessly integrated* means that you can use the software's different functions together in one document without switching programs. Not impressed yet? Wait till you get into this seamless stuff! You don't have to start a separate drawing document to create a picture — you can draw right there in the middle of your letter to Aunt Barbara or right on top of your sales spreadsheet.

Word processing (typing)

Perhaps the most-used function of AppleWorks is word processing. That's not just writing simple letters. The word-processing function pops up all over the place: when you're creating a spreadsheet and need to enter an introduction; when you're creating a slide in a presentation; or when you're entering a block of text into a drawing document to create a newsletter or flier.

Are you wondering why it's called *word processing* and not just *typing?* If you're used to a typewriter and this is your first introduction to word processing, you're in for a treat. A word processor enables you to do far more than just enter text. You now have the full ability to *manipulate* the text you enter. For example, you can type your text, move it anywhere you like, style it in many ways, check spelling, find synonyms in a thesaurus, count your words, use footnotes, change margins and indents, wrap or justify text, search for and replace words, and much more.

If you are a student, you may have found out (the hard way) that your teachers were right, and work is easier when you devise a plan. For those of you who still haven't figured this out (but will someday), AppleWorks also offers outlining, an easy way to list the main points of your document and then organize and build upon them.

Word-processing documents can do one more thing that may surprise you. They can become Web pages. All you have to do is create a document as you normally would. When you save it, select HTML as the file format. AppleWorks has built-in translators that convert your document for you and pack it up, graphics and all, into a neat folder ready to place on the Web. You don't have to learn a thing about HTML if you don't want to. But, in case you do, or in case you want more control over your HTML output, you can customize these translators. If you have the HTML bug and want to learn even more, check out *HTML 4 For Dummies,* 2nd Edition (IDG Books Worldwide, Inc.), by Ed Tittel and Stephen Nelson James.

Drawing

Like word processing, drawing can pop up almost anywhere. The drawing functions of AppleWorks provide line tools and shape tools to help you create graphics. Additionally, AppleWorks gives you palettes full of colors, editable patterns, gradients, and textures to complete your image.

You can create a drawing document on which you create a page layout or an entire work of art. Or you can take advantage of the drawing functions within other document types to create a letterhead or fliers in a word-processing document, make maps and diagrams, add graphics to a database, and much more.

When you use the AppleWorks drawing tools, lines and shapes are composed of points and invisible, behind-the-scenes mathematical formulas. When you resize drawings or move graphic objects on top of one another, the images still look good on-screen and print with crisp lines and smooth curves. You also can easily change your drawings at any time.

Painting

Before you get your hopes up, we have to tell you that this painting is limited to what you do on-screen. Even a great program like AppleWorks can't make your computer paint your house (although it can help you hire a painter, chart the progress, and send out fliers announcing the paint job).

The paint feature gives you electronic pencils and brushes to create your works of art and colors to fill your shapes and color your lines.

Just as you can't rearrange real paint after you apply it, you can't rearrange what you do with AppleWorks painting tools. This is because instead of working with the easily edited lines of a drawing program, painting tools work with the smallest possible elements, called *pixels*. Imagine that you're coloring a sheet of graph paper and each square on the graph paper is a pixel on your computer's screen. To create a painting, you either color in a square or leave it empty. If you make a shape and then need to make it larger, you uncolor some squares and color in new ones.

You can also add text to a painting. Doing so "paints" the text in — the text turns into dots that are part of the painting instead of individual characters that you can edit. You can use the paint functions to design logos, manipulate clip art, or edit scanned images. AppleWorks even enables you to select any part of a painting so that you can move, rotate, stretch, or slant it — creating interesting effects — better than you can do with real paint, huh?

Spreadsheets (calculating and more)

You may be thinking, "Spreadsheets — sheesh, I'll never use those. They're just for accountants!" After you're comfortable with AppleWorks, however, you may be surprised by the uses you find for a spreadsheet. Okay, you may not be into things like creating business invoices, maintaining financial statements, tracking stocks, and balancing your checkbook, but one day you may need to make that recipe for 100 into a recipe for 9, and you may just find yourself saying, "Hey, I can do that with a spreadsheet!" (Honest, it could happen. But only if you cook to begin with.)

As a matter of fact, anything set up in rows and columns is fair game for a spreadsheet. How about your daily schedule or a monthly calendar?

Do you like visualizing trends with graphs and charts? Just enter the data into a spreadsheet, and AppleWorks does the rest. You can choose from many types of charts. You may need to graph data from a chemistry experiment, for example, or you may need to chart profits.

Databases (filing and maintaining data)

You can use a database anytime you want to store, search, or sort information such as addresses, the contents of a baseball card collection, a business inventory, or any other collection of information. The number one way to use the AppleWorks database function is to put your address book or client list into a data file. You can then use a database document as your electronic Rolodex.

AppleWorks enables you to customize databases to work with information in any way you like. Because of the integration features of AppleWorks, you can use the graphics tools to add color and pictures to your database files. After you organize and sort information, you can easily print it on standard labels.

One of the most useful database features is the ability to merge information from your database into any text area or spreadsheet. This feature makes printing personalized forms or letters a cinch. Ed McMahon's notices saying that you may have already won a prize pale in comparison to what you can do.

Communications

The communications capabilities within AppleWorks 6 are now more than ever before a program-wide integration with the World Wide Web.

This hot and spicy form of communication connects you to the Internet's graphical splendor. You can place links or buttons in any AppleWorks document, so that all your clients and friends have to do is click and go. Their Internet browsers launch and connect them to the Web site you want them to see or automatically launch their e-mail program to send you a message.

If your friends and colleagues aren't using AppleWorks, you can still open and look at documents that they sent and take advantage of all your communications features. For example, if you're not using a document that has a link, just add a couple of buttons to your button bar, then click one of these buttons at the top of your screen: One button launches your browser, and another takes you directly to any Web address that you highlight within a document. You (or an associate) can even create custom buttons that take you directly to specific Web sites.

Presentations

AppleWorks 6 now includes a dedicated Presentations environment. Although you could create presentations and slide shows using drawing documents, you won't have the various transition effects — fade-in/out, shutters, and so on — unless you use a Presentation document. You can even keep different variations of the same presentation in one document and just set alternative groupings of your slides for your various audiences.

Bringing These Things Together (Integration)

The real strength of AppleWorks is its unique ability to mix its parts together — easily. How? By using the concept of frames.

A *frame* is sort of a window from one kind of AppleWorks function (or *environment*) into another. AppleWorks uses the term *environment* to refer to each of its main application or document types. When you choose a document type, you indicate the environment in which you predominately want to work.

The frames you can choose from are drawing, painting, word processing, spreadsheet, and *tables*. Tables are new in AppleWorks 6. Here's some more information about frames:

- ✔ You can use only one frame at a time.

- ✔ When you're in a frame, you are fully within that frame's environment.

- ✔ When you're not in a frame, the frame is just another graphic object that you can reposition by dragging.

- ✔ The one frame type that does not have its own document type is the table.

- ✔ Just because you've chosen a main environment for an AppleWorks project doesn't mean that you can't use as many others as you want. You access other environments by creating frames within a document.

The best way to explain frames is with an example. Say that you're preparing a report. Reports are mostly words, so you begin with a word-processing document. Then you want to include a table to display data. Simple enough.

You *could* use the Tab key to make the numbers line up in columns, but if you later edit that data in any way, it becomes quite a mess. If you have tab-separated columns, AppleWorks lets you select this data and convert it to a table.

If you need to perform calculations on some of the tabular data, you can create a spreadsheet frame. If you need more versatile formatting than a spreadsheet provides, use a table.

"But wait," you say, "I'm in a word-processing document, right?" Yup, you are, but AppleWorks enables you to use all the functions of a spreadsheet right there, smack-dab in the middle of your word-processing document.

To create a spreadsheet frame, simply select the spreadsheet tool and drag it to the place you want to put the table. Now you're in spreadsheet mode, with full access to the commands and functions you use for spreadsheets.

If you click your mouse in an area outside the spreadsheet, though, this frame becomes just another object, so that you can move or resize the spreadsheet and even have your text flow around.

The same concept applies when you add text to a draw document. To add words to your graphics, drag the text tool to where you want the text, creating a text frame. Within that area, you can access all the text tools that you have in a word-processing document, including text styles and the spell checker. You can even nest text frames within a word-processing document, for example, if you wish to create a sidebar.

You can add as many frames to a document as you like. Of course, you can add different kinds of frames within a document. For example, use a draw document as your main environment to lay out your invoice; add your company logo in a paint frame, your address in a text frame, and a tally for the charges in a spreadsheet frame. The spreadsheet actively calculates your costs and fees, so that you can truly prepare your invoices within one document!

Frames aren't linked with any particular line of text or spreadsheet cell. Instead, they're floating objects that you can move around anywhere in the document. You can see what we mean when you edit the data in the main document and find your frame overlapping. That's when you click the frame and move it into place in relation to your recent edits. Of course, you can embed a frame into a line of text if you prefer. That way, the frame moves as you edit your text. We show you more about embedding frames and graphics into a line of text in Chapter 7. The guys at Apple call these embedded frames *inline frames*.

Frames only apply to word-processing documents, presentations, spreadsheets, tables, and drawing. The other environments don't need frames because the draw tools are available at all times. Database data gets inserted into documents by a technique called *merging*, which inserts database data into special placeholders you set up in your documents. Paintings are just collections of dots (called *pixels*), so frames don't make sense there. This may sound difficult, but it's really simple. We explain the details in Chapter 12.

Exploring Other AppleWorks Features (Neat, Helpful Stuff)

In the preceding sections, we show you the major things that AppleWorks does. The following sections show you some of its bells and whistles.

Assistants

Sometimes you seem to spend a lot of time re-creating the same types of documents, except with different content or formatting. Respecting your valuable time, AppleWorks gives you an *assistant* — a little helper that asks you a few focused questions and then presents you with a preformatted document that's ready to use.

Templates

Templates can be another great timesaver. Templates (previously known as Stationery) refers to the good, solid, ready-made starting points for specific types of documents. AppleWorks comes with many document templates to cover your needs. You can also create your own templates.

Document passwords

At any point in a document's life, you may decide that you're more comfortable assigning a password to the document so that prying or curious eyes can't see what they shouldn't. You can assign a password to any AppleWorks document at any time. You also can change the password as needed — as long as you know the current password!

Buttons

Buttons are shortcuts to common tasks. They not only provide one-click access to commands, but they also give you visual clues as to what you can do from where you are. Nine buttons make your travel on the Internet superhighway smooth driving. Another dozen build a chart for you in a jiffy. The rest mostly help you with document formatting. And then you can set up other buttons that launch other programs, open other documents, take you to specific Web sites, or perform other tasks. The more creative you are with buttons, the more time you save.

Chapter 2

How AppleWorks Works

*I*f AppleWorks were a car, this is where you would take it out for a little spin and try to figure out how to work the gearshift. This chapter gives you the information you need to handle the basic stuff common to all AppleWorks document types — things like opening a new document, saving, and printing. So dig in and don't forget to fasten your seat belt!

Starting AppleWorks

First things first. Before you can use AppleWorks, you need to start it up, or launch it. How you do that depends on how your system is set up.

Whether viewing by icon or as a list, open the AppleWorks 6 folder, locate the AppleWorks icon, and double-click it to start. You can also use the Launcher if you are so inclined and wish to add AppleWorks to a Launcher page, or if you have an AppleWorks alias on your desktop, double-click it. For maximum efficiency, add an AppleWorks alias to your menu, and launch the program by selecting it from there.

If you can't find AppleWorks, try these tips (your setup may be different):

✔ AppleWorks is on your hard drive, which is represented by an icon in the upper-right corner of your desktop (called Macintosh HD by default). You can find it in the AppleWorks 6.0 folder, which may be in a folder called Applications if your computer came with AppleWorks pre-installed. The application is called AppleWorks.

✔ If you still can't find AppleWorks, use your system's Find feature (probably called "Sherlock" or "Sherlock 2") to locate it. After that, if you *still* can't find it, pick up a copy of Bob LeVitus's *Mac OS 9 For Dummies*, published by IDG Books Worldwide, Inc.

Creating a New Document

Each time you launch AppleWorks, the program presents you with a Starting Points window like the one shown in Figure 2-1. You see buttons for the six document types when the Basic tab (the default) is showing. Click a document type to open a new document.

Figure 2-1:
The Starting
Points
window.

After AppleWorks is running, it no longer displays the Starting Points window, even if you switch to another program and then switch back to AppleWorks, unless you choose Show Starting Points from the File menu (⌘-1) or close all your open documents. You have two other options to create a new document:

✔ Click the button in the button bar for the type of document you want to create.

✔ Choose File➪New and choose the document type you wish from the hierarchical menu

The only difference between these options is that the Starting Points window gives you the option to use Assistants or Templates, which we cover in Chapter 3.

If AppleWorks is already running and you switch to another application and back again, AppleWorks gives you a clue that you're back. The clue is the Application menu in the upper-right corner of your screen, where you can see the AppleWorks icon (and the word AppleWorks, too, in OS 8.5 or later if you have your Application menu extended to show program names). Additionally, you can see the button bar, unless you turned it off.

After a while, you don't always want to start from a new blank document; you develop your own stationery *templates* to launch instead. After you develop a document that you like, you can save time by making it a template. When you want to use that style document, you can just open it, rather than formatting a whole new document. You also have the option of using an Assistant to help you create a custom template. Find out about Assistants in Chapter 3.

Choosing Your Primary Environment

Which type of document you want to begin with depends on the kind of work you primarily plan to do. As we go into detail about each document type throughout this book, you get a better idea of when to use each one. Meanwhile, here's a quick reference guide:

- Use a *word-processing document* for jobs that are mostly text — for example, a letter, a school report, or an outline.

- Use a *draw document* to create graphics like maps, diagrams, and plans. You can also use draw documents for laying out pages that combine graphics with blocks of text and/or spreadsheets, such as newsletters or manuals.

- Use a *paint document* for creating logos, freehand pictures, and special effects with graphics and text.

- Use a *spreadsheet document* to display information in columns and rows — schedules, financial reports, or calendars, for example.

- Use a *database* to store information. Addresses, product inventory, and things that you want to print on labels are good candidates for a database.

- Use *presentation documents* for creating hard-copy or on-screen presentations.

The document type that you choose is your primary environment, but you aren't limited to that type of function. Remember, you can use one kind of function within another by creating a frame. (See "Tools," later in this chapter.)

Opening Existing Documents

You can open existing documents in a couple of different ways; we give the basics here.

Launching as you open a document

A common way to launch a file is to open the folder in which the document resides and double-click the document's icon. If AppleWorks isn't running yet, this method launches it while opening your document. If your computer's hard drive icon is covered, preventing access to your folders simply reduces the size of your document.

A more efficient way to get to documents is to create an alias of any project that you work on often and place it in the menu.

Opening a document from within AppleWorks

Most people prefer to open documents by double-clicking them, as we explain in the preceding section. The other way to open a document is to use the Open dialog box.

Here's how it works:

1. **Choose File⇨Open.**

   This brings you to what Mac users call the Open dialog box shown in Figure 12-2.

   If you're not running System 8.5 or later, your Open and Save dialog boxes may look different from those displayed here. AppleWorks 6 uses the Navigation Services versions of these dialogs if they are available, as they are beginning with MacOS 8.5.

2. **Navigate to the folder that contains the document you want to open.**

3. **First click the document you want, to highlight it and then click the Open button.**

   You can also open the document by double-clicking it.

   If you don't see the document that you want to open, select All Available from the File Type pop-up menu.

Choose File➪Open to open a document that was created in another application. The dialog box method translates the document as it opens it. You can also simply drag a file onto the AppleWorks icon to have AppleWorks translate and open it.

The contents of the KathyStuff folder

Look here to find out where you are

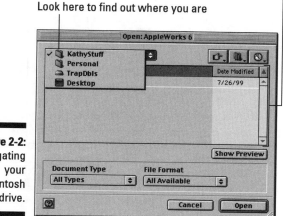

Figure 2-2:
Navigating
your
Macintosh
hard drive.

You can look for a specific type of AppleWorks document by choosing that type from the Document Type pop-up menu in the Open dialog box. You can also narrow your selections to a specific file format by choosing that format from the File Type pop-up menu in the same dialog box. If the folder you're looking in contains tons of files, you can use these menus to locate a specific document more quickly.

Getting to Know the AppleWorks Interface

Interface . . . such a designer's term. *Interface* is the technical term for the look, feel, and controls of something. Your car's dashboard or the buttons on your microwave are interfaces. In AppleWorks, the interface consists of the windows, buttons, menus, and tools. Figure 2-3 shows the Macintosh interface.

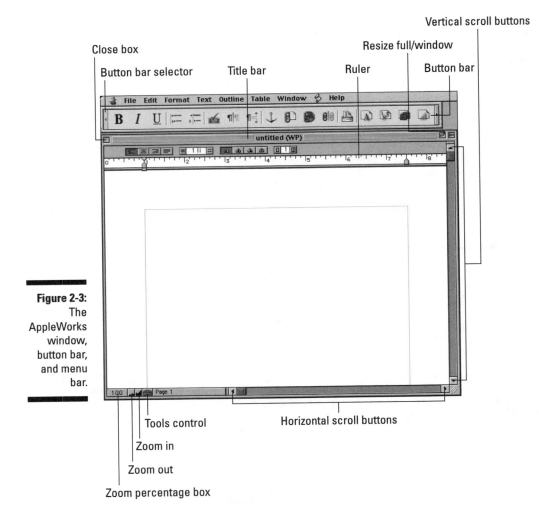

Figure 2-3:
The
AppleWorks
window,
button bar,
and menu
bar.

View controls

We assume that, as a computer user, you have some experience with the general window controls for your system. In addition to those controls, Apple has a few of its own that make working in AppleWorks more pleasant.

  ✔ **Zoom controls:** Three zoom controls reside at the bottom of your window. Zoom In, which looks like big mountains, doubles the magnification of your document each time you click it. Zoom Out (little mountains) does the opposite. The percentage box next to the controls tells you at what size your document is currently displayed. The box is also a pop-up menu. Click, hold, and drag to choose from a list of commonly used percentages. "Other" brings up a dialog box that enables you to enter any percentage you like. Don't confuse these zoom controls with the Zoom or Resize buttons in the top-right corner of the window. Those change the size of the window. These buttons change the magnification.

✔ **Tools panel toggle:** This button, located next to the zoom controls, shows or hides the Tools floating window. The Tools window contains one panel of frame-creation tools and one panel of drawing, painting, and table-editing tools. You can find more information about the tools later in this chapter.

✔ **Page indicator:** You can tell which page(s) you're working on by looking at the page indicator. Double-clicking it calls up the Go to Page dialog box. Type a page number in the box and click OK to be instantly transported to that page.

✔ **Pane controls:** These are the thick strips above the vertical scroll bar and to the left of the horizontal scroll bar. You can split the window into multiple "panes" by positioning your pointer in the strip, clicking, and dragging either down or right (depending on the pane). You can divide the window into as many as nine smaller sections, each of which can display different parts of the document.

Pane controls are handy if you want to look at the start of a report as you compose a summary at the end. Or maybe you have a large diagram and want to keep an eye on the left edge as you finish the right. To resize any split, click the split line and drag. To unsplit, double-click the split line. These strips are black.

Other window controls

While we're on the subject of windows, here are some commands that also help you view your documents:

✔ To view several documents at once, click the Tile Windows button on the button bar or choose Window⇨Tile Windows. Tiling resizes all open AppleWorks documents to fit them all on-screen at once.

✔ You can also choose Window⇨Stack Windows to reposition all open windows so that you see all title bars at once. Click any title bar to bring that document forward and work with it.

✔ To work in the normal full-screen mode, but switch between documents, use the Window menu to bring a document forward. All open AppleWorks documents are listed in the Window menu.

Button, button, we've got the button

Granted, moving your mouse to a menu and selecting a command is really simple. But buttons are even easier. They provide immediate access to frequently used menu commands. One of the best things is that the AppleWorks buttons are *dynamic* — these function-specific buttons change, depending on the environment in which you're working. For example, text commands are only appropriate when you are word processing, so their buttons only show at that time.

The button bar floats freely as a horizontally resizable palette. If you don't see the document that you want to open, select All Available from the File Type pop-up menu.

Buttons can really save you time. For example, our favorite, Show/Hide Invisibles, toggles the invisible formatting characters (spaces, tabs, and returns) on and off so that you can see what you're doing and then get the invisibles out of the way. To do this manually, you have to open the Preferences dialog box and click the option each time you want to hide or show the formatting characters. You can choose from several button bar button sets, but only one can or will be displayed at a given time. The most common is the *Default,* which contains the buttons you'll probably use most often. Don't let them fool you — these are just the bars for unopened documents. When you open a document, you get the document's function buttons, too.

What do all those buttons do? Move your mouse over any one and a description appears to tell you in a balloon. If you find the descriptions annoying, you can turn them off in Edit⇨Preferences⇨Button bar or by choosing Customize Button bar from the contextual menu which appears when you ⌘-click the button bar.

AppleWorks enables you to edit the button bar to remove the buttons you don't use often and add new buttons. We tell you all about editing buttons and button bars in Appendix A.

You may not always see all the buttons on your current button bar. Some may be hiding. To check or remedy this, scroll through the buttons by clicking either the darkened left or right scroll arrow. You can also click the resize area at the lower-right corner of the button bar to lengthen (or shorten) it.

Tools

Tools do exactly what their names imply — they get things done. You can access the Tools window any time in all six environments. When using a database document, there is also a special panel containing database-specific tools in the main window.

If the tools are hidden, just click the Tool toggle button in the lower-left corner of the window to show them, or choose Window➪Show Tools.

When you use the paint environment, the set of painting tools is enabled. Similarly, when you are working with a table, the table-editing tools become enabled. Both versions of the Tools panel are shown in Figure 2-4. Notice the eight extra painting tools. We go over each tool in detail in Part III.

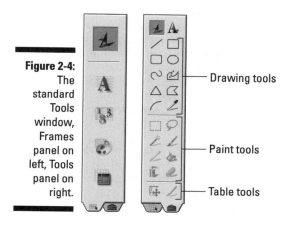

Figure 2-4: The standard Tools window, Frames panel on left, Tools panel on right.

— Drawing tools

— Paint tools

— Table tools

The *frame tools* are the five tools on the Frames panel of the Tools window. You use these tools to create or edit a frame within a document. Frames are the secret to the AppleWorks magic. You read a lot more about them as we cover each function of AppleWorks. For now, here are some quick descriptions and a few pointers.

Arrow pointer — the one o'clock-pointing arrow

This is the arrow that looks like a mouse pointer, pointing to one o'clock rather than ten o'clock. Use this tool to select, move, and resize frames or the graphics you made by using the draw tools. The arrow pointer is the key to the power of AppleWorks. When you use the arrow pointer to click a frame or a drawn object, you select it as an object. Keep the mouse held down and you can drag the frame, as an object, within your document. But when you double-click a frame or drawn object, it enters the environment within the frame. Each time you change environments, the pointer changes. For example, if you want to edit a spreadsheet frame and you're using the arrow pointer, click twice in the spreadsheet frame to edit the data in the cells. The first click selects the frame, and the second changes the pointer to the spreadsheet tool.

You know that any object (or frame) is selected because four (or eight) small, black boxes appear at its corners. These are called *handles.* Clicking a handle and dragging it resizes the object or frame. Be careful with resizing: It can distort graphics and hide or expose rows and columns in spreadsheets. For proportional graphic resizing, press the Shift key before you click the handle, and hold the Shift key as you resize the graphic.

Text tool — the letter A

Clicking the text tool changes your pointer to an I-beam. Use the I-beam to position the text insertion cursor, which, in a word-processing environment, enables you to select text or enter new text. The I-beam is also used to place a text frame within a drawing, presentation, or spreadsheet document, or on the layout of a database document. To create a text frame, click the text tool to select it. Then, move your mouse onto your document and click and hold down the mouse button as you drag within the document to define your text area. The text stays within the side boundaries you define, and the area grows longer to accommodate your text. You can always reshape this text block later.

The *text insertion cursor,* or the *cursor* as its friends call it, is the flashing vertical line that tells you where each character you type will appear in your document. Characters that you type always appear to the left of the cursor and push that cursor to the right (unless you're using a language kit, such as Arabic or Hebrew, where text flows from right to left).

Text frames can be handy even when you're already in a word-processing document. They let you add a caption to a graphic or a spreadsheet frame that is independent of the body of text, enabling you to move it along with the graphic or spreadsheet frame. To add a text frame to a word-processing document, choose the text tool and press the Option key as you drag to create the frame.

Text frames act differently in a painting environment. As soon as text is entered, it turns into paint-type pixels, and cursor-type editing is no longer available.

Spreadsheet tool — the numbers against a grid

The spreadsheet tool enables you to create or edit spreadsheet frames. Spreadsheets are most commonly added to word-processing or drawing documents to create certain types of tables, reflect calculations, or create charts or graphs. To add a spreadsheet frame to a document, click the spreadsheet tool, move your mouse (don't drag) onto your document, and then click and drag within the document to define your spreadsheet.

Spreadsheets behave differently in a painting environment. You can enter data into cells initially, but clicking outside the spreadsheet turns that spreadsheet into paint-type pixels; editing is no longer available. Instead, create spreadsheets in a text or draw document and then paste them into the paint environment.

If you're working in a spreadsheet document, holding down the Option key while dragging the spreadsheet tool creates a spreadsheet frame. You can place the frame anywhere in the document because it's not tied to a specific cell. See Part IV of this book for more information on spreadsheets.

Paint tool — the painter's palette

As you've probably figured out by now, the paint tool is for creating a paint frame within your document (unless you're already in a paint document, of course). All you do is click the paint tool, move your mouse (don't drag) onto your document, and then click and drag within the document to define your painting area. After the area is defined, special paint tools activate in your Tools panel. From there, you select your specific paint tool and create to your heart's content.

Table tool — the colorful grid

As you've probably figured out by now, the table tool is for creating a table within your document. All you do is click the table tool, move your mouse (don't drag) onto your document, and then click and drag within the document to define your table area. After the area is defined, special table tools activate in your Tools panel. You can even put tables within tables.

Nesting tables is how many Web pages organize things into columns and sections. You can place text, drawings, paintings, spreadsheets and other tables into your table cells.

Draw tools

The ten draw tools are elite because they are almost always available. Unlike the word-processing, paint, table, and spreadsheet tools, the draw tools don't need a frame to make them active. Whenever you select a draw tool, you automatically switch to the draw environment. You can create objects wherever you want them. Look back at Figure 2-4 to see the draw tools. We look at them in detail in Chapters 10 and 11.

Paint tools

The paint tools are available only when you use the paint environment. If you're an artist, you'll become very familiar with them. If you're a business user, you may never even see them enabled. In Chapters 9, 10, and 12, we talk more about them.

Accents window

The Accents floating window contains five panels: colors, patterns, wallpaper (these used to be called textures), gradients, and lines. These let you customize graphics, lines, and text by using different colors, patterns, fills, and styles. You can see the different panels in Figure 2-5.

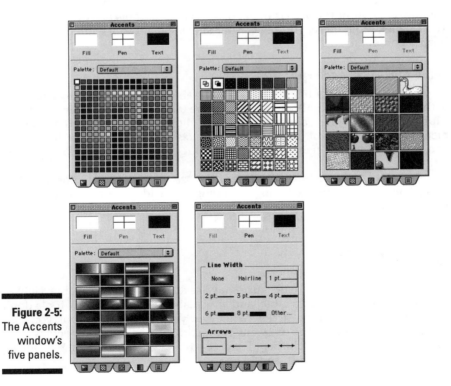

Figure 2-5:
The Accents window's five panels.

Menu Tricks

The menus in AppleWorks work pretty much like they do in any other program. They just do tricks from time to time, changing to suit what you're working on. We want to make sure you're comfortable with this.

Magical morphing menus

Probably the most confusing thing for new AppleWorks users is that the menu bar changes when you change environments. Which menus appear in the menu bar depends on what you're doing. Because of this, you may find yourself thinking, "Hey, just a minute ago, I had Font, Size, and Style menus, and now they're gone!" In that case, you've changed from the word-processing environment to one of the others. Font options are still available, but they aren't a priority, so they become submenus under the Format menu.

We promise that you'll get used to these ever-changing menus. They're a good thing and really cool after you're used to them. For more information on the specific menu options in each environment, skip to the chapters that describe each AppleWorks environment.

Your mouse pointer is the key to knowing in which environment you're working. If it's a drawing tool or an arrow, you're in drawing mode. If it's an I-beam, you're in word-processing mode. It it's a fat plus sign, you're in spreadsheet mode. If it's a piece of graph paper, you're in table-editing mode. If you see a pencil or other paint tool, you're in painting mode in the painting environment.

Menu constants

No matter which environment you work in, five menus are always in the menu bar: the File, Edit, and Window menus plus an AppleScripts menu and the Help menu. We don't want to go off on long, boring descriptions of what every command under every menu does — and you probably don't want us to. Instead, we just do a quick overview of the sorts of things you can expect to find in these menus. The rest of the book explains how to use the commands in the menus, presented in the context of trying to get something done rather than in the abstract.

The File menu

This menu's commands don't put all your papers in the filing cabinet for you, but they do help you handle your AppleWorks documents. The File menu is where you work with your document in a very general way — opening it, closing it, saving changes, printing it, or exiting (quitting) AppleWorks. In case you mess up, the File menu also has the Revert command, which puts your document back to how it was the last time you saved it. The File menu also has commands for inserting other documents into yours and merging database information into your document. Because the Starting Points window is for opening and creating documents, the command to display it is also in the File menu. Don't worry if you're not familiar with some of these things; we cover each as it is called for throughout the book.

The Edit menu

The Edit menu contains everything you need to edit your documents. You may not think this is a big deal, but some applications scatter edit-type commands like spell-checking all over the place in arcane menus so that you never know where to find them.

The queen of the Edit menu is the Undo command. This miracle command can undo the very last thing you did in AppleWorks. If you accidentally click somewhere and screw up your document, use Undo to fix it. There's a catch, though. It only undoes the very last action you took, so if it took you ten steps to muck up your document, you still have to deal with the first nine on your own (unless you can use File⇨Revert).

In addition to the standards such as Cut, Copy, and Paste, the Edit menu is home to the spell checker and replacement feature. Look for them in the Writing Tools submenu.

The Window menu

We prefer a view of the Matterhorn. Alas, this menu doesn't let you choose what you see out of your room's window, but it does help you work with AppleWorks windows. It lets you arrange windows on-screen, bring open documents to the front, and show or hide the tools, accents, button bar, and ruler. The Window menu is also where you access the presentation tools to display your document as an on-screen slide show or presentation. Read more about Presentations in Chapter 14.

The AppleScript menu

Apple provides you with a very powerful tool called AppleScript for use with those applications which respond to AppleEvents. AppleWorks 6 is one of those responsive programs and, in this release, you get access to AppleScripts stored in the Scripts folder inside your AppleWorks Essentials subfolder of the

AppleWorks folder. Apple has even gotten you started with some sample scripts to perform common tasks. AppleEvents are the messages that one program can send to another program or itself, and AppleScript is the language that Apple created so that people like you could customize your software and systems. You can find out more about AppleScript in general at `http://www.apple.com/applescript` and about using AppleScript with AppleWorks 6 at `http://www.tandb.com/appleworks`.

The Help menu

Apple provides both Balloon Help and HTML help for AppleWorks 6. You can read all about your help choices in the next chapter.

Page Setup

Page Setup not only tells the computer how to print your document, it also sets up your page. If you like the page's orientation when you open your new document, never mind. Otherwise, use this command.

In Page Setup lingo, *portrait* is vertical (tall) and *landscape* is horizontal (wide). Most of the time, you'll want portrait. For a spreadsheet with many columns or a draw document with a wide picture, choose landscape. Presentations (slides) are also often displayed in landscape orientation.

From here, you also choose paper size and paper source, as well as whether to enlarge or reduce your image. Any time that you change printers, come back here, make sure it all looks right, and then click OK. This tells AppleWorks about your new printer.

Saving Your Work

We're putting Save immediately after Page Setup for a reason: As soon as you begin your document and enter something worth keeping, save it! Simply choose File⇨Save (⌘-S). This command opens the Save dialog box shown in Figure 2-6. Type a name for your document, but don't be so quick to click Save! First take a good look at where you're saving to. In this case, we're saving to the Letters folder, wherever that is.

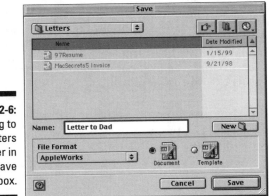

Figure 2-6:
Saving to
the Letters
folder in
the Save
dialog box.

The keyboard shortcut for Save is ⌘-S. Make this a reflex! You hear tons of advice on when to save. We say, whenever you do something you like, save it! Not only will you be grateful in the event of a power outage or a computer freeze, but when you totally muck up your document, you can simply use File⇨Revert to revert to your last saved version. AppleWorks 6 will let you set an AutoSave interval and will save working copies to its AutoSave folder at those times, but the AutoSave doesn't affect your main document — only you do that when you choose Save.

Where to save?

When you save your work, a dialog box enables you to specify where you want to save your document. Paying attention to where the document gets saved is *really* important. The first time you save a particular document and whenever you choose the Save As command, the Save dialog box appears. Never mind where AppleWorks wants to save your work. Before you click Save, navigate to where *you* want it to go.

To avoid a nightmare when you reinstall or update any program, *never* store documents in the folder that contains a program. Instead, create a logical filing system that helps you find your work. Create new folders by project to store your documents. You should make sure not to store anything in the System folder. Creating subfolders within the Documents folder may be a good choice.

Save versus Save As

After you save your document initially, use the Save command to include any changes you have made since your last save. The Save dialog box doesn't appear because you're just updating the same document. Use Save As when you want to create a new document to work on and safely put away the version you have so far. Give the new version a different name so it doesn't replace the first version.

For example, perhaps on Monday you create a new document and save it with the name Bob's Doc. You work on that file on Tuesday and Wednesday and save your changes as you go each day. If you save your document using the Save command, come Thursday you have one file named Bob's Doc that includes all the changes you've made so far. But if you save your work once a day using the Save As command and name each document with a version number, you have three files: Bob's Doc1, Bob's Doc2, and Bob's Doc3. In this way, Save As enables you to keep a history of changes you made to a document or use a previously saved document as a starting point for creating a new document without changing the original.

Don't use Save As unless you specifically want to have separate documents. If you create several documents with the same material and same name, especially if you don't pay attention to where you save them, you're bound to have a hard time knowing which one you worked on last.

Saving in other file formats

Another option in the Save dialog box is saving your document in another format. For example, you can save a draw document as a PICT or JPEG document to give to a friend. When you conjure up the Save dialog box, you see a pop-up menu offering several file types. The default is AppleWorks (as shown in Figure 2-6). To choose another file type, just select it from the pop-up menu of choices, name your new document, and then Save as usual. The file types with [QT} reference formats that are saved via calls to QuickTime 4.

Saving as a template

If you find yourself setting up the same document formats over and over or retyping the same information again and again, try saving a document as a template. A document saved as a template always remains intact. Instead of opening that document, AppleWorks actually opens a new, untitled copy — the original is never changed. It's like designing a form for a tear-off pad: Each time you open a template, you tear off a form from the pad to fill out with new information. Some people — and programs — call this document *stationery*. Same thing.

To create a template, set up the elements that should always appear in future documents. Constant elements may include headers and footers, a logo and company information at the top of the first page, return address information, and "boilerplate" text, such as a standard greeting and closing. Set your font and font size as desired. Be sure to position your cursor exactly where you want it to be when the new document opens.

After all common elements are in place, choose File➪Save As to open the Save As dialog box. Type a name for your template in the File Name text box. Then set the document type to Template. Click the radio button next to the icon labeled Template. Then click Save.

If you want your template to appear in the Templates panel of the Starting Points window, save it in the Templates folder inside the Starting Points sub-folder of your AppleWorks 6 folder. AppleWorks saves templates there automatically. Some people prefer to save templates in a separate folder and open the template from that folder whenever they need it. Better yet, place that folder under the menu. You can get the best of all these by saving the template in one place and aliases to it in the other two.

One template that's very powerful is a default document you can create that opens whenever you open a new document of that type. For example, to set up a new drawing document, turn off the Grid and Autogrid. Turn on Page View and Rulers. Set the rules to Text for handy text editing. Then — this is the key — call it AppleWorks DR Options and save it as a template to the Templates folder. Every new draw document comes up with those settings. Don't like them? Change the settings and save the document as a new template or replace the old template. You can have one template (or stationery) for each environment. Just substitute the *DR* with *WP* for the word-processing default, *PT* for the paint document, *SS* for spreadsheet, *DB* for database, or *PR* for presentation.

Printing Documents

Computers are supposed to create a paperless world, but we often need to present our work on paper. To print, you basically just choose File➪Print or use ⌘-P. However, that assumes that your target printer is already selected. In case it isn't already selected as your default printer, read the following sections.

Select your target printer

You can print to any printer that's hooked up to your computer or network. In order to select it, though, it has to be turned on and ready to print.

Choosing a printer on a Mac is pretty simple. If icons for your printers appear on your desktop and your target printer's icon has a black outline, that printer is already selected. If the icon is on your desktop but not selected, click the target printer icon once and select Set Default Printer (⌘-L) in the Printing menu that appears. (If you want one full copy printed, without opening your document, drag the icon for your document onto the desktop printer icon. If you don't have a desktop printer icon, choose ⌘⇨Chooser, and then select the printer and close the Chooser window.)

How many, please?

If you want to print one copy of the entire document, just open the Print dialog box and click Print. To print multiple copies, enter the number in the Copies box. To print just one page, type the same page number in the From and To boxes. For example, for page three, From: 3 To: 3 should be displayed. To print from a certain page through the end of the document, type the starting page in the From box and leave the To box empty. To print up to a certain page number, enter that number in the To box and leave From empty.

In each printer's print dialog box, you also find the option to print only the left or right pages. Examples of when this is handy are when you wish to print on both sides of the paper to create a book or when creating a presentation. See Chapter 14 to get the idea.

Setting Document Passwords

At any point in a document's life, you may decide that you're more comfortable assigning a password so that prying, or curious, eyes won't see what they shouldn't. You can assign a password to any AppleWorks document at any time. You can also change the password as needed — as long as you know the current password.

To add a password, choose File⇨Properties. Click the Set Password button. A dialog box comes up, asking you to enter the password to use. Type it in and click OK. The same dialog box comes up again. AppleWorks isn't being dense — just careful. Enter your password a second time to ensure that you typed it correctly.

The next time anyone tries to open that document, AppleWorks requires the password.

If you want to change your password, follow these steps:

1. **Choose File⇨Properties and click the Set Password button.**
2. **Enter your current password in the first dialog box, and then click OK.**
3. **Enter your new password in the second dialog box, and then click OK.**

   Each dialog box looks exactly the same, which may be confusing.

4. **Enter your new password again in the third dialog box, and then click OK.**
5. **Click OK to leave the Document Summary dialog box.**

Closing a Document

When you're done working with a document, do a final save and then click the close box at the top-left of the title bar or use ⌘-W or choose File⇨Close.

Closing AppleWorks

When you're ready to call it a day and put AppleWorks to bed, just choose File⇨Quit or ⌘-Q. That's it. AppleWorks asks if you want to save changes to any open documents before closing the application.

Chapter 3

Help: It's Not Just a Beatles Movie Anymore

1sn't there a saying about help coming in all shapes and sizes? If not, there should be. As you use AppleWorks, you'll undoubtedly have questions. You can find answers several ways:

- Read this book. (We like that, and we wanna help.)
- Check the AppleWorks Help menu.
- Use Apple Online Help on the Web, available through the AppleWorks Web site: http://www.apple.com/appleworks.
- Find independent sources of help on the Web — things like users groups and e-mail lists.

All these types of help are great for showing you how to do things yourself, but sometimes, you may enjoy having someone do the dirty work for you. That's where AppleWorks templates, Assistants, and Help Menu Assistants step in.

Because we care so much about you, we use this chapter to point you in the right direction so you can find the type of help you need. Accept our help — you may just avoid having to explain ink splotches to a fancy-schmancy doctor who charges $100 an hour.

Helping You Use AppleWorks

Whether you want to explore the AppleWorks Help menu, access Apple technical support on the Web, or trade tips with other AppleWorks users on a users group or e-mail list, this section helps you help yourself.

Using the AppleWorks Help menu

The Help menu is located at the right end of the AppleWorks menu bar and hosts more than the help you usually expect in a manual. The Help menu also provides an overall introduction to AppleWorks and to AppleWorks Assistants.

AppleWorks Help runs separately from the other AppleWorks applications on your machine, and you can't use it until you select the Help command. If you plan to seek help often, you should keep it running. If you're running MacOS 8.5 or later, this application is the Apple Help Viewer. If you're running an earlier version of MacOS, Help appears in your default Web browser. So if you are running an older system and you want to use the available help, you're going to need a Web browser (unless you're really adept at reading HTML).

The Help menu offers you several options, some of which are shown in Figure 3-1.

Here's what they do:

- **About Balloon Help:** Believe it or not, this is a Help file about getting help. Honest. If we don't make everything clear enough, check this out.

- **Show Balloons:** Balloons? Yep. One of the Mac programmers must've had a fondness for comic books. With Balloon Help on, you point to an item on-screen and a cartoon-style text balloon appears with a brief explanation of what that item is or does. Select Help⇨Show Balloon to turn on the balloons. The menu then toggles to Hide. Help⇨Hide Balloons turns them off.

- **AppleWorks Help:** This option offers a compendium of Help topics and pages, tied together via on-screen links, a Table of Contents, an Index, a Search function (if you're using MacOS 8.5 or later), and lists of related topics at the end of each topic. This topic is also accessible via ⌘-? or by using the Help key on your keyboard.

Figure 3-1:
Balloons
and
AppleWorks
Help.

Help
About Balloon Help...
Show Balloons
AppleWorks Help   ⌘?

You can always access help by clicking the question mark icon from within any dialog box sporting one (and almost all do) to get help that is specific to that dialog box's topic.

Accessing the AppleWorks Newsletter on the Web

For the most up-to-the-minute help, you can also access Apple's AppleWorks Newsletter on the Web via a button on the Starting Points Web panel. This button connects you to the Web (if you have an Internet connection available) and takes you directly to the AppleWorks Newsletter for tips and late-breaking news. From there, you have access to any updated information, some updated downloads, and responses to timely questions.

Finding independent sources of help on the Internet

The folks at Apple can be very helpful, but sometimes you want a little help from your friends. The following two Internet communities will make you feel right at home.

AppleWorks Users Group

The AppleWorks Users Group, or A*WUG, brings together more than 15,000 AppleWorks users from 52 countries. For a $39 annual membership fee, you get ten issues of the 24-page *AppleWorks Journal*, full of tips and techniques; free telephone support from volunteer consultants; and access to the Members Helping Members online database. You can also download AppleWorks templates, graphics, fonts, and utility programs. You can learn all about A*WUG at its Web site (http://www.awug.org) or by sending an e-mail to orders@awug.org or calling (734) 454-1969.

TIP

Using help tips that suit all your personalities

No matter what kind of help you need, there's a tip for finding help that suits you. Check out these tips for using the Help system and make your own diagnosis:

✔ Hearing voices? Use the Search commands! Search for the specific word or phrase in your head and the Help system reveals all the information you need.

✔ Use your Web browser, starting at the TOC. htm file, to be able to set bookmarks/favorites. You'll find the AppleWorks Help files in System Folder: Help:AppleWorks.

✔ Paranoid? Keep a paper trail! Choose File⇨ Print and you can print and save all the snippets of important information you receive. Read it to yourself, and *they* won't hear anything through the bug planted in your ear.

ClarisWorks list-serv

Before it was christened with its new name, AppleWorks was called ClarisWorks. The software's name may have changed, but folks are still faithful to the program and willing to help fellow AppleWorks users. If you have an e-mail account, you can join some of the faithful on this free ClarisWorks *list-serv*, a moderated e-mail list. After you subscribe, e-mail messages from other list members come to you. You can simply read and learn from them, or, if you know an answer or want to ask a question, you can post a message to the list. To learn more about the list or to subscribe to it, visit the Web site at `http://listserv.temple.edu/archives/claris-works.html`.

Doing It for You

AppleWorks Help is great for showing you how things work and how to accomplish tasks yourself. But sometimes doing something yourself is just plain silly — especially when it has already been done for you. And with templates, it *has* been done for you.

Using AppleWorks templates

AppleWorks *templates* are prepared documents. When you open a template, you actually open an automatically generated copy, so the original remains intact. You can save or discard the copy you create without worrying about changing the original. The templates that come with AppleWorks include business aids, business letters, event aids, address lists, and presentations. You can use templates right away by filling in your own information or customizing the template to suit your needs.

To select a template, follow these steps:

1. **Choose File⇨Show Starting Points.**

   The Starting Points window opens.

2. **Click the Templates tab.**

   You see the panel shown in Figure 3-2.

3. **Click your template choice once.**

   Your new document opens, ready for you to work with it. Directions are incorporated into each document.

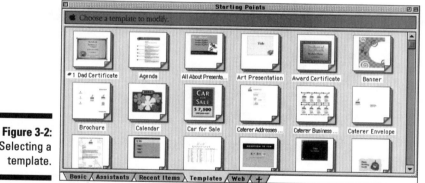

Figure 3-2: Selecting a template.

Using AppleWorks Assistants

You access the Assistants from the Starting Points window (refer to Figure 3-2) to create brand new documents for you.

These AppleWorks Assistants are like "smart templates." As you use an Assistant, you create a new document by providing information about how you want the document to look and what you want it to say. The Assistant, after asking one or more "pages" of questions, creates a new custom template tailored to your needs. Assistants are available for creating several types of documents. You select an Assistant on the Assistants panel of the Starting Points window. Click the Create button when you're ready to see your new document.

Part II
Working with Text: The Keys to Success

The 5th Wave — By Rich Tennant

"OK, TECHNICALLY, THIS SHOULD WORK. JUDY, TYPE THE WORD 'GOODYEAR' IN ALL CAPS, BOLDFACE, AT 700-POINT TYPE SIZE."

In this part . . .

Whether you're new to word processing or have been doing it for a while, there's stuff for you to discover here. AppleWorks is a powerful word processor. This part shows you not only the basics of working with text, but also how to do some fun stuff.

Would you like some graphics to jazz up your pages? How about free-rotated graphics — and free-rotated text! Need to add a table or chart to your document? No problem. How about an outline? It's all easy in AppleWorks — and it's all right here in this part.

Chapter 4

Using the Word Processor: It's Not Your Father's Smith-Corona

The word-processing environment is probably the most used of all the AppleWorks environments. In this chapter, we cover the basic word-processor functions — the baby steps of text entry on a computer. If you're accustomed to a typewriter, you have to start over and unlearn some habits that don't translate very well to the computer world. If you never learned to type, this chapter helps you figure out how to put words where you want them on the screen. After all, you have to crawl before you can walk!

Knowing When to Use Word-Processing Documents

When should you use a word-processing document instead of another kind of document? As a rule of thumb, choose word processing when the bulk of your document is text — for example, a letter or report. Sometimes your master environment is obvious; at other times, you can go with one of two or more environments. A case in point would be a newsletter, which is an obvious candidate for the word-processing environment but is much more flexible within the drawing environment.

When you sit down to write to Mom or create the great American novel, go for a new word-processing document. And when you're not totally sure, go for word processing. Copying the text and pasting it into any other document later on is a cinch.

Entering Text

Before you can process words, you have to get the words into your computer. So that's the natural place to start. The following sections tell you the very least that you need to know if you're new to the world of word processing.

The insertion point

When you begin a new word-processing document, AppleWorks presents you with a page containing only a thin blinking line. Your creation is waiting to happen. To put your pen to paper (metaphorically speaking), simply begin typing.

The blinking line lets you know where your text will appear. You may hear this called the *insertion point*. We prefer its friendlier name — *the cursor*.

Every time you type a character, you push the cursor farther toward the end of the document. Whatever you type appears to the left of the cursor.

The keyboard

Unless you have a fancy speech-to-text dictation program, you use a keyboard to enter text into your computer. You don't need to know how to type to use a computer, but knowing how to type makes things a lot easier. If your typing skills are nil, treat yourself to a typing instruction program.

For the most part, all keyboards are the same. Macs, however, use the ⌘ (Command) and Option keys. The key you press to go to a new line or paragraph is called Return. Because its function is to create a new line, like the Return key on a typewriter, we use Return. When entering data, another key comes into play: the Enter key on the number pad. Luckily, this is marked Enter for everyone. (On some laptops, this is squeezed next to the spacebar.) We call that the Enter key. Just get to know the keyboard you use most, and you'll be fine.

Text wrap

No, text wrap isn't a new, more intellectual form of rap music. Text wrap is what happens when you reach the end of a line when entering text. If you learned to type on a manual Underwood, you may remember smacking the carriage return when your line approached the right side of the paper, and you knew this because the typewriter had a bell that dinged at you when you got close to the right margin. In more modern times, you may have used an electric typewriter with a Return key. You spent entire days of typing class hitting Return at the end of a line. Now you get to unlearn that. In a word-processing document, the computer magically transports any word that doesn't fit to the next line. Pressing Return at the end of every line is not only unnecessary, it's bad and can cause you problems later.

Don't press the Return key at the end of a line. The only appropriate time to press Return is when you want to end one paragraph and begin a new one. In word processing, returns are for ending paragraphs, not lines. Don't press the spacebar twice at the end of a sentence, either. Just press it once. AppleWorks knows how much space to put at the end of a sentence. With very rare exceptions, typewriters made all characters take up the same amount of space. Only a few of the fonts that you'll use behave in this way.

Navigating the Seas of Text

The best thing about using a computer rather than a typewriter or paper is that you can get all your thoughts out while they're hot in your head. Then, after you let them all flow out, you can go back, organize, edit, and rethink to your heart's content. This is the true power of word processing. So get ready for a brave new world. Break those habits. And have fun!

Mouse tales

Before the mouse was invented, the only way to move around in your document was to use the arrow or page scroll keys, pressing and pressing until you finally got where you needed to be. The mouse makes jumping anywhere in the document at anytime easy. Using a mouse takes a bit of getting used to, but hang in there. In a short time, you'll be hooked.

Have you done a bit of mousing on-screen? Start a word-processing document and notice that when you move the pointer into the text area of the document, the pointer changes to what's known as the *I-beam* pointer, shown in Figure 4-1. We call this cursor the I-beam because it looks like a cross section of a steel I-beam used in construction.

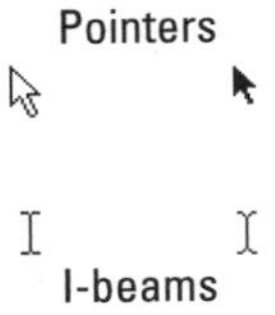

Figure 4-1:
The Pointer
and I-beam
cursors.

Pointers

I-beams

The I-beam is a type of pointer that places the cursor at a different location on the screen. To move the cursor, move the I-beam to where you want the cursor to be, and then click the mouse button to place the cursor. For maximum speed, use the up and down scroll bar to move between pages, and then click the I-beam to place the cursor on that page.

The I-beam is a guideline, not the actual cursor. You have to click to place the cursor in your document. If you just position the I-beam and start typing, your text appears where the cursor really is, which is not necessarily where your I-beam is! Remember: Click to place the cursor.

Keyboard kicks

If you feel more efficient keeping your fingers on the keyboard, you can use the keyboard shortcuts instead of mousing. You can move the cursor with the keyboard using the four arrow keys. You can also use the modifier keys to affect how the arrow keys work. (See Table 4-1 for a list of modifications.)

Table 4-1	Moving the Cursor with the Keyboard
To Do This	*Press This*
Move right one character	→
Move left one character	←
Move up one line	↑
Move down one line	↓
Move right one word	Option-→
Move left one word	Option-←
Move to beginning of paragraph	Option-↑
Move to end of paragraph	Option-↓

To Do This	Press This
Move to end of line	⌘-→
Move to beginning of line	⌘-←
Move to beginning	⌘-↑
Move to end of document	⌘-↓
Move down one screen*	Page Down
Move up one screen*	Page Up

*This is not recommended because the cursor doesn't move; only your view of the page does.

You must be careful when using the Home, End, Page Up, and Page Down keys on the Mac's extended keyboard. These keys do not move the cursor — only your view. The Home key takes you to the beginning of your document, and the End key takes you to the end of it. If you press the End key and start typing, however, your text isn't added to the end of your document. Whatever you type is inserted where you left the cursor — which may not be where you want to insert the text. If you use these keys, remember to place the cursor before you start typing.

Selecting, Deleting, and Replacing Text

Selecting, deleting, and replacing text are very important to the editing process. So are chocolate, highlighters, and cola. We can help you with selecting, deleting, and replacing, but for the others . . . our publisher said no food was allowed in the bookstores.

Selecting text

Did your mom tell you that it pays to be selective? And then later that you're too selective? Well, this is one of those cases where it does pay to be selective. You can't change anything until you tell the computer what you want to change. In other words, if you want to make a change to your text, select it.

After you're used to positioning your cursor, you're halfway to selecting text. You can use the mouse or the keyboard, depending on your preference. When you select something, the background of the selection changes color to let you know what you have selected. This change of color is called *highlighting*.

Mouse selection

Here, now, for your computing pleasure, are some mighty mousing selection techniques:

- **Clicking:** One way to select things with the mouse is to click something — a lot:
  - *To select a word:* Double-click the word.
  - *To select a line:* Triple-click anywhere in the line.
  - *To select a paragraph:* Quadruple-click anywhere in the paragraph.

- **Dragging:** The most common way to select a chunk of text is to drag over it. To do this, position the I-beam cursor at one end of the chunk, click to position the cursor, and then, holding the mouse button down, move (or *drag*) the I-beam to the end of the text that you want to highlight. When the text is selected exactly to your liking, release the button. Don't release the mouse button until it's right. Until you release the button, you can always change it. Remember to begin at one end or the other. You can't begin in the center and go in two directions at once.

A faster way to select a long chunk of text is to position the I-beam at one end of what you want to select. Release the mouse button and move the I-beam to the other end of your desired selection, press the Shift key, and then click where you want the selection to end. All text between the two clicks is highlighted. You can make the first click and then scroll anywhere before positioning that last click. It's way faster than dragging over a bunch of pages to select all that text. It even works from character to character, not just in whole word or in whole line chunks. Pretty slick click trick, eh?

Keyboard selection riffs

The Shift key is a secret tool that can help you make a selection with the keyboard. Uh-oh, we feel a table coming on. Table 4-2 lists nifty key selections. You can also use the mouse and keyboard in combination to really gang up on your text. For instance, if you drag over a block of text and find that you forgot a word or picked up an extra space at the end, you can add or subtract from your selection with the keyboard combinations.

Table 4-2	Selecting Stuff with the Keyboard
To Select	*Press This*
Right, one letter at a time	Shift-→
Left, one letter at a time	Shift-←
Up, one line at a time	Shift-↑

To Select	Press This
Down, one line at a time	Shift-↓
Right, one word at a time	Shift-Option-→
Left, one word at a time	Shift-Option-←
From cursor to beginning of paragraph	Shift-Option-↑
From cursor to end of paragraph	Shift-Option-↓
From cursor to end of line	Shift-⌘-→
From cursor to beginning of line	Shift-⌘-←
From cursor to beginning of document	Shift-⌘-↑
From cursor to end of document	Shift-⌘-↓
Every bit of text in your document	⌘-A or Edit⇨Select All

Deleting text

To completely erase your text, use the Delete key, located in the upper-right corner of the letter keys. On some keyboards, it is labeled Backspace and has an arrow pointing backwards. Don't be fooled by the word Backspace. It doesn't simply move your cursor back. It removes all the text it backs over.

Your Mac has a Delete key, but many also have a key that has an X over a right-pointing arrow (and sometimes says del). Most people call this the *forward delete key.*

For greater efficiency, select the block you want to remove and then press Delete. The entire selection is removed from your document with one press of a button. Carried to the extreme, you can select all your text and clean out your entire document at once!

It's easy to select text, scroll to another part of the document, see something you want to delete, and press Delete without repositioning the cursor. This wipes out the block of text you previously selected, even though you don't see it on-screen. At least you'll have a clue, though — the section containing the cursor jumps into view — momentarily. Needless to say, that's a bad thing. Always make sure that you know where your cursor is before you delete. But, if you do accidentally delete something, use the Undo command *right away* to get it back. Click the Undo button on the default button bar or choose Edit⇨Undo; we talk more about it in the next section.

Replacing text

Replacing is way cooler and faster than deleting. It's sort of an auto-delete. To replace a block of text with something new, don't waste a key action deleting the selected text. Just select the text you want to delete and start typing your new stuff. That's it. The selected text disappears and whatever you type appears in its place. You can do this with one character or an entire page.

Undoing, Cutting, Copying, and Pasting

These commands live happily together in the Edit menu, ready to help you shuffle your text around.

Undo

If you happen to delete the wrong text, fear not! Don't press anything for a moment. Take a few deep breaths. Then click Undo on the default button bar or choose Edit⇨Undo. Your text returns as if nothing happened.

As its name implies, Undo undoes the last action you did. Don't get too comfortable, though. *Last* is the operative word. You get only one shot with Undo — right after you make a mistake. If you accidentally delete the wrong chunk of text, you can undo it right away. But, if you delete that text, type a few lines, and then realize you want the deleted text back, you're out of luck.

There are some things that not even the magic Undo can help you with, though. For example, you can't undo an action after you use the save command or close your document, and you can't unsave a document. When you can't undo your last action, Undo is grayed out in the menu.

Cut

If you took out your trusty scissors and cut out a word from a printed document, it would be gone and you'd have the word waiting to be pasted elsewhere. That's the way Cut works on-screen, too — except that you don't need the scissors, which is good because they'd just scratch the screen anyway.

As with the Delete key, you first have to select what you want to cut. But that's where the similarity ends. When you delete, the text is removed from your document. Unlike deleted text, cut text gets moved to a safe haven — the Clipboard.

To cut, choose Edit⇨Cut or use ⌘-X. The text you selected disappears.

Copy

Copy leaves your selected text where it is but makes a copy of it to paste into another location. Copy makes it easy to duplicate frequently used or difficult-to-type text. If only it worked with $20 bills!

To copy text, select it and choose Edit⇨Copy or use ⌘-C. It doesn't look as if anything happens, but a copy of the selected text goes to the Clipboard to await a Paste command. (See the sidebar "The Clipboard" for more information about the Clipboard.)

Paste

Paste takes whatever is on your Clipboard and places it into your document. Usually, you want to paste something in a different location from where you picked it up. After cutting or copying the desired text, just position the cursor where you want the text to appear and choose Edit⇨Paste. That's ⌘-V.

You can also replace text using the Paste command. First, select the text you want to replace, and then choose Paste. Your selected text disappears and is replaced by whatever you previously cut or copied.

There's one more command, called Clear. Like Cut, it removes your text. But unlike Cut, it doesn't place it on the Clipboard. The text is just gone . . . forever. Why use Clear? You use it only when you want to delete text but leave the contents of the Clipboard intact. Basically, it's just like using the Delete key. It isn't used very often.

The Clipboard

When you cut something, whether it's text or graphics, it doesn't disappear into nothingness as when you delete. Instead, it's transferred to an invisible storage container called the *Clipboard.* The Clipboard enables you to move and copy by combining the Cut or Copy command with the Paste command. By first cutting text out of your document and placing it on the Clipboard, you can paste the text back into a different spot. Or you can copy something and then paste it into several locations — not just one — to save typing or graphic creation. You can only have one thing on the Clipboard at a time, so whatever you've cut or copied to the Clipboard stays there until you replace it by cutting or copying something else. The really cool thing is that the contents of the Clipboard carry over to most other applications, so you can copy and paste between documents running in two different programs!

This Cut, Copy, Paste, and Undo stuff is pretty universal. After you master these commands, you can use them with almost any word-processing application.

You can drag and drop text (or graphics) between most documents and even between programs. Open two files. Select what you want to move in one document and drag it over to the other document. You can even drag from one place in a document to another place in the same document. This bypasses the Clipboard. Remember this when you want to copy a second object but leave the contents of the Clipboard untouched for further pasting.

Staying Out of Word-Processor Hell (Spaces, Tabs, and Returns)

If you aren't into reading about formatting, we want at least to impress these major rules on you. These rules should be etched onto the front of every computer monitor.

Don't get spacey

Never, ever, use the spacebar to align columns of text. Using the spacebar to align text is one of the most common mistakes people make when they start using a word processor (almost as common as pressing the Return key at the end of a line). Although this works on a typewriter, it fails on a computer. On the typewriter, the spacebar moves the carriage a set space. A computer has no need for physical carriage movement. Most computer fonts (typefaces) use variable-width letters. For example, an *i* is narrower than a *w*. Therefore, no matter how many spaces you add in front of a column of text to line it up with the text above or below it, unless the text in both lines is identical, you can't make the text line up. It may look right on-screen, due to the limitations of the screen, but on a printer, the funkiness shows up.

Monospaced fonts like Courier and Monaco are exceptions to this rule. Although you still shouldn't rely on spaces for alignment, these fonts mimic the typewriter so that an *i* takes up the same space as a *w*.

The rule of tabs

Tabs solve the problem of how to align text. A tab is always measured by how far it is from the margin. Tabs are exact measurements and therefore always line up, both on-screen and in print. That brings us to another common mistake: pressing Tab several times in a row to indent text. The correct rule is one tab per indent or jump on a line. We go into more detail on this in Chapter 5.

The rule of returns

No, we're not talking about taking your computer back to the store when you get frustrated — although that option may be tempting at times. Earlier in the chapter, we say not to press the Return key at the end of a line. That's what *text wrap* is for. The only time to press the Return key is at the end of a paragraph. Think of the Return key as the "new paragraph key." Use it to create a new paragraph, and for that reason only.

Keyboard shortcuts

Have you noticed that some of the menu commands have symbol and letter combinations to their right? These are called *keyboard shortcuts* — another way to choose a command. Keyboard shortcuts are quicker to use than choosing a command from a menu. We explain the shortcuts for Undo, Cut, Copy, and Paste in this sidebar, but AppleWorks has plenty more.

You don't have to memorize these shortcuts. They're listed in the menu every time you select a command. You can pick them up one at a time at your own pace.

Sometimes the shortcut key is the first letter of the command and sometimes it isn't. Basically, sometimes logical keys were available and sometimes they were already taken. Use these mnemonics to help you:

- ✔ **Z for Undo:** Zee what you did! Undo that right now! Also remember that Z is the last letter of the alphabet and Undo undoes the last thing you did.

- ✔ **X for Cut:** Think of it like x-ing out something, or the visual of an open pair of scissors.

- ✔ **C for Copy:** C is the first letter of the command — easy and logical!

- ✔ **V for Paste:** Well, you've got us on this one. Suffice it to say that this one is right next to all the rest.

Chapter 5

Fun with Text Formatting

The combination of a good computer and good word-processing software makes it easy to format your text to look sharp. A variety of fonts, the use of boldface and italics, and all the other ways you can format text give you quite a bit of creative power. Do be careful, though; with so many formatting options, you may find yourself producing documents that look more like ransom notes. This chapter shows you how to format your text. We leave it to you to find your own level of grace and style.

To set your document's paper size and orientation, choose File⇨Page Setup. This controls whether the document prints in the tall direction (portrait) or the wide direction (landscape) on the paper. (We cover the Print/Page Setup dialog box in Chapter 2.)

Text Preferences

Preferences are more important here than in any other AppleWorks environment. In other places, they're convenient. Here, they're downright necessary — at least if you ever quote someone or use contractions. In word-processing documents, Preferences are your first line of formatting. They control how your quotation marks look, how the date appears when it's automatically entered, and more. Edit⇨Preferences is the magic door into the Preferences dialog box. If you open it now, you can follow along.

When you open Preferences from the word-processing environment, the Text preferences come up automatically. As shown in Figure 5-1, a pop-up menu enables you to select a category of preference settings to work with. If you're following along, but opened Preferences from another environment or without any document open, just click the Topic pop-up menu to get to the text preferences to see what we're talking about.

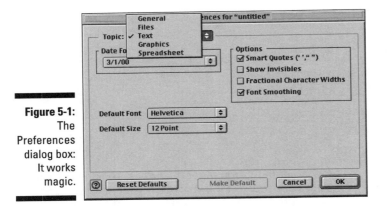

Figure 5-1:
The
Preferences
dialog box:
It works
magic.

And now . . . the grand text preference tour:

- **Date Format:** Determines how you want the date to appear in your document when AppleWorks automatically inserts the current date (see "Page numbers and other placeholders" later in this chapter). You have five choices. To pick one, click the radio button next to it. You can come back to change it anytime.

- **Smart Quotes:** Types printers's curly quotes and apostrophes (" " ' ') instead of the dumb "tick" marks the computer normally types. We recommend that you keep this box checked because curly quotes look much better than inch marks do — unless you really mean to show inch and foot marks (' "), in which case you should uncheck this box temporarily.

- **Show Invisibles:** Displays the invisible formatting characters hiding in your document, which makes it easier for you to see your tabs and other formatting. (We discuss them later in this chapter.) And it's great to notice that you have two spaces between words before you print your page! This option is normally unchecked, but some people (us!) like to see invisible characters all the time.

- **Fractional Character Widths:** Fine-tunes the space between letters, which is good for printing on a laser printer when using Adobe Type Manager (ATM), but bad for seeing your text on-screen because it scrunches it all up (due to the resolution limitations of your monitor). Most people keep this box unchecked.

✔ **Font Smoothing:** Smoothes font display by using anti-aliasing: filling in gaps and jagged areas with lighter-shaded pixels. If you have font smoothing enabled in your Appearance control panel, you will probably want to turn this off.

✔ **Default Font:** Selects the font in which all your text will be typed when you select New Document for word processing or any text — unless you create an entire default document as shown in Chapter 2.

✔ **Default Size:** Sets the size to be used for the default font (above).

Formatting Letters and Words

It's time to give your document some finesse. This task is easy and fun, because you can try anything, see the effect immediately, and keep experimenting until you love what you see.

Bold, italic, and underline

When words are spoken, inflection adds to their meaning and interpretation. Left alone, the printed word is rather unemotional. By adding a bit of texture to your words, you can help your reader see your inflections.

Here are a couple of quick tips on when to use each attribute:

✔ **Bold text stands out.** Bold type demands attention and looks important. In typewriter days, our closest option was typing in all caps. With word processing, that's definitely out now. In fact, with the advent of electronic mail *(e-mail),* caps are considered very rude because they're the equivalent of yelling. For extra emphasis, you can also italicize bold text.

✔ *Italic text emphasizes without being overly obtrusive.* It also replaces all the times you used to underline with a typewriter. Although hard to read on-screen, italic text prints nicely. For extra emphasis, you can also bold italicized text.

✔ Underlining is *out* as a way of emphasizing text. For one thing, underlined text is hard to read when underlines distract you from the words. (That's why highlighters have replaced the ancient method of underlining text to mark it.) Also, the World Wide Web has changed the way we interpret underlines. These days, an underline indicates a hypertext link, which means that clicking the text sends you to another, related place.

You can apply these text attributes as you go (as you enter the actual text) or after the fact (by going back to a word or phrase after you enter it).

Typing your text first and going back to it later offers you the benefit of making sure that your formatting is consistent. It also enables you to get all your thoughts on track, without getting hung up on the look.

You have four ways to choose bold, italic, or underline:

- Choose the attribute you want from the Text menu's Style submenu.
- Press the keyboard shortcut for the menu command.
- Select the attribute from the pop-up Style menu located on the button bar, but you'll have to add it to the button bar first. It looks like an italic capital S with a little arrow indicating that it has a submenu.
- Click the attribute's button.

Here's how to apply formatting attributes:

- **Apply as you go:** Turn on the attribute, type your text, and then turn off the attribute.

  Style commands are controlled in a *toggle* fashion — like a light switch. If the command is off when you choose it, you turn it on. If the command is on, selecting it turns it off.

- **Format later:** Type, type, type. Get all your thoughts out. When you're finished, select the text you want to format and apply an attribute. Jump to the next chunk, select, format, and move on. This is faster because you don't have to turn the attribute on and then off again.

You can mix and match styles to make your word both bold and italic, or bold, italic, and underlined if you really want to induce eyestrain. Just activate one style after the other. If you check the Style menu, you can see that the styles currently in use have check marks next to them.

Choose Text⇨Style⇨Plain Text (⌘-T) to turn off all special styles at once. ⌘-B, ⌘-I, and ⌘-U toggle **bold**, *italic*, and underlining respectively.

Text size

Sometimes you want to write LARGE. Sometimes you want to write very small. (You never know when you'll need to create legal contract fine print. Just don't ask us to sign anything.) The most commonly used size for text is 12 point, or sometimes 10, depending on the font and how much text you need to cram on a page. (Publishers even sneak down to 9 point or less.)

We don't mean *point* as in "What's your point?" Nope, this point is a special measurement used by printers and typesetters. One point equals ½ of an inch — an awkward number, but it goes way, way back to before inches. And inches aren't very logical anyway.

You apply a font size like any other formatting — either as you go or later. Here's how you tell AppleWorks that you want a different font size:

- ✔ **Menu bar:** Choose your size from the Text menu's Size submenu. The menu offers common sizes from 9 to 72 points, as well as Other so that you can type in any size from 4 to 255 points. It also includes a command for smaller and larger, which decreases or increases text size in increments of one point at a time.

- ✔ **Button bar:** Choose the size you want from the Size pop-up menu after you've added it to the button bar. This menu contains the same options as the Size submenu.

- ✔ **Button:** Click the Increase Font Size and the Decrease Font Size buttons. These are the buttons with an up arrow for increasing size and a down arrow for decreasing size. Each time you click one, the font changes one point size.

The little-known keyboard shortcuts for increasing and decreasing font size by one point in either direction are Shift-⌘-> and Shift-⌘-<. Select some text and try them!

Changing fonts

Changing the font is like applying a text attribute, except you use the Text menu's Font submenu or the Font pop-up menu located in the button bar. As with other formatting, you can apply it as you go or after you type your text.

- ✔ To apply as you go, select the font you want to use from the Font menu and start typing.

- ✔ If you want to change the font of text you already typed, select the text, and then choose the font you want from the Font menu.

Nothing could be easier. A word of warning, though: Limit yourself to just a couple of fonts per document. Your document looks more classy that way. Also, the more fonts you use, the longer your document takes to print because the font information must download to the printer. (This only applies to *PostScript* printers. If your printer doesn't use PostScript — the resolution-independent page description language created by Adobe — it doesn't matter how many fonts you use.

Changing font colors

Changing the color of any text is a breeze. As with any other changes, you select the text first. Then simply pick a color from the color panel of the Accents window (with Text selected at the top of the panel). It's the one with the colors on it — easy to recognize. Or, you could add the Text Color button (and its pop-up menu) to the button bar.

Using styles

Style is a commonly misused word. People use it to refer to bolding a word when bold is more accurately defined as an attribute. The ambiguity is compounded by the Style submenu, which is more accurately defined as an Attribute submenu. A *style* is actually a *set* of formatting properties. After you choose the font, size, and attributes, you can group all this information together, create a style to reflect it, and then apply that style to other parts of your text with just one click of the mouse. This action can save you a lot of time because you don't have to apply each attribute to each piece of text over and over again.

The AppleWorks stylesheet window is universal to all the environments. Show Styles is available under the Format menu, where you find five types of styles: Basic, Paragraph, Outline, SS-Table (Spreadsheets) and Table. The first two styles are options for word processing, so we cover them in this chapter. The third style, Outline style, is a function of the word processor. We cover outlines in Chapter 8. Table styles apply to tables, so we tell you about them in Chapter 7.

The Basic style enables you to create a style that includes font, size, text style, and color. (It doesn't include paragraph indents or tab stops. We get to those attributes later in this chapter.) The most efficient way to create a Basic text style is to follow these steps:

1. **Apply formatting to one chunk of text until it's the way you want it. Then select it.**

2. **If the Styles window is not already showing, choose Format⇨Show Styles (Shift-⌘-W) or click the Styles button (after adding it to the button bar), which features a pair of Ss, separated by a blue vertical bar.**

   You should now see the Styles window (see Figure 5-2).

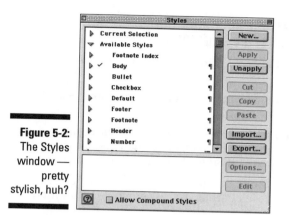

Figure 5-2:
The Styles
window —
pretty
stylish, huh?

3. **Click the New button at the top right of the window.**

   Doing so brings up the New Style dialog box (see Figure 5-3).

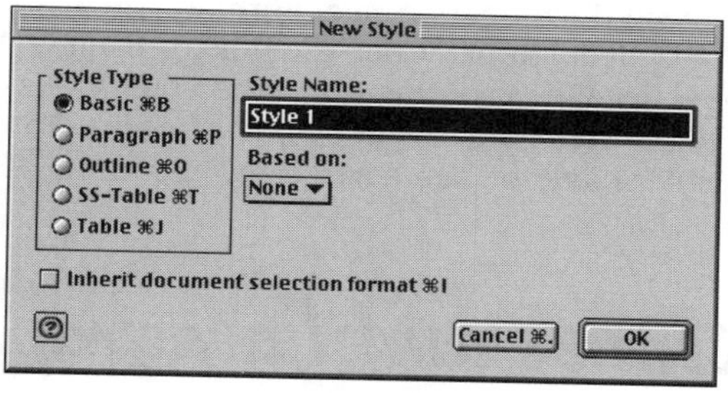

Figure 5-3:
Get your
styles here!

4. **Type a name for your new style.**

   AppleWorks automatically fills in something like Style 1, but you should use a meaningful name, like **The Big Giant Heading.**

5. **Use the following settings in the New Style dialog box:**

   - Click the Basic radio button.

   - Check the Inherit Document Selection Format checkbox.

   - Choose Default in the Based On pop-up menu or choose None. If you choose None, you start from scratch, free and clear. If you base it on default, your new style builds upon the preset style, and any changes you make to the default style affect this new style.

Check out your default style's properties: When you finish with this style, select Default in the list of styles in the stylesheet window and click Edit. Click Done after you've had your peek.

6. **Click OK to create the style.**

   Your new style now appears in the Styles window.

   From now on, to apply that style to your existing text, choose from the following methods:

   - **Styles window method:** Select the text and then click the desired style from the Styles window.

   - **Pop-Up Styles button method:** Make sure to add the Styles button to your button bar, then select the text and then choose the desired style from the pop-up Styles button in the button bar.

   - **Format as You Go method:** Just choose a style before you start typing. Remember to deselect that style when you don't want it anymore.

An alternative to creating a style from formatted text is to create a new style and then select its attributes from the menus. We cover that later in this chapter in the "Paragraph styles" section.

You can copy styles between documents. Select Format➪Show Styles, and then in the Styles window select Export. Click the box for each style that you want to export, and then click OK. Save this export as you do any other document. To import, reverse the steps and begin by using Import. You have the option to replace styles that have the same name.

Formatting Sentences and Paragraphs

After you have some of the formatting basics down, you can move on to formatting lines, sentences, and paragraphs.

You can either format as you go or apply formatting changes to text you have already typed.

Using the text ruler

The text ruler in AppleWorks is an on-screen ruler that shows you where your text appears across the page. The ruler also includes some handy formatting buttons. If you don't see the ruler at the top of your page, choose Format➪ Rulers➪Show Rulers (Shift-⌘-U).

Aligning text

If your text is out of alignment, you feel a lot of vibration when you drive on the freeway. No, wait, that's when your front end is out of alignment. Text alignment has to do with how your text lines up on the page.

You can align text in various ways:

- **On the left:** This method is the standard alignment for Roman text-based languages such as English. It's called *flush left, left-justified,* or *ragged-right.*

- **On the right:** This choice is the standard for some languages, but it's mostly decorative in English. Called *flush right, right-justified,* or *ragged-left,* right alignment may be used for dates and other items in headers and footers. It may also be used to align numbers at times.

- **On both sides:** This way is common in many American books and newspapers. It's called *justified, force-justified, fully justified,* or *right-and-left-justified.* Justified text can look really good or really bad because the text is expanded or contracted to line up on each side of the page. The trick to using justification is to use it only for wide columns (or narrow margins). If your columns are too narrow, the gaps between words create rivers of white space that distract the reader and/or cause the need for too many hyphens.

- **From the center:** This method is used decoratively, in headers and footers, or in headlines. This justification is simply called *centered.*

To align text, place your cursor in the paragraph you want to align, or, if you are aligning several contiguous paragraphs, select at least part of each of those paragraphs and then use one of these methods:

- **The text ruler:** The ruler has buttons that depict each type of alignment. Click the button for the one you want to apply. (If the text ruler isn't visible, select Format➪Rulers➪Show Rulers.)

- **The button bar:** Click the button that depicts the alignment you want to apply.

- **Keyboard shortcut:** Use one of the shortcuts in Table 5-1 to apply an alignment.

The buttons look the same in the ruler and in the button bar. Figure 5-4 shows you what they look like.

Table 5-1	Keyboard Shortcuts for Aligning Text	
To Do This	**Click This Button**	**Keyboard Shortcut**
Align left		⌘-[(left bracket)
Align right		⌘-] (right bracket)
Center		⌘-\ (backslash)
Justify		Shift-⌘-\ (backslash)

Unlike applying an attribute such as bolding, coloring, or changing fonts, you don't have to select the text you are aligning. Why not? Because aligning applies to the entire paragraph in which your cursor is pointing.

Indenting

Denting is what you'd like to do to the side of your computer with a baseball bat when you get frustrated. Indenting is when you shove the first line of a paragraph over a bit so that readers know it's a new paragraph.

Of course, the simplest way to indent the first line of a paragraph is to press the Tab key. The problem is that if you're typing a ten-page report you probably have to press Tab about 40 or 50 times. Then, when you need to change the indent, you have to change it 40 or 50 times! Naturally, AppleWorks has a way to save you from those 40 or 50 keystrokes: Just use the indent markers in the text ruler. Figure 5-4 shows you where the indent markers live.

On the ruler are two arrows, one hanging from the top and one resting on the bottom. The top arrow controls the first line of any paragraph. The bottom arrow affects all subsequent lines within that paragraph. Each time you begin a new paragraph by pressing Return, your cursor jumps to the point of the top arrow, called the first line indent. AppleWorks continues laying text on that line until the cursor gets to the single arrow on the bottom right of the ruler. At that point, it automatically moves the next word to wherever the bottom arrow on the left is positioned. Text is placed between the two bottom arrows until you press Return to begin a new paragraph.

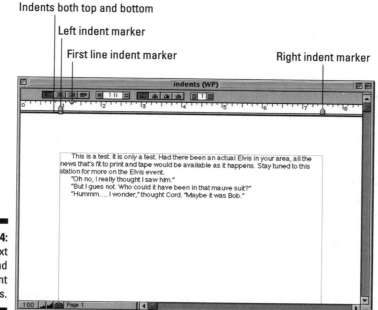

Figure 5-4:
The text
ruler and
the indent
markers.

Position the cursor in the paragraph that you want to indent before you slide the markers. Each paragraph has its own indent setting, so you need to tell AppleWorks which paragraph you want to indent by positioning the cursor in that paragraph. To affect more than one paragraph, select at least a part of each paragraph.

When you click any of the ruler arrows, a dotted line appears up and down your page all the way to the ruler. This guideline helps you align your text. The guideline moves along as you move the arrow.

To indent the first line

To indent the first line, drag the top arrow (the first line indent marker) to the right as far as you want the first line to indent:

- ✔ If you set the first line indent for a new paragraph, just start typing; the first line starts at the indent point.

- ✔ If you set the first line indent in an existing paragraph, the first line moves over when you move the indent marker in the ruler. Maybe some of the following text will move as well, so be aware that your page may break at a different point.

Here's another typewriter habit to break. The half-inch indent we're used to is a holdover from typewriter days. Check out a few professionally printed books and you notice the proper spacing is smaller. It's an *em-space* to be precise — the width of a capital letter *M* in the font you're using. On the AppleWorks text ruler, that's about a notch or two.

To indent the whole paragraph right or left

Notice that the bottom arrow has two parts: the point and a small rectangle that rides along the ruler's bar. Moving that rectangle moves both left arrows together. So, to indent the entire paragraph from the left, move the small rectangle under the bottom arrow along the ruler.

If you click and drag the bottom arrow, you move only the bottom arrow, leaving the first line of the paragraph unaffected. That creates a hanging indent, which we cover very soon.

Moving the right arrow causes all text in a paragraph to wrap at that point, rather than at the document's right margin.

To make a quotation or passage of text stand out — called *blocking text* — indent that text on both sides. Just slide both the right and left bottom arrows toward the center as far as you like.

You can indent every paragraph in your document by choosing Edit➪Select All (⌘-A) before you slide the indent marker.

Tab stops

If you really want to push your text around, use tab stops. Remember typewriters? You slid a doodad across the carriage to where you wanted the Tab key to take you. You then hit the Tab key, and the carriage jumped to the tab stop to begin typing there. Word-processing tabs are similar.

You can have as many tab stops on a line as you want. In fact, although you don't see them, there are default stops every ½-inch. But maybe you already knew that. Have you ever lined up a column 1½ inches inward by pressing tab three times before typing? On each line, you did the same thing: Tab, Tab, Tab, type, Return, Tab, Tab, Tab, type, and so on.

That was the wrong way to align your text. The right way is to only press the Tab key one time for each jump along the ruler, and then to place a custom tab stop along the ruler at the point you want the column of text to begin. With that in mind, look at the possibilities in the following sections.

Formatting text is much easier, especially tabs, when you can see where you place the tabs in your document. To see tabs and other normally invisible characters on-screen, click the Show/Hide Invisibles button. The tab marker is the black arrow. The section called "Invisible men and other characters," later in this chapter, tells you more about viewing invisible characters.

The four types of tab stops

AppleWorks has four — count 'em, four — types of tab stops for you to choose from. Lots of power. Tabs work a lot like text alignment, except the text alignment begins at the tab, not the margin. Figure 5-5 gives you a quick breakdown of the different tab stops.

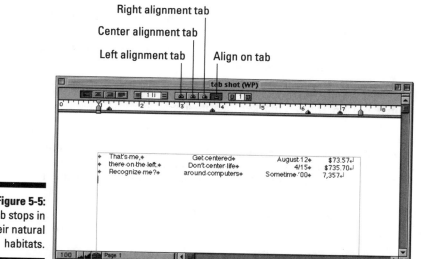

Figure 5-5:
Tab stops in their natural habitats.

Here's what each type of tab stop is good for (with Figure 5-5 to illustrate):

- **Left-aligned:** This alignment is the "regular" tab stop. All text starting at one of these tab stops is aligned flush left.

- **Center-aligned:** Your text is centered at the point of the tab stop. It lets you do a little inline alignment, so that you can center your text off-center. Use this tab when you need to have a few short lines of text centered relative to each other, but not necessarily in the center of the page.

- **Right-aligned:** This alignment pushes text out to the left so that the right edge of the text always lines up with the tab stop.

- **Align on**: This choice is the coolest and most flexible tab stop. By default, it awaits a decimal point and places that decimal point at the tab stop. (If you don't insert a decimal, the tab stop aligns the end of the text on the tab. This tab stop is perfect for invoicing or listing costs.)

If you choose the Align On tab option, double-click the tab to open the Tab dialog box. In the box, you can change the symbol that the tab lines up on. Simply type a character into the field that appears next to the choice. Experiment and be creative.

Setting tab stops using the ruler

Here's the easy way to set tab stops — visually, using the ruler:

1. **Position your cursor in the paragraph you want to affect.**

2. **Click the symbol for the type of tab you want and drag it to the spot on the ruler where you want the tab stop.**

   A guideline appears in order to help you place it perfectly.

   The tab stop snaps onto the bottom of the ruler. That's when you can let go of the mouse button.

3. **After the tab stop marker is in place on the ruler, slide it back and forth to fine-tune your tab stop.**

If you want to remove a tab stop, just drag it off the ruler. When you release the mouse button, the tab marker disappears.

Rather than dragging the tab stop to the ruler, you can just click the spot on the ruler where you want the tab to land. The type of tab that's selected above the ruler is the type that appears when you click. This method is a timesaver when you're placing more than one tab stop of the same type.

Setting tab stops using the Tab dialog box

You can also set tab stops the hard way — with the Tab dialog box:

1. **Position your cursor in the paragraph you want to affect.**

2. **Choose Format⇨Tabs.**

   This brings up the Tab dialog box (see Figure 5-6).

Type the character on which to align here

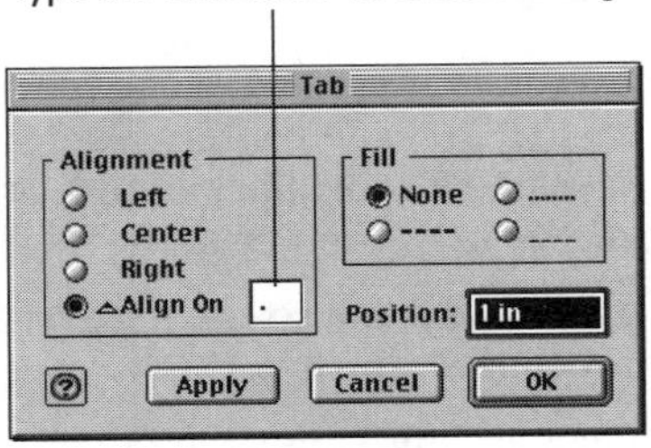

Figure 5-6:
Just put
it on my
tab —
the Tab
dialog box.

Tab
Alignment **Fill**
○ Left ● None ○ ⋯⋯
○ Center ○ ---- ○ ___
○ Right
● ▲ Align On [.] Position: [1 in]
? [Apply] [Cancel] [OK]

3. **Choose a type of tab from the Alignment selections on the left.**

4. **Type in the position where you want the tab to appear.**

   This position corresponds to the numbers on the ruler.

5. **Click the Apply button to place that tab stop.**

6. **To add another tab stop on that line, enter another position and click Apply again.**

7. **Click OK when you finish adding tabs for that line.**

If you want to copy your tab stops into other paragraphs you've already typed, see the section titled "Applying a ruler," later in this chapter.

Filled tabs

One other tab option is Fill. You can choose from three fill characters — dash, dot, and understrike — and the one you choose fills the normally empty space of the tab (with dashes, dots, or understrike characters).

You use a filled tab to set up a table of contents or a theater program. Figure 5-7 shows an example of formatting with filled tabs. Notice the tab stop in the ruler. Here are a few tab tips:

✔ Use the Tab dialog box to fill a tab with any of the four fillers.

✔ Programs usually look best with right-aligned tabs.

✔ Tables of contents look best with left-aligned tabs.

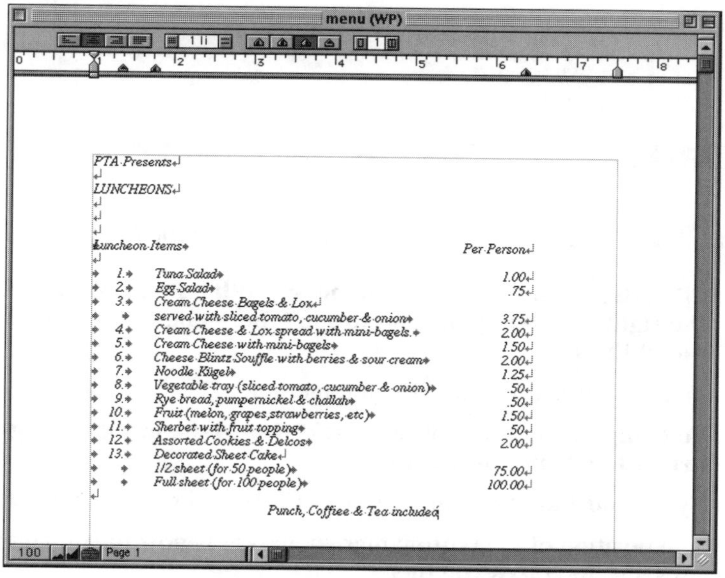

Figure 5-7: Make this mouth-watering menu with tasty, filled tab stops!

To modify a tab stop that's already on the ruler, double-click it. The Tab dialog box appears. Select a new type of tab or select a fill. You can also use the dialog box to reposition the tab stop, but simply sliding the tab stop along the ruler is much easier, although not necessarily as precise.

There are two parts to the formula. Make sure you have both parts in place. Be sure that you have placed the tab mark on the ruler and that you have pressed the Tab button to tell the text to jump into place at the next tab stop.

You can insert several tabs in any line. Simply press the Tab key once for each tab stop you set in the ruler. The first tab symbol (from the Tab key) moves the text to the first tab stop. The second tab symbol moves the text to the next tab stop, and so on.

Hanging indents

A *hanging indent* makes the first line of your paragraph stick out to the left. What's a hanging indent good for? Take a look at the number four in Figure 5-8. You can use a hanging indent to create numbered steps, a bulleted list, several lines set off with check marks, or whatever.

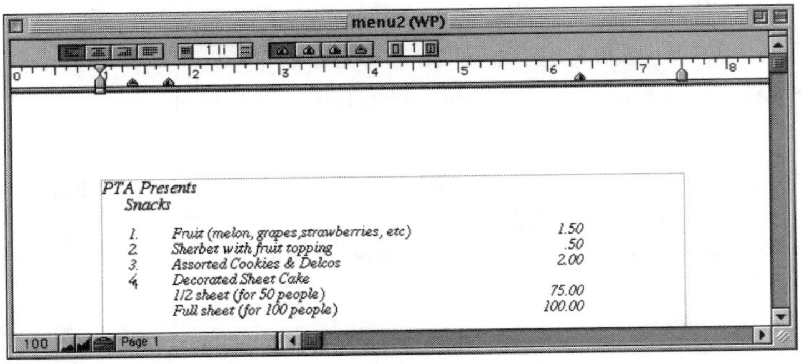

menu2 (WP)

Figure 5-8:
An indent
hanging out
for cake.

PTA Presents
  Snacks
  1.   Fruit (melon, grapes,strawberries, etc)   1.50
  2.   Sherbet with fruit topping   .50
  3.   Assorted Cookies & Delcos   2.00
  4.   Decorated Sheet Cake
       1/2 sheet (for 50 people)   75.00
       Full sheet (for 100 people)   100.00

A hanging indent is easy to create — after you get the *hang* of it. Here's how:

1. **Click the small rectangle that moves both left arrows and drag it to the right to where you want to start the second line and all subsequent lines.**

   You can't bring text past the left margin.

2. **To bring the first line of text back toward the margin, drag the top arrow to where you want it.**

3. **Type your bullet or number, press Tab, and then type your body text.**

   The position of the bottom margin marker is now the default tab stop, so pressing Tab takes you there.

If you're applying this hanging indent to a paragraph you already typed, perform Steps 1 and 2, and then insert the bullet or number and a tab at the beginning of the first line.

For a really sharp list, insert a right-aligned tab stop between the top line arrow and the bottom line arrow. Now type a tab, the number, and another tab. This way, if your list goes into the double digits, you always have the same amount of space between the number and the body of the paragraph. Look back at the ruler in Figure 5-7 to see an example of how this is set up.

Here's a little secret: AppleWorks has a built-in style to do this for you. Select the text to which you want to apply this style and then select Number from the Styles window. The built-in style also auto-numbers your lines as long as you keep the style applied. It doesn't really create a hanging indent. You can also choose a built-in Bullet style.

Invisible men and other characters

Formatting is always easier when you can actually see what you're doing. Instead of leaving formatting characters invisible, let 'em show themselves. Just click the Show/Hide Invisibles button to show them. Click it again to hide them. You can also show the invisible characters with the Preferences dialog box: Select Edit➪Preferences➪General, click the Text pop-up, and then check the box next to Show Invisibles. Figure 5-9 shows you the various formatting characters and what they do.

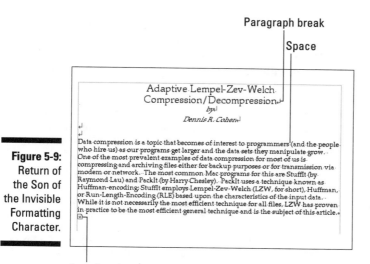

Figure 5-9: Return of the Son of the Invisible Formatting Character.

Line spacing

Line spacing is what happens to actors when they forget their lines on stage. More important, in a text document, it's how much white space you place between lines of text. This is called *leading* in typographical terms because typesetters used to place a blank strip of plain lead between text lines to set them apart. You can create as much line spacing as you like simply by using the ruler. Experiment and you notice that changing the leading can set apart sections, thoughts, and so on. The spacing also affects the feeling of the page — called *color* by typographers.

Figure 5-10 points out the line spacing controls. Notice that the current line spacing is displayed in the box between the text alignment and tabs. The spacing increment is half a line at a time. As you click the Increase Line Spacing button (right), the line spacing goes up from 1 line to 1.5 to 2, and so on. The spacing can also be set to point and other increments by going to Format⇨Paragraph. . . . The box displays the unit of measurement.

Decrease line spacing

Increase line spacing

Figure 5-10: Spacing your lines . . . uh, what was I going to say?

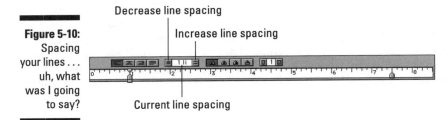

Current line spacing

To change the line spacing, just position the cursor anywhere in the paragraph you want to affect and click the Increase or Decrease button. Your paragraph should expand or contract, depending on which button you click.

To change the unit of measurement to adjust line spacing by points, double-click the box that reports the current spacing. The Paragraph dialog box that we show you in the next section pops up, enabling you to change from lines to points. The dialog box also lets you choose inches, millimeters, centimeters, and picas.

Space between paragraphs

You're probably used to pressing Return an extra time or two to add an extra line or two before or after a paragraph. Although pressing Return works decently in short documents, such as one-page letters, it can become problematic in larger documents. Here's how to space between paragraphs the professional way.

With your cursor in a paragraph you want to affect, choose Format⇨ Paragraph or double-click the box on the ruler that shows the current line spacing. You should see a Paragraph dialog box like the one in Figure 5-11.

Here's an example of how to use the dialog box to add space between paragraphs: Say you have a document currently all single-spaced and want to add an extra line between each paragraph. Just choose Edit⇨Select All, open the Paragraph dialog box, and enter **1** in the box next to Space After, after first making sure that the measurement is by line.

Click Apply to see the effect without leaving the dialog box. Click OK if you like the result. The document is nice and tidy, and all of the paragraphs are now separated by blank lines, and you don't need to press Return twice after each paragraph.

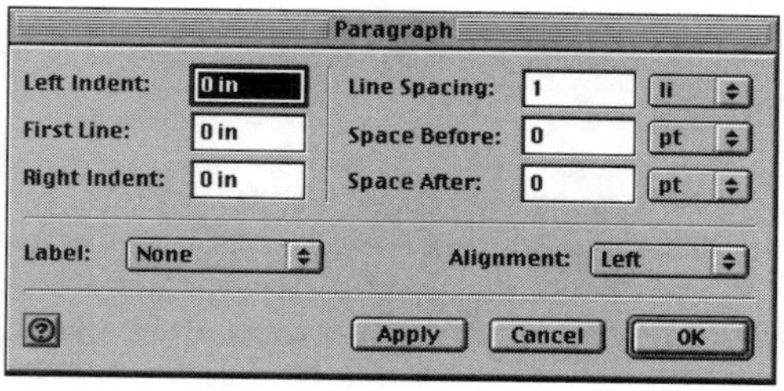

Figure 5-11:
The
Paragraph
dialog box
lets you
change all
kinds of nifty
things.

Paragraph		
Left Indent: `0 in`	Line Spacing: `1`	`li`
First Line: `0 in`	Space Before: `0`	`pt`
Right Indent: `0 in`	Space After: `0`	`pt`
Label: `None`	Alignment: `Left`	
	Apply	Cancel	OK

If you're working on a document that runs long, line spacing can really help you out because you can select all your text again, open the Paragraph dialog box, and decrease the line spacing to make all the text fit on the already full pages. Switch to the points measurement. If your text is in 12-point type, the box now says 12. Type **11** instead, click Apply, and check your result.

Applying a ruler

No, we won't rap your knuckles for positioning text on the page with the spacebar. In AppleWorks, applying a ruler means to copy the ruler settings from one paragraph and paste them into another paragraph. After you set up a paragraph the way you like it, you can copy the tab stops, the indents, the line spacing, and the space between paragraphs — all the settings in the Paragraph dialog box — and paste them into any other paragraph. Here's how:

1. **Start by formatting one paragraph the way you want it.**

   Remember to place the cursor in the paragraph you are formatting. Include all tab stops, indents, and line spacing.

2. **With the cursor in that paragraph, choose Format⇨Rulers⇨Copy Ruler or Shift-⌘-C .**

3. **Move the cursor to the paragraph to which you want to add the settings. To apply the ruler to several paragraphs, select those paragraphs.**

4. **Choose Format⇨Rulers⇨Apply Ruler or press Shift-⌘-V.**

The shortcuts are easy — the same as Copy and Paste, plus the Shift key. Copying and applying a ruler doesn't copy the text style. To copy and apply a set of formatting such as font, style, and size, use a custom style, mentioned in "Using styles" earlier in this chapter.

If you set your tabs, indents, line spacing, and so on in a paragraph and then press the Return key at the end of that paragraph, in front of the invisible Enter character, you carry the formatting into the next paragraph you create by pressing Enter.

Paragraph styles

Paragraph styles save a set of formatting choices that includes text and ruler settings. That means you can apply custom formatting, indents, tab stops, and line spacing in one step. You can also change the formatting on every paragraph in your document that uses that paragraph style simply by changing the style itself.

Think about it — you decide to change all the body text in your document from Helvetica to Times. Just change the paragraph style settings, and all the paragraphs (in that document) that use that style are updated automatically. To create a paragraph style, do this:

1. **If the Styles window is not showing, choose Format⇨Show Styles or Shift-⌘-W.**

   You should now see the Styles window. Refer to Figure 5-2 for a picture of the Styles window.

2. **Click the New button at the top right of the window.**

   This action brings up the New Style dialog box, as shown in Figure 5-3.

3. **Type a name for your new style.**

   AppleWorks calls it Style 1, but you should use a meaningful name, like Chapter Heading or Caption.

4. **Click the Paragraph radio button under Style type.**

5. Choose a style to be the starting point for your new style from the Based On pop-up menu.

You can use any existing style for the basis of your new style. If you want to start completely from scratch, choose None. To start with the normal default formatting, choose Default.

If you use one style for the basis of another, any future modifications to the first style also apply to the second style. For example, if your first style includes Arial as the font, so does the second style. If you change Arial to Courier in the first style, the second style also changes to Courier.

6. Uncheck the box next to Inherit Document Selection Format.

7. Click OK.

Your new style now appears in the Styles window.

Now the pointer changes to an outline S with an arrow in the upper-left corner.

8. Choose the settings for your new style from the menus, ruler, buttons, or button bar formatting controls.

Use the S pointer to choose the formatting options for your new style. The choices you make show up when you option-click the disclosure triangle next to the style's name, as shown in Figure 5-12.

You can see a miniature representation of how your style looks by clicking the Edit button in the Styles window.

9. Click Done.

Your new style appears in the styles list.

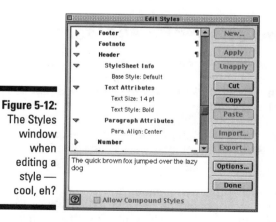

Figure 5-12:
The Styles window when editing a style — cool, eh?

You can also create a style based on a selected paragraph. First, select a paragraph and do Steps 1 through 4 in the previous list. Then skip to Step 6 and check the box labeled Inherit Document Selection Format. Click OK and then click Done in the Edit Style window. Your new style now appears in the stylesheet palette.

Formatting Pages and Documents

After you whip your text and paragraphs into shape, look at the big picture — the document as a whole.

Page breaks

Suppose that you're typing along, and you get to the middle of the page and decide that your next thought would look really good at the top of the next page, rather than there in the middle of this page. You can press Return or Enter dozens of times to get you there (as the ghost of formatting past whispers, "That would be bad"), or you can insert a page break (which would be good). To insert a page break, position your cursor where you want the break to occur, and then choose one of these two options:

- Press Shift-Enter. The Enter key is the one on your number pad. On a PowerBook, the Enter key is next to the spacebar. If your Enter key and Return key are one and the same, this option may not work.

- Choose Format⇨Insert Page Break.

Page numbers and other placeholders

We can all use a little magic in our lives. How about a magic command that automatically numbers the pages in your document? No problem. AppleWorks can take care of that for you, as well as time and date stamps that are automatically updated every time you open your document.

Where can you find these wonders? In the Edit menu, in the guise of three commands: Insert Date (Fixed or Auto-Updating), Insert Time (Fixed or Auto-Updating), and Insert Page #.

Actually, the auto-updating versions of these commands and the page number choice don't insert the real date, time, or page number. Instead, each inserts a placeholder — a special invisible character that tells AppleWorks that it needs to look up the current time, date, or page number at the placeholder.

Just position the cursor and choose the command you want from the Edit menu. The time, date, or page number appears and is automatically updated the next time you open the document. The page number is updated when pages are added or removed.

Here are some handy tips for working with placeholders:

✔ If you want a date or time stamp but don't want that information updated when the document is next opened, choose the Fixed version of the command from the Edit menu. (Inserting a date this way is faster than typing the time, day, month, date, and year.)

✔ If you want the page number, time, or date to appear on every page, insert the placeholder in a header or footer (which we get to in a moment).

✔ You can start the page numbers at any number. This option is handy if you have broken up a long work into several smaller documents, such as chapters. You can start page numbering in your current chapter where the numbering left off in the last chapter. The starting page number option is in the Format⇨Document dialog box. You need to set the number separately in each document.

✔ Insert Page # also enables you to insert the section number, section page count, and document page count. Thus, your page can say "page 2 of 4" and always be correct. See "Sections," later in this chapter, for more information about, well, sections.

Headers and footers

Headers and footers are like hats and shoes for your document. You wouldn't want your document running around without matching accessories, would you? A *header* is an area of text at the top of the page that repeats on every page of the document. A *footer* is an area of text at the bottom of the page that repeats on every page of the document. You can put the same stuff in a footer as in a header.

Typical header/footer contents are

✔ Your name

✔ The date and time of the document's creation

✔ The page number and page count

✔ The title of your work

✔ Ribbons, barrettes, and little pink beads

To add a header or footer to your document, choose Format⇨Insert Header or Insert Footer. After you insert one, the Format menu changes from Insert to Remove, in case you want to remove it later. Here are some more things to keep in mind about headers and footers:

- ✔ Anything in the header or footer appears on every page, at least for that section. The headers and footers remain that way unless you choose to mirror facing pages and tell AppleWorks that they're to be different — more about that in the section on facing pages, below.

- ✔ You can format header and footer text using all alignment and styling techniques that apply to any other text. Tabs are common here, so you can left-align the date, center a page number, and right-align your name.

- ✔ Choose Format⇨Section and check the box next to Title Page to keep the header and footer from showing up on the first page of your document — which you can use as a title page.

If you're using a title page and don't want it to count in the total number of pages in your document, choose Format⇨Document and type **0** in the Starting Page # or Start at Page box. That way, the second page of your document counts as page one.

Sections

Remember one-room schoolhouses? The whole room was a school, but a few rows were one grade, and the next few rows were another grade learning entirely different things. That's what *sections* are like in a word-processing document. Within a section, you can change the header and footer, the number of columns, and the page numbering. You can even start a section with its own title page. Sections are a great way to break up chapters in a document or to have different numbers of columns on the same page.

Here are a few tips for working with sections:

- ✔ To start a new section, position the cursor where you want the new section to start and choose Format⇨Insert Section Break or press Option-Enter.

- ✔ To delete a section, show Invisibles, select the section break, and press Delete or choose Edit⇨Clear.

- ✔ To change a section's formatting, position the cursor anywhere in that section and choose Format⇨Section. You should see the Section dialog box, as shown in Figure 5-13.

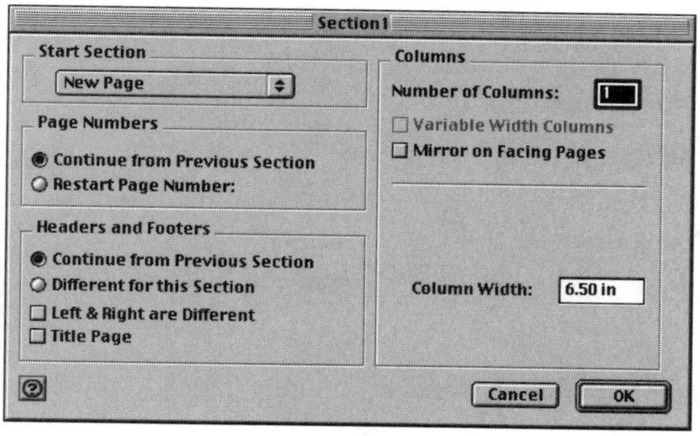

Figure 5-13:
Is this a nonsmoking section? The Section dialog box.

We cover column options later in the chapter. For now, just notice the left side of the dialog box. Most of the options are pretty straightforward, but a couple need a little bit of explaining:

- At the top is the Start Section pop-up menu. Your selection here tells AppleWorks where the next section should start after the section break. If you choose New Page, the current section starts on the line below the previous section. If you choose New Left Page or New Right Page and you're using facing pages, you may wind up with a blank page between sections.

- In the Headers and Footers area, you can choose whether to use different headers and footers in this section and whether to use a title page. If you check the box next to Left & Right Are Different, you can use different headers and footers on facing pages.

Facing pages

There comes a time in everyone's life when you have to stand up and face the pages. Oops . . . that would be music. Well, here we face pages, or talk about pages that face each other. Use facing pages if you want your document to end up on double-sided pages. This way, you can set up headers and footers so that the page number — or other important information — always appears at the outside corner of the page.

You can also leave space at the inside edge of the page to accommodate a binding for your document. This space is known in page-layout circles as a *gutter.*

Here's how you set up facing pages:

1. **Choose Format⇨Document.**

2. **Check the Mirror Facing Pages box.**

   Notice that in the Margins area of the dialog box, the boxes labeled Left and Right have changed to Inside and Outside.

3. **(Optional) Increase the size of the inside margin to leave a gutter for binding.**

Here are a couple of tips for working with facing pages:

✔ To see two pages side by side on your screen, go to the Document dialog box's Page Display area and click the button next to the Facing Pages Side-By-Side option.

✔ To use different headers and footers on left and right pages, choose Format⇨Section and select the box labeled Left & Right Are Different in the Headers and Footers area. This selection enables you to keep the page number at the outside corner of every page.

Footnotes

Footnotes are (a) letters you write with your toes or (b) comments that can appear at the bottom of the page and contain references, information sources, or other explanations.

To insert a footnote, position the cursor where you want the footnote marker to appear and choose Format⇨Insert Blank Footnote, Shift-⌘-F. If you have added the Insert Citation button (found in the Word Processing group of buttons) to the menu bar, clicking it walks you through an Assistant to create a detailed footnote, citing your reference sources. We recommend exploring it. When you use the Insert Blank Footnote command, AppleWorks automatically inserts a footnote marker and takes you to the bottom of the page to type your footnote. Press Enter (on the number pad) to go back to your body text when you finish typing your footnote.

AppleWorks is set up to automatically number your footnotes. When you insert a footnote marker, AppleWorks puts in the correct number for the new footnote. If you want to use a symbol (like * or †) instead of a number, here's what you do:

1. **Choose Format⇨Document.**

2. **Uncheck the Automatic Numbering Start At box in the Footnotes area of the Document dialog box.**

That's it. The next time you insert a footnote and automatic numbering is turned off, AppleWorks displays a dialog box asking you to choose a symbol for the footnote. This symbol is automatically displayed as superscript in your body text, just like numbered footnote markers.

You can also tell AppleWorks to start the footnotes at a number other than one. This option comes in handy if you have broken up a long work into several smaller documents, like chapters. That way, you can have footnote numbering in one chapter start where it left off in the last chapter.

If you happen to move a footnote marker during your editing, AppleWorks automatically updates the number and order of that footnote, relative to the other footnotes in your document.

Margins

Margins are to your document what the shoulder is to a freeway. They're important, but nobody ever notices them. The clean, white space in the margins helps to offset the densely packed action of the body text. By default, AppleWorks sets the margins to 1 inch all around. This is a pretty good setting for most documents. In fact, it works well with most preprinted business letterheads. But you may find that 1 inch is too much space.

To adjust the margins, choose Format⇨Document.

Just enter the margin you want in the appropriate boxes. Use decimals, not fractions, as shown in Figure 5-14. You can use any unit of measure you want by simply entering the number and the unit. AppleWorks converts it to whatever unit you're currently using in the ruler. For example, if the ruler is using inches and you type **3 cm** for the top margin, the 3 cm converts to 1.18 inches.

Don't set your margins smaller than a ½ inch because most printers need a minimum of a ½-inch margin to ensure that the edges of your document aren't cut off. This is the same as US Letter (small) in the Page Setup dialog.

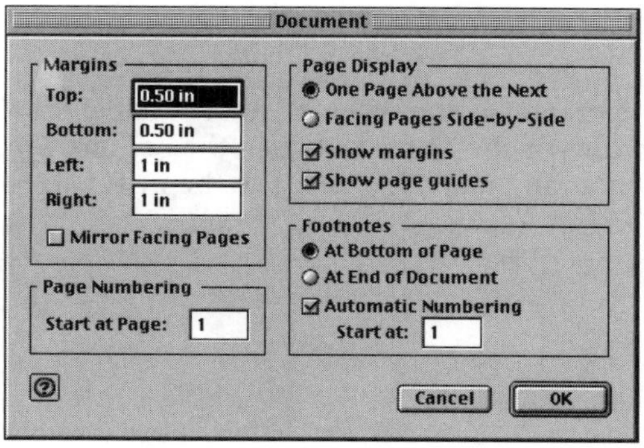

Figure 5-14:
The
Document
dialog box.

Document

Margins
Top: `0.50 in`
Bottom: `0.50 in`
Left: `1 in`
Right: `1 in`
☐ Mirror Facing Pages

Page Numbering
Start at Page: `1`

Page Display
⦿ One Page Above the Next
◯ Facing Pages Side-by-Side
☑ Show margins
☑ Show page guides

Footnotes
⦿ At Bottom of Page
◯ At End of Document
☑ Automatic Numbering
Start at: `1`

Cancel · OK

The gray lines at the edges of your document are the page guides. Anything inside the lines is your document; anything outside is margin. You can turn off the page guides by choosing Format⇨Document and deselecting the Show page guides checkbox. To actually see the white margin space as you work, select the Show Margins checkbox. We recommend keeping both options checked.

While you've got the Document dialog box open, look at one more option you can set: how pages are displayed on-screen. Normally, the setting is One Page Above The Next, so you scroll down to see the next page. Alternatively, you can choose the Facing Pages Side-By-Side option. This can be handy when you're designing a layout for your text. You still scroll down to see subsequent pages, but you see two at a time, side by side.

Columns

AppleWorks really does columns right. All you need to do is click the Add Column button in the text ruler. One click and your document is divided into two columns on each page. Need another column? Just click the Add Column button again — now you have three columns. Keep going if you want. And to remove a column? The Remove Column button makes that just as easy.

You can see which button is which in Figure 5-15. You can have up to nine columns on a page. Of course, you'd better use very short words with nine columns, because with standard margins, each of the nine columns is only 0.57 inch across.

Remove Column

Add Column

Figure 5-15:
Columns,
anyone?
Just click a
button.

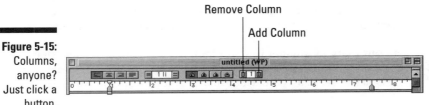

The Add Column feature creates columns that are of equal width. If you want to change the column width or the space between the columns, you can use the mouse or type information in a dialog box. See the next two sections for more information.

To change columns with the mouse

After you have added columns, you can change them with your mouse. To do so, press Option and move the mouse over the column guide. The pointer changes to two arrows pointing in opposite directions. Move the pointer around a bit and notice that when the mouse is over the page guide lines at the edge of the column, the cursor has two lines between the arrows, but when the mouse is in the middle of the space between the columns, the cursor has a box between the arrows.

If you want to change the column width and leave the space between the columns the same, press Option and move the pointer between the two columns so the two arrows have a box between them. Then hold down the mouse button and drag the column guide lines to change the column width.

If you want to change the space between the columns, hold down the Option key and move the pointer over one of the column guide lines so that the arrows have two lines between them. Then hold down the mouse button and drag the column guide line to change the space between the columns.

To change columns with the Columns dialog box

For those of you who prefer to enter numbers in a dialog box: Choose Format⇨Section. Columns are controlled from the Columns area of the Section dialog box.

If you have more than one column, you can select variable-sized columns. To change the size of a column, just select the column you want to change from the pop-up menu and type a width into the Column Width box. Do this for any columns you want to change. The space between columns depends on how much space is left after you assign all the column widths.

When you're finished, click OK to apply the changes. If you don't like the new widths, just undo the changes by clicking the Undo button on the default button bar or by choosing Edit⇨Undo.

Chapter 6

The Text Tools — Editor in a Drum

In This Chapter

▶ Checking spelling

▶ Finding and changing text

▶ Counting words

▶ Looking up synonyms

▶ Hyphenating

*Y*ou've typed all your text, moved it around, set up your tab stops, and applied styles; now comes the hard work: the editing. Luckily for you, AppleWorks includes a whole slew of functions that help you hack your way through even the densest jungle of text.

Using the Spellchecker

The spellchecker can save you a lot of embarrassment. A simple misspelling can make even the most polished report look like it was written by a monkey chained to a computer. If a former vice president had used a spellchecker, he wouldn't have ended up looking like Mr. Potatoe (sic) head.

You can check your entire document at once or check a specific block of text.

To check your entire document, choose one of the following methods:

✔ Choose Edit⇨Writing Tools⇨Check Document Spelling.

✔ Press Control and click in the text to bring up a contextual menu. Select either Check Document Spelling or Check Section Spelling from it.

✔ Use the keyboard shortcuts: ⌘-=.

To check a block of text, select the text you want to check and then choose one of the following methods:

- ✔ Choose Edit⇨Writing Tools⇨Check Selection Spelling.
- ✔ Use keyboard shortcuts: Shift-⌘-Y.
- ✔ Press the Spellcheck button. It has the letters a..z and a red check mark as its icon.

Regardless of how you initiate your spell check, the next thing you should see is the Spelling dialog box shown in Figure 6-1.

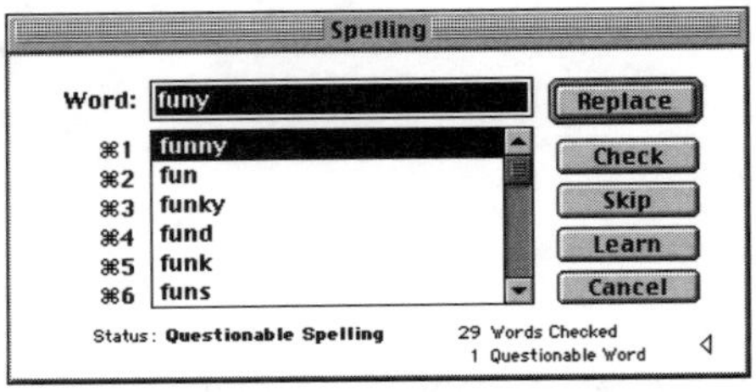

Figure 6-1:
Do you spell funny? The Spelling dialog box.

The spellchecker starts at the beginning of the document or selection and checks each word in that document or selection. When it finds a word it doesn't recognize, it displays the word at the top of the dialog box and lists possible corrections below. You can replace the questionable word with one of the words in the scrolling list below in several ways:

- ✔ Double-click the word you want to use (in the scrolling list).
- ✔ Use the mouse to select a word in the list, and then click Replace (or press the Return or Enter key).
- ✔ Use the up- and down-arrow keys to select a word in the list, and then click Replace (or press the Return or Enter key).
- ✔ Press ⌘-1 through ⌘-6 to select the word that appears next to that number on-screen. For example, for the misspelled word in Figure 6-1, press ⌘-5 to replace it with the word *funny*.

Sometimes the spellchecker offers more than six suggestions for replacement words. You can scroll through the list with the scroll bar or use the up- and down-arrow keys. In case you're wondering, no matter where you scroll in the list, the number shortcut always selects the word currently next to that number on-screen.

If you don't see the correct spelling in the list, just type the word as it should be spelled and then click Replace. If the spellchecker flags a word you know is spelled correctly, it means that the word in question is not listed in the built-in AppleWorks dictionary. You have two choices:

- ✔ If this is a word that you seldom use, click the Skip button to leave the word as is and move on to the next misspelling.

- ✔ If you use this word often or it appears several times in your document, click Learn to add the word to a custom user dictionary. After the word is in the user dictionary, AppleWorks knows it.

Here are some other useful hints about the spellchecker:

- ✔ Handy things to add to the user dictionary are foreign words, proper nouns like street names, acronyms, and frequently used e-mail addresses.

- ✔ If you want to check the spelling of a word that's not in your document, choose the Check Document Spelling command. When the Spelling dialog box appears, type in your word and click the Check button.

- ✔ To see the misspelled word in the context of your sentence, click the Context button or the triangle thingy at the lower-right corner of the dialog box. The dialog box expands to include a line of text that shows the word in context. Click the same button again to get rid of the line of text.

- ✔ When the spellchecker finishes checking your document, the Replace button changes to Done. In short documents with no misspellings, you may think that the dialog box starts out with the Done button because it changes from Replace to Done so quickly. Click the Done button to dismiss the Spelling dialog box.

- ✔ If you're not into spell-checking at the moment and want to call it off, just click Cancel.

English is a tricky language. Many words have different spellings and meanings but similar pronunciations. Spellcheckers don't know the context of your word usage, so they don't pick up on these errors. *Sew, dew ewe no watt wee mien?* Another common error that isn't fielded is when you transpose letters or mistype a word and the result is a real word other than the one you wanted. *Hate you field this information for future reference?*

Find and Go Change

AppleWorks loves to play hide-and-seek. It goes seeking anything you ask it to, and it's just as accommodating when you want it to change something.

Finding text

To open the Find/Change command dialog box shown in Figure 6-2, choose one of these options:

- ✔ Choose Edit⇨Find/Change⇨Find/Change.
- ✔ Press ⌘-F.

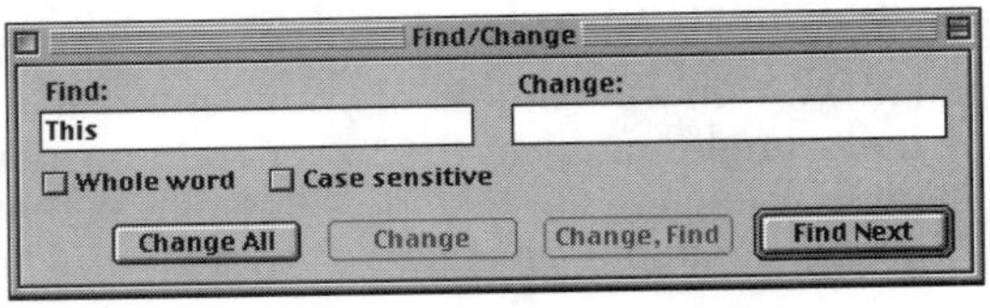

Figure 6-2:
Find that which you seek with the Find/Change dialog box.

You have three ways to find text:

- ✔ Bring up the Find/Change dialog box, type the text you seek in the Find what text box, and click Find Next (or press Enter/Return).
- ✔ Select an example of the text you seek, and then bring up the Find/Change dialog box. AppleWorks automatically enters the text you seek into the Find what text box.
- ✔ Copy the text you seek and then choose File⇨Find/Change⇨Find Selection (Shift-⌘-E), and then paste the copied text into the Find/Change dialog box. (The cursor is already in the Find/Find What field, awaiting your paste command.) AppleWorks automatically looks for the next chunk of text in your document that matches what you selected.

AppleWorks starts looking to the right of the current selection (or wherever the cursor is positioned) and continues to the end. If it doesn't find a match, AppleWorks starts over at the beginning of the document. If it finds no match anywhere in the document, a message appears to let you know.

If you decide that you need to find the next match for the same text again but have already closed the Find/Change dialog box or deselected the text, use Find Again, located in the same submenu. (Of course, you can use ⌘-E, too.) If you're good at keyboard shortcuts, you may prefer using Find Selection and Find Again to find all matches for your text without ever seeing the Find/Change dialog box.

You have a couple of options to narrow your search a bit:

✔ Check the box labeled Whole Word in the Find/Change dialog box only if the text is a separate word. For example, if you type **and** in the Find text box without checking the Whole Word box, AppleWorks finds the *and* in S*and*y, comm*and*, and b*and*. If the box is checked, only the word *and* is found.

✔ Check the box labeled Match Case to find only those words that match upper- and lowercase with the text in the Find box. If you type **AT** into the Find text box and check the Match Case box, you get *AT&T* but not *Attention* because the case doesn't match.

✔ You can check both boxes at once to narrow your search even further.

Changing text

You may have noticed the Change To text box in the Find/Change dialog box in Figure 6-2. After finding your text, AppleWorks can turn it into anything you like. Change can come in handy if you decide halfway through your latest romance novel that Cord is a much more romantic name than Bob. (Sorry, Bob.) Choose Edit⇨Find/Change⇨Find/Change in order to open the Find/Change dialog box. Type **Bob** in the Find What text box and type **Cord** in the Change To text box. Click Change All to give Bob an instant name change throughout your document.

Here's another way to use Find/Change: If you're writing a report and don't have all the information at hand, you can insert an arbitrary placeholder like %%% or **XXXX** for a name or figure. Later, when you get the information, use Find/Change to locate your placeholders and change them to the real thing. Just make sure to keep track of which placeholder you use for each bit of information.

After you type what you want to find and what you want to change it to, you have several options for conducting your search-and-replace mission:

✔ To find the next occurrence of the text in the Find text box, click Find Next (or press Return or Enter because that's the default choice).

✔ To change the text you see highlighted in the document to the text in the Change box, click Change.

✔ To change the highlighted text and find the next occurrence of the text in one very efficient, safe step, click Change, Find.

✔ To change every occurrence of the text in the Find text box to the text in the Change box, click Change All.

Use the Change All button with caution. You can't undo the changes you make with it. AppleWorks warns you about this. Most of the time, you should check the Whole Word option before you click Change All. That way, you change *Bob* to *Cord* but not *Bobbing* to *Cordbing* or *Shishkabob* to *Shishkacord*. You may also want to check the Match Case option to be even more specific. Make sure that you carefully consider how the Change All button will affect your document before you click the button. (Or make a copy of your document using the Save As command before you attempt this trick at home.)

Are you having problems breaking the habit of placing two spaces between sentences? Just type two spaces into the Find text box, type one space in the Change text box, and then click Change All. AppleWorks finds all instances of two consecutive spaces and replaces them with one space. Cool, huh?

At some point, you may need to find other invisible formatting characters. Table 6-1 shows you what to type in the Find field to find them.

Table 6-1	How to Find Invisible Formatting Characters
To Find This	*Type This*
Space	Space
Nonbreaking space	Option-space
Tab	\t or ⌘-Tab
Return character	\p or ⌘-Return
Line break*	\n
Column break	\c or ⌘-Enter (num)
Page break	\b
Section break	\-Option-6
Discretionary hyphen**	\- or ⌘+—(Command+dash)
Date placeholder	\d

To Find This	Type This
Time placeholder	\h
Page number placeholder	\#
Backslash***	\\

*A line break tells AppleWorks to move the next text to the following line instead of wrapping it at the right indent marker or margin.

**See the "Hyphenating" section, later in this chapter, for more details.

***Because the backslash is used as part of the code to find formatting characters, you need to type two backslashes to find just one.

Counting Your Words

Use Word Count to get a complete report on how many characters, words, lines, paragraphs, and pages your document has. To use the Word Count command, choose Edit⇨Writing Tools⇨Word Count or select it from your ever-trusty contextual menu. A window appears with a complete accounting of how many of everything you have in your document. Click OK to dismiss the window when you're finished. You can also count any block of text by selecting the block before bringing up the Word Count window. Checking the Count Selection box changes the word count from a count of the total words in your document, to the total words in your selection.

Finding Synonyms

You may be typing along without a care in the world when, suddenly, you want to say that something is "spiffy." Spiffy really isn't the word you are looking for, but that's all you can think of. Your train of thought gets completely derailed, flinging mental boxcars everywhere. To get back on track, select the word that caused the trainwreck and choose Edit⇨Writing Tools⇨Thesaurus. That's Shift-⌘-Z or you shortcutters out there. It's also available via contextual menus for those of you whose finger hovers above your Control key. The Word Finder Thesaurus dialog box shown in Figure 6-3 comes to your rescue.

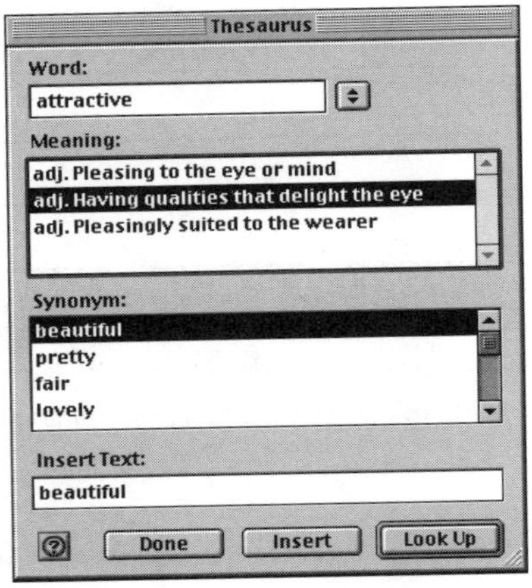

Figure 6-3:
The deadly,
synonym-
eating
thesaurus!

Here's how you use the thesaurus:

1. **(Optional) Select the word in question.**

2. **Bring up the thesaurus by choosing Edit⇨Writing Tools⇨Thesaurus.**

   Your word appears in the Find box at the lower left. (If you didn't select a word in your document, enter a word in the Find box yourself.)

3. **Click Look Up (or press Return or Enter since Look Up is the default).**

   You are rewarded with a list of definitions (if there are any) to choose from and for each of those you select you receive a list of synonyms from which to replace your original word.

4. **When you find a word you like, click it once to select it and then click Replace. You may select any word from the list of synonyms.**

   The Thesaurus dialog box vanishes, and your original word is replaced with the synonym you selected.

   If you didn't select a word before you chose the thesaurus command, clicking Replace inserts the new word in your document at the cursor.

If one of the words in the synonym list intrigues you and you want to delve into it, select it and click Lookup. Synonyms for that word now appear. You can keep looking up words until you find one you like.

If you decide that you liked one of the words you looked into, click the pop-up button next to the topmost text box for a list of the last few words you looked up since opening the Word Finder Thesaurus. Select the one you want and click Look Up again to bring back this word.

Hyphenating

Hyphenating comes in handy when you're working with columns of text. Hyphenating a column of justified text breaks the words up into smaller chunks and helps even out the spaces between words. The result can be a smoother-looking column of text — unless the column is too narrow and ends up with too many hyphenated words. You can hyphenate text three ways:

- ✔ To add a hyphen that always appears in the word, no matter what, just type a regular dash or minus sign.

- ✔ To add a hyphen that only appears if the word moves to the end of a line, type ⌘- – (that's Command and a dash). This character is known as a *discretionary hyphen*. (Discretionary hyphens don't appear when you show invisible formatting characters.)

- ✔ To automatically hyphenate an entire document or text frame, choose Edit⇨Writing Tools⇨Auto-Hyphenate. This method is the easiest way to hyphenate columns of text.

•

Chapter 7

Adding Tables, Charts, and Pictures

*V*ariety is the spice of life, right? This chapter shows you how to add variety — and, therefore, spice — to your text documents. Your documents will positively sparkle when you know how to place and position images, create and position spreadsheets, and add charts and tables. Why, with what you're about to learn in this very chapter, we daresay you may never create another bland, dull page again!

Adding Images (Charts and Graphs, Too)

AppleWorks doesn't care whether you're adding a chart, graph, clip art, QuickTime video, drawing, table, or even a spreadsheet that's hanging out on your Clipboard. You can do all of the above and add them to an AppleWorks word-processing document or frame. Images can behave in one of two ways, neither of which are very image-like. You may add an

✔ **Image that acts like text:** When the cursor is blinking, AppleWorks expects text, so it attaches anything inserted *inline* as if it's a character. As you edit the text, the graphic moves along with the text. You can move the graphic to another line by pressing Return and then align it by using the text alignment options. You can select the graphic by dragging the cursor over it, as you would with text.

To tell AppleWorks where you want to place an inline image, simply place the cursor where you want the graphic to appear, and click the mouse.

✔ **Image that acts like an object:** When you see no cursor and the arrow pointer is the active (selected) tool, AppleWorks expects graphics — which are *object-based* — so it inserts the graphic as an object. Objects happily remain separate entities from text; you can select an object with the arrow pointer and drag it anywhere in the document. You can *wrap* (flow) text around objects, overlap an object with other objects, and so on. For more on working with objects, see Chapters 10, 11, and 13.

> **TIP** To help you understand objects, think of transparent plastic sheets stacked on top of each other. Your text is on one layer, and each image or graph is on its own layer on top of the text.

We give you everything you need to know about inserting an image as an object in the following section. But before you get started, you first need to select the arrow pointer tool. If your Tools window isn't showing, follow these steps:

1. **Click the Tool toggle icon at the bottom of the document's window (next to the page number).**

   The Tools window becomes visible.

2. **Click the arrow pointer tool on either tab**

   The text cursor disappears, and the arrow pointer appears. AppleWorks thinks in terms of objects rather than text, even though you're still in a word-processing document.

   You're ready to insert an object.

Popping in a picture

The previous section shows you how to control the placement and behavior of your graphic. This section shows you various ways to add images to your document:

✔ **Use copy and paste.** To copy a graphic from an existing document into your document, follow these steps:

1. **In the source document, select the graphic you want and choose Edit⇨Copy, or press ⌘-C.**

2. **Switch to the document to which you want to add the graphic and choose Edit⇨Paste, or press ⌘-V.**

✔ **Use the Insert command.** To insert an existing graphic from your hard drive, follow these steps:

1. **Choose File⇨Insert.**

   A modified open file dialog box appears

2. **Navigate to the desired file, and click Insert.**

   To more easily find your image files, use the Show pop-up menu to choose the type of document you seek. Doing this filters out all other types of documents.

✔ **Use MacOS drag and drop.** This method mbines the previous two capabilities. You can drag graphics or files (at least of the types AppleWorks can open) from other open AppleWorks documents, from other drag-aware applications, or from the Finder.

✔ **Use AppleWorks Clippings.** These Clippings are located via a floating window that enables you to browse and drag clip art into your document from elsewhere on your disk, a CD, or even off the Internet. See Chapter 13 for more on Clippings.

✔ **Draw a graphic.** Grab a draw tool and start drawing. Draw graphics are easy to make, and they look good when you print them. We cover them in Chapters 10 and 11.

✔ **Paint a graphic.** Click the paint frame tool to create a paint frame, and then paint away to your heart's content. Check out Chapters 10 and 12 for more on painting.

Here's how to get rid of the rectangular border around a paint frame (or any other frame): Select the frame (so that you see the handles at the corners). Then click the pen icon (on the Lines panel of the Accents window), and select None from the Line Thickness box. No more border — on-screen or in print.

Aligning with the baseline

When a graphic is inline with text, it sits on the baseline of the text line. This setting often doesn't look good, so you may want to move the graphic above or below the baseline. Here's how:

1. **Click the object to select it.**

2. **Choose Format⇨Descent.**

   A simple dialog box, with only one entry option, appears.

3. **To move the graphic's base below the baseline of the text line, enter a positive number. To move it above the baseline of the text line, enter a negative number.**

   To help you select a number, the dialog box tells you the height and width of your graphic in points.

You can also resize a graphic, even when it's inline with text. First, select the graphic. Then drag the handle that appears on the lower right of the graphic, or choose Format⇨Scale by Percent from the menu and enter the percentage by which you want to scale. For more on resizing, see Chapters 11 and 12. (Don't be surprised later when Scale by Percent shows up under the Arrange menu instead. That's where it is for free-floating objects.)

Wrapping text

The main problem with graphics or frames floating around as objects within a word-processing document is that your text continues on its merry way, unaware that a table or image is on top of it. The graphic simply covers up any text that happens to be underneath it. The best way for you to remedy this is to wrap the text around the object.

To tell the text to wrap around an object, follow these steps:

1. **Click your graphic to select it (with the arrow pointer).**

   The graphic is selected when you see black *handles* at the corners. If the graphic is a table or spreadsheet and you entered data in the spreadsheet environment, click outside the table to switch environments and leave it selected. (You can do the same for a painting.)

2. **Choose Options⇨Text Wrap.**

   This menu choice brings up the Text Wrap dialog box shown in Figure 7-1.

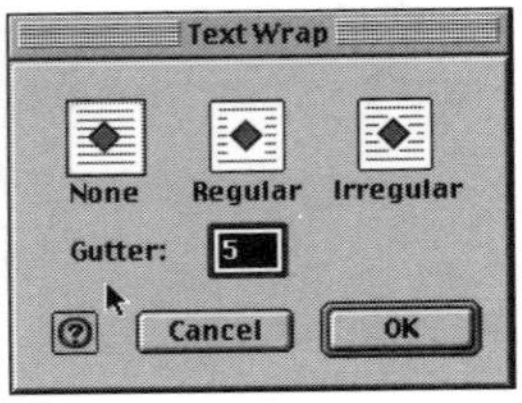

Figure 7-1:
Rapping about how your text wraps.

| Text Wrap |
| None | Regular | Irregular |
| Gutter: 5 |
| Cancel | OK |

3. **Pick a text wrap style and set the gutter:**

   • **None:** This selection is actually no text wrap. Select it to cancel previously added text wrap.

- **Regular:** This selection wraps the text in a rectangular shape, as if an invisible rectangle is around the object.

- **Irregular:** This choice is the most fun. It wraps the text to fit the object's shape. Of course, if your object is a table, a spreadsheet, or a rectangular image, the outcome is the same as selecting Regular wrap. Remember one tricky thing, though: Sometimes your image doesn't look rectangular, but the wrap thinks it is. Select your graphic and use Arrange⇨Ungroup to let the text flow around the individual components.

The *gutter* is the space between your text and your graphic. Enter a number, in points, to determine this space.

Now your text obediently flows around your graphic — whatever shape the graphic may be. As you edit the text or move your graphic, the text reflows.

Remember that you can select the graphic as an object — regardless of what it is — and position it anywhere you like. Nudge the object around until the text flows nicely. Sometimes the tiniest nudge makes a huge difference. If *nudging* (using the arrow keys) moves in larger chunks than you think, the autogrid may be on — choose Options⇨Turn Autogrid Off (⌘-Y) to deactivate it.

Changing behaviors (of the graphic, not yourself)

To bring a free-floating item inline with your text:

1. **Click your object (with the arrow pointer) to select it.**

   The object is selected when you see black handles at the corners. If you select a table, spreadsheet, or painting and you are still in that environment, click outside of that object's borders to switch environments and select the object.

2. **Choose Edit⇨Cut.**

   Doing so removes your object and saves it in the Clipboard.

3. **Position the cursor in your text where you want the object to appear.**

   If your object is a table, chart, or something similar, putting it in its own paragraph provides the best results. That way, you can center the table with the text alignment buttons and have the text around it aligned however you choose.

4. **Choose Edit⇨Paste to put your object into place.**

   After you paste the object into the line of text, you use the text-alignment buttons in the ruler or button bar to line up the object on the page.

To make an inline item free-floating:

1. **Click the object (table, spreadsheet, painting, or any object) to select it.**

   The object is selected when you see a dotted line around it, along with a black handle at the bottom right. If you're still in the object's environment, click outside the object to switch environments and leave the object selected.

2. **Choose Edit⇨Cut.**

   Doing so saves your table to the Clipboard for safekeeping.

3. **Click the arrow tool from the tool palette.**

   The cursor is gone.

4. **Choose Edit⇨Paste.**

   The item appears as an independent object somewhere in the center of your screen or page. Position it as you like.

Creating Tables

Before word processors had fancy table commands, you had to set up tables by using tab stops. Using tab stops is still a quick-and-dirty way to line up a few columns of text in your document, but not if any line needs to wrap to another line. In that case, you end up with a heck of a pain in your tab finger. The table in Figure 7-2 shows how much money the PTA has raised.

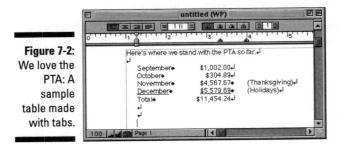

Figure 7-2:
We love the
PTA: A
sample
table made
with tabs.

Notice in Figure 7-2 that the line indent controls bring in the first column, and then the ruler has a tab stop for the next two columns. The first tab stop (on the left) is an *align on* or *decimal* tab, which is most appropriate for the column of numbers there. The next tab stop is an *align left* tab to place the comments text flush left. Chapter 5 gives you more information on the different kinds of tabs and on setting tab stops.

Tables with a click

Okay, you want a table with a little more flair — with more formatting options than you have with tab stops. No problem. AppleWorks integration to the rescue! Until AppleWorks 6, AppleWorks tables were actually spreadsheets. But now you don't have to deal with all the spreadsheet-like stuff, like typing into the entry bar instead of the cell. Now, you see only a table into which you type information. With AppleWorks 6, you can still use spreadsheets for your tables, but there is a new Table frame type with many formatting options unavailable to spreadsheet frames.

Let's talk about the new tables first.

The New Table button

 The New Table button is the economy-class way to put a table in your document. Although it offers no frills, the New Table button acts in a single click and presents a short dialog asking the number of rows and columns you want in your table. The New Table button corresponds to the first item in the Table menu and is displayed in the margin here.

To create an empty table, just position the cursor where you want the table to appear, and click the New Table button. We suggest putting the table in a paragraph by itself and centering it with the Center Align button in the ruler. If you need to add or remove rows or columns, click the table (which selects it as an object) and drag the handle (the little black square) in the lower-right corner.

If you've already begun aligning rows of text to create a table using tabs, such as the one in Figure 7-2, select your text and then select Table⊅Convert to Table to automatically convert the text to a table in one click.

The table frame tool

The table frame tool is for those of you who either haven't added the New Table button to the button bar or would rather drag something into position than go up to the Table menu. Just click the table frame tool and drag it onto your page where you want the table to appear. The same short dialog box asks how many rows and columns you want.

Entering data into a table

Each cell of your table is just like a word-processing frame. You can embed pictures, sounds, movies, hypertext links, outlines, bulleted lists, or most other frames. Unfortunately, you can't embed table frames in a table cell.

When your data starts to overflow the cell, it automatically resizes to accommodate the added information, unless you turn off Auto Resize by selecting Table➪Auto Resize, removing the check mark. This operation is irreversible. If you subsequently delete the data that caused the cell to grow, it does not shrink back.

You can use some keyboard shortcuts for navigating from one cell to another in a table. If you hold down ⌘ and press any arrow key, you move to the next cell in that direction, wrapping to the next/previous row or column when you reach the edge of the table.

Do you need another row (or column) in your table? Select the entire row above which you want the new row and choose Table➪Insert Cells. Is there a wasted row? Select it and choose Table➪Delete Cells. Both of these choices are only available when the selection is rectangular and a full row or column.

Combining and splitting table cells

On many occasions, you may want cells in one row or column to be combined. For example, when you're creating column headers you might want to have a header over a group of columns. AppleWorks 6 makes this easy. Just select the cells you want to combine and choose Table➪Merge Cells (⌘-M). If each of the cells contained data, tabs now separate the data blocks.

You can even get the visual effect of embedding tables within tables by highlighting the cell or rectangular group of cells you want replaced and choosing Table➪Subdivide Cells (⌘-J). Doing this brings up the dialog box shown in Figure 7-3. Notice that this dialog is very similar to the New Table dialog, albeit with smaller default numbers of rows and columns. You can also use the cutting tool to subdivide cells, but then you have to do it one line segment at a time.

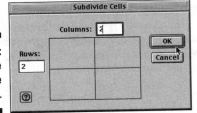

Figure 7-3: One subtable coming up.

If you have data in the cells you're subdividing, the new cells may be unequally sized. This result is due to AppleWorks automatically resizing cells to accommodate data (see above). If you want the cells to be equally sized, turn off Auto Resize before subdividing.

You can also widen just one cell in a column or heighten just one in a row. Choose Table⇨Line Segment Selection and then move just the border you want.

Decorating your table

In addition to all the graphic adornment available through the Accents window, tables give you some extra decorating capabilities.

You can put various frame borders around your cells by selecting from the Table⇨Line Styles submenu.

Do you want a diagonal line to extend from the top left to bottom right corner, or top right to bottom left, or both? No problem. Just select Table⇨Diagonal Line and choose the line, color, pattern, and width you want. Why not just use the line tool, you ask? That would work, if the cell never grows or shrinks; however, the table's diagonal line will resize as the cell resizes.

Do you want your text to hug the top of the cell, the bottom of the cell, or do you want it to be centered vertically in the cell? Again, just choose from the Table⇨Vertical Alignment submenu.

The vertical alignment choices are preserved as VALIGN directives if you save to HTML; however, you will lose the border adornments (other than width) and the diagonal lines.

Spreadsheet tables

This section shows you how to create a spreadsheet frame in your text document:

1. **Bring up the Tools window by clicking the Tool toggle button in the lower-left corner of the document window, by choosing Window⇨ Show Tools, or by pressing Shift-⌘-T.**

2. **Click the spreadsheet frame tool to select it.**

    The spreadsheet frame tool looks like a grid with some numbers above it.

3. **Move your cursor (which now looks like a fat plus sign with a hole in the center) to the place you want to put the table. Hold down your mouse button while dragging to create a rectangle that is the size you want. Then release the mouse button.**

A spreadsheet now fills the rectangle you just made. Or . . .

4. **Click the spreadsheet frame tool and drag it onto the page.**

This gives you two columns and eight rows.

Entering Data into Your Spreadsheet Table

Entering data into a spreadsheet is a bit different from typing in a word-processing document. For one thing, you don't type the information directly into a spreadsheet cell, you type it into the data entry bar near the top of the document window, just above the ruler. Figure 7-4 shows the data entry bar and the entry buttons. After you type the text that you want to appear in the cell, you can click the check mark or press the Enter key on your numeric keypad to accept it. You can also accept it and move to the next cell horizontally by pressing the Tab key (Shift-Tab moves you to the previous cell) or press Return to go down a cell (Shift-Return to go up). To delete what's on the entry bar, click the X button.

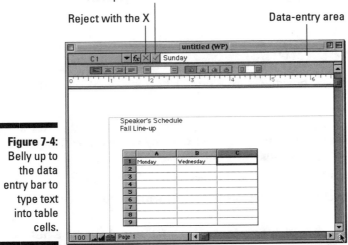

Figure 7-4:
Belly up to
the data
entry bar to
type text
into table
cells.

In addition to the check mark button, you can use several keys to enter text in the cell:

- Pressing the Return key enters the text and moves down one cell in the column.
- Holding down Shift and pressing Return enters text and moves up one cell.
- Pressing Tab enters the text and moves one cell to the right.
- Holding down Shift and pressing Tab enters text and moves left one cell.
- Pressing Option plus any arrow key enters text and moves one cell in the direction of the arrow.

To enter text in adjacent columns or rows, select the entire block of cells you want to enter text into, and then use Return to enter text in columns or use Tab to enter text in rows.

When you use Tab to move around within the selection, you move to the end of a row and then skip back to the beginning of the next row. The same applies to Return: You first move down to the bottom of a column; then you skip back to the top of the column to the right. The cell that remains white in the selected block is where the text you type is entered.

A set of Spreadsheet Preferences is located under the Edit⇨Preferences⇨ General menu when you select Spreadsheet from the pop-up menu in the resulting dialog. These preferences enable you to alter the way the arrows and the Return or Enter key behave. That's handy if you are used to these keys behaving differently. For more information on Spreadsheet Preferences, see Chapter 15.

Formatting a Spreadsheet Frame

You can use these formatting tips regardless of how you create the spreadsheet frame. Because you're actually working in the spreadsheet environment when you format your table, you may notice that the menus change. Don't be alarmed. They change back to what you're used to when you go back to the text environment.

Make sure that you're using the spreadsheet frame tool (the fat plus-sign pointer) before you try to select cells. If you try to drag a spreadsheet frame without the spreadsheet frame tool, you just end up moving the table. (If you move the table, select Edit⇨Undo Move.) The fastest way to get the spreadsheet frame tool is to double-click the table.

Quick tips for formatting spreadsheets

If you want the complete story on formatting spreadsheets, see Chapters 15 and 16. For now, here are some quick tips:

✔ You need to select the cells you want to format before you apply formatting commands.

✔ You can select one or more cells, columns, or rows, or select the whole table to format. (You can select blocks of cells in a rectangular shape only.)

✔ A selected cell has a heavy border around it.

✔ A group of selected cells is highlighted.

✔ The cell in the corner where you start your selection stays white, but it's still selected. The heavy border around the highlighted cells tells you which ones are selected.

Here's how you select cells in a spreadsheet frame:

✔ **To select a single cell,** click it. (Remember that you're actually double-clicking if this is the first time you're accessing the cells with a pointer cursor.)

✔ **To select a row,** click the number at the left side of that column. The numbers show only if you made the table from scratch or if you choose to have them show by using Options⇨Display.

✔ **To select a column,** click the letter at the top of that column. The letters show only if you made the table from scratch or if you choose to have them show by using Options⇨Display.

✔ **To select a row or column** if you used the button and the letters and numbers aren't visible along the top and side, just drag through an entire row or column.

✔ **To select a block of cells,** place the fat plus-sign pointer in one corner and drag to the diagonally opposite corner of the group of cells that you want to select. Alternatively, you can click one corner and then hold down Shift and click the diagonally opposite corner.

After you select the cells, you can apply formatting commands by using menus, keyboard shortcuts, or buttons. Remember that the menus change to the spreadsheet environment menus when you are working in a spreadsheet frame. All the text formatting commands are now located in submenus in the Format menu, including the commands for text size, style, alignment, font, and color. All keyboard shortcuts for the formatting commands remain the same, though. Speaking of buttons, they also change to be spreadsheet-specific.

Because you're working in the spreadsheet environment, all the number formatting and calculation abilities of a spreadsheet are available in your table. See Chapters 16 and 18 for more information on number formats and spreadsheet formulas.

You can draw attention to all or part of your table with color. Select the cells you want to color (you enter spreadsheet mode) and select a fill color. (If the tools aren't visible, click the Tools button next to the page number at the bottom of the document window.) You can find out more about the fill palette in Chapter 10. The stylesheet also provides predesigned table styles that you can use to create eye-popping tables.

Changing column width and row height

To change the width of your columns or the height of your rows, you can use the Column Width or Row Height dialog boxes or drag the column or row with the mouse.

To use the Column Width or Row Height dialog boxes:

1. **Select a column or row by clicking its heading (if visible).**

   For rows, the heading is the number on the left; for columns, the heading is the letter at the top. You can also select multiple columns or rows and change them all at once.

2. **Choose Format➪Column Width or Format➪Row Height.**

   The Column Width or Row Height dialog box appears. The Row Height dialog box is shown in Figure 7-5, but the two dialog boxes look the same.

Figure 7-5:
The two ways to change row height and column width.

3. **Type the new value in the field, or check the box labeled Use Default.**

   The default is 72 for column width and 14 for row height. Click OK when you finish.

To change the row height or column width manually with the mouse:

1. **Make sure that you're using the spreadsheet frame tool (the fat plus sign).**

   Select the spreadsheet frame tool from the Tools window's Frames tab if necessary.

2. **Move the pointer to the line between the rows or columns of the spreadsheet; click and drag that line to change the row height or column width.**

   The pointer changes to a double-headed arrow with a line in the middle. To see the pointer, refer to column A in the image on the right in Figure 7-5.

Hiding and showing column and row headings

After you format your table, you may want to get rid of the column and row headings — the numbers and letters at the top and left sides. Or perhaps you want to show the column and row headings to make formatting an existing table easier. Either way, here's what you do:

1. **Choose Options⇨Display.**

   If you don't see an Options menu, enter the spreadsheet environment first. Double-click the table with the arrow pointer tool to enter spreadsheet mode.

   You should now see the Display dialog box shown in Figure 7-6. You're interested in the top two checkboxes on the right side — the ones labeled Column Headings and Row Headings.

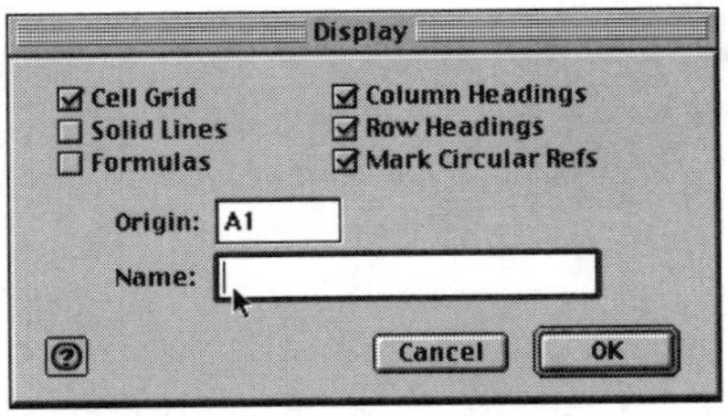

Figure 7-6:
The Display
dialog box
lets you turn
off row and
column
headings.

Display
☑ Cell Grid   ☑ Column Headings
☐ Solid Lines ☑ Row Headings
☐ Formulas   ☑ Mark Circular Refs
Origin: A1
Name:
Cancel   OK

2. **Uncheck Column Headings to make the letters disappear from the tops of the columns.**

3. **Uncheck Row Headings to make the numbers disappear from the left sides of the rows.**

4. **Click OK.**

 As an alternative to using the Display dialog box, you can simply click the Show/Hide Headers button. You can bypass the dialog box for other tasks as well: Click the Show/Hide Gridlines button to turn the gridlines on or off. (If you want to change the gridlines from dotted lines to solid lines, however, open the Display dialog box and check the Solid lines option.) If these buttons aren't already on your spreadsheet button bar, see Appendix A to find out how to add them.

Positioning your spreadsheet frame

You can have your table inline with your text or as an object (floating above your text on its own transparent layer). Just be aware of the text cursor or lack thereof when you create your table. Regardless of how the table comes in, you can cut and paste it to behave as you like.

If you want your spreadsheet-style table to operate independently from your text, leave it as a floating frame.

To make a caption for your floating spreadsheet table that sticks to your table like bubble gum on a mustache, create a text frame in your text document. You can do this in two ways. One way is to select the text tool (the A) from the Tools panel, and then press Option as you drag a box to create a text frame. Now type a caption for your table. The other way is to type your caption anywhere in your text environment, and then cut this text and paste it in as an object (by activating the arrow pointer instead of the cursor). Either way, after the caption is typed, click outside the frame to select it as an object and position it. To make life easier, select the two items as objects and select Arrange⇨Group. (You can find more about selecting multiple items and grouping in Chapter 11.)

 Remember, here we're assuming that you are working in a word-processing document. In a drawing document, your tables, spreadsheets, and text blocks are all free-floating objects, so this stuff about text getting in the way won't happen. Of course, you could have a text frame on a drawing document and attach a spreadsheet inside the frame. Or you could make blocks of text wrap around the spreadsheet or table. You will come up with many ideas of your own as you explore the various chapters in this book and experiment with AppleWorks yourself.

Creating Charts

You have two ways to put a chart in a document: Copy and paste a chart from a separate spreadsheet document, or create a chart from a spreadsheet frame right there in your document. (If you need to brush up on your spreadsheet skills, take a look at Chapter 15 before you try your hand at creating charts.) This section shows you how to create a chart from a spreadsheet frame in your document because that method takes about the same effort as the other method — and it gives you more flexibility to update the chart if your numbers change.

1. **Start by creating a spreadsheet frame in your document.**

   If you already have a table or spreadsheet in your document, skip to Step 2 or 3. If you don't, select the spreadsheet frame tool and drag a box, which creates a new spreadsheet frame.

2. **Enter the data for your chart into the spreadsheet.**

   The number of columns of data determines what kind of chart works best for you. This example creates a pie chart, which needs only one column of numbers.

3. **Select the block of cells containing the data for your chart.**

4. **Click the button that represents the chart you want.**

Voilà, your chart is done. Is that cool, or what? Figure 7-7 shows you the spreadsheet and the pie chart.

The only thing left to do is tidy everything up so that your chart appears where you want it.

Charts, of course, can be either inline or floating. Flip back to the "Adding Images (Charts and Graphs, Too)" section for more information on how to keep your chart inline or make it float. And to fine-tune the look or colors, see Chapter 17, which covers more than you ever thought you'd need to know about charts.

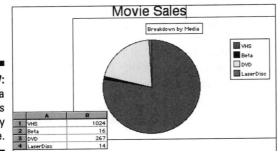

Figure 7-7:
Making a
pie chart is
as easy
as pie.

Chapter 8

Outlining: You Gotta Start Somewhere

Making an outline enables you to brainstorm the structure of your document before you fill in the details. The AppleWorks outliner enables you to do cool stuff, such as rearrange the order of your topics, assign subtopics to other topics, and expand and collapse your outline to get the big picture. Believe it or not, many people who don't have AppleWorks shell out big bucks for special outlining applications to get the features you already have.

When you use an outline, paragraphs become *headings,* or *topics,* in your outline. Topics that are indented under another topic are *subtopics.*

Most people don't give outlining a chance because they take a quick look, get frustrated, and move on. Outlining in AppleWorks is actually pretty simple to do, but unlike plain word processing, outlining has no real-world counterpart. Most people can see how word processing is like a typewriter, but they've never used a tool that lets them easily change the structure of their outline.

Think of an outline as a bunch of sticky notes, with one topic on each note, that you put up on the wall and move around until you like the flow. Outlining goes beyond that analogy, though, because you also can collapse your outline to see just the top-level structure and then expand it again to fill in or view the details.

Take a quick look through this chapter to get an idea of how AppleWorks outlining works. Then, the next time you have to give a speech, do a presentation, or write a report, give it a try.

Setting Up an Outline

With AppleWorks, you can add an outline anywhere in any text document or frame or even in a table cell. All you have to do is use an outline style. You find these styles in the Styles window (Format➪Show Styles or ⌘-Shift-W). You can either select the text you want to use in an outline and apply a style, or choose a style and start typing.

The outline styles are grouped together at the bottom of the Styles list. You can choose from three predefined outline styles, Diamond (for you blue-bloods), Harvard (pronounced "Hah-vud"), or Legal (we won't go there for fear of litigation). You can also create your own outline styles.

Here are the basics for setting up an outline:

- ✔ To create a new topic at the same level as the present topic, press the Return key.

- ✔ To create a subtopic under the current topic, choose Outline➪New Topic Right or press ⌘-R. Doing so indents the topic to the right.

- ✔ To create a new topic that's one level higher in the outline than the current topic, choose Outline➪New Topic Left, or press ⌘-L. Doing so moves the topic to the left. (You can't create a new topic at a higher level than the main level. If you try, nothing happens, except maybe an error beep.)

- ✔ To change a topic you already created into a subtopic, choose Outline➪Move Right➪With Subtopics, or press Shift-⌘-R. The topic becomes a subtopic, even if no higher-level topic is above it. You can also press the Demote button on the button bar. If you don't want the topic's subtopics to move, choose Outline➪Move Right➪Without Subtopics.

- ✔ To move an existing topic one level higher, choose Outline➪Move Left➪With Subtopics, or press Shift-⌘-L — if you don't want the subtopics to move, you don't get a command key equivalent. Alternatively, you can press the Promote button on your button bar.

Figure 8-1 shows you a sample outline in the Diamond format. Topics that don't have subtopics have empty diamonds, topics with subtopics under them have filled diamonds, and topics that have subtopics that are collapsed and not visible have shaded diamonds. For more information on the Diamond format and other outline styles, skip ahead to the section "Outline Formats and Custom Outline Styles" in this chapter.

Figure 8-1:
Today's
topic:
Outlines and
the traveling
women who
love them.

```
◇ Turkey
◆ Thailand
      ◇ Chang Mei
      ◇ Bangkok
◆ India
      ◇ New Delhi
      ◇ Ledak
      ◇ Shrinigar
      ◇ Vanaress
```

Rearranging outline topics

When you see your ideas for topics and subtopics on-screen, you'll undoubtedly want to rearrange them and move sections around. The AppleWorks outliner gives you the flexibility to restructure your ideas, which is why you use it instead of formatting your outline manually.

Moving text around works a little differently in an outline view. When you move a topic that has subtopics under it, the subtopics move with the main topic — unless you force AppleWorks to leave the subtopics behind. You can move your topics up and down within your outline in several ways: with the mouse, with keyboard shortcuts, or with menu commands.

To move topics up and down with the mouse, move the pointer to the left of the topic that you want to move, and press the mouse button. The pointer changes to a bar with up and down arrows, as shown in Figure 8-2. (You have to drag the mouse a tad before the moving pointer materializes.) Now drag the topic up or down. A black bar at the left edge of the document shows you where the topic ends up. Release the mouse when the topic's black bar is where you want it.

Unfortunately, you can't move topics right or left by using the mouse or any special buttons. You need a menu command or a keyboard shortcut. We list keyboard or menu commands for shuffling your topics in Table 8-1. If you want to find out more about commands for collapsing and expanding outlines, see the table in the next section.

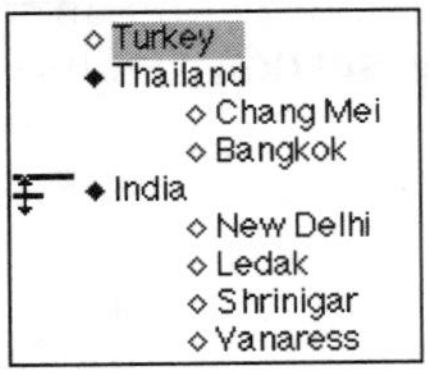

Figure 8-2:
Using a
mouse to
move a
topic.

◇ Turkey
◆ Thailand
   ◇ Chang Mei
   ◇ Bangkok
◆ India
   ◇ New Delhi
   ◇ Ledak
   ◇ Shrinigar
   ◇ Vanaress

Table 8-1	Commands for Rearranging Your Outline Topics
To Make This Happen	*Do This*
Collapse a topic	Choose Outline⇨Collapse or double-click to the left of the topic.
Expand a topic	Choose Outline⇨Expand or double-click to the left of the topic.
Move a topic up in the outline	Choose Outline⇨Move Above or press Control-↑.
Move a topic down in the outline	Choose Outline⇨Move Below or press Control-↓.
Move a topic right in the outline	Choose Outline⇨Move Right or press Shift-⌘-R or Control-→.
Move a topic left in the outline	Choose Outline⇨Move Left or press Shift-⌘-L or Control-←.
Move a topic only, without its subtopics	Press Option and choose a move command from the Outline menu, or press Option-Control and an arrow key.
Select a topic and its subtopics	Click the topic's label (the number, letter, or symbol at its left). Drag to reposition.
Select a topic without its subtopics	Click anywhere in the topic's text.

Collapsing and Expanding Outlines

One of outlining's most powerful features is the capability to collapse subtopics and look at only the top-level headings. When you look at just top-level headings, you can get an overview of the structure of your document and make changes without the lower-level topics cluttering up the page. If you move a topic with collapsed subtopics under it, the subtopics follow along. Table 8-2 shows you how all this collapsing and expanding works.

Table 8-2	Expanding and Collapsing Subtopics
To Make This Happen	*Do This*
Collapse subtopics under a topic	Choose Outline⇨Collapse or double-click the topic's label.
Expand subtopics under a topic	Choose Outline⇨Expand or double-click the topic's label.
Expand or collapse the entire outline	Choose Outline⇨Expand To and type a level number in the Expand To dialog box.

If you need to expand your outline to show all subtopics, bring up the Expand To dialog box and type **16**. That's the maximum number of levels AppleWorks allows, and it expands your outline to the lowest level. To collapse the outline again, type a smaller number, like 2 or 3.

Outline Formats and Custom Outline Styles

The diamond style is cool because it shows you which topics have subtopics under them, even when the subtopics are collapsed and not visible. However, you may be used to another outline style, or you may need to use another style because of the requirements for your document. AppleWorks includes three built-in outline styles, and you can create as many more as you like. The different formats use different kinds of labels for the different levels of topics.

Built-in formats and labels

The three built-in outline formats are Diamond, Harvard, and Legal. Diamond is the default; we use this format as an example earlier in this chapter.

Here's a quick breakdown of the formats and what each is good for:

- **Diamond format:** A straightforward format that easily helps to whip your outline structure into shape.
- **Harvard format:** The one to use if you're a student. It's what most of us think of when we hear the word *outline*.
- **Legal format:** The one to use if you're a lawyer. It's like the numeric paragraph format but more precise. Using the Legal format, topic 4, subtopic 2 is labeled 4.2. If three more subtopics fall under 4.2, you have 4.2.1 through 4.2.3. This format makes it easy to be precise — just what lawyers like.

Custom labels

Apply one outline style or format to your whole outline — or change the label or style format for specific topics within an outline. This section shows you how to change the labels on isolated topics. (To change the label for all topics on a specific outline level, skip to the next section, "Custom outline styles.")

Suppose that you have a Harvard outline but need a checklist somewhere within it. No problem. Or what if, within your diamond outline, you have a group of subheadings that need to show the order of steps in a set of instructions (a numbered list)? Again, no problem.

To apply a different type of label to a topic or topics, follow these steps:

1. **Select one topic by clicking in the topic text. Select several topics by dragging through their text.**

2. **Choose the style you want from the Text Style pop-up button (if you put it on your button bar) or the Styles window.**

Turning an ordered outline style into an unordered style such as bullets or a checklist jumps that section back to a level one topic. You can move the section back. Just be sure to note where the sections are at the time you apply the new style.

You can make a topic into plain body text by selecting the topic and applying the body — or any other body text — style.

Custom outline styles

Because AppleWorks has only three real outline styles built-in, you may feel a bit limited in your options. Fear not! You can create a custom outline style the same way you create a custom paragraph style. Here's how:

1. **If the Styles window is not showing, choose Format⇨Show Styles, or press Shift-⌘-W.**

2. **Click the New button at the top right of the window.**

   The New Style dialog box appears.

3. **Enter a name for your new style.**

   AppleWorks automatically fills in something like Style 1, but it's best to use a meaningful name, such as *Chapter Heading* or *Caption*.

4. **Click the radio button next to Outline, under Style Type.**

5. **Choose a style to be the starting point for your new style from the Based On pop-up menu.**

   You can use any existing style for the basis of your new outline style. If you want to start completely from scratch, choose None. To start with the normal default paragraph formatting, choose Default.

   If you base your outline style on another paragraph style and later change the formatting of that paragraph style, your outline formatting changes, too.

6. **Uncheck the box next to Inherit Document Selection Format.**

   Unless you want your outline style to use the formatting of some selected text, make sure that this box is not checked.

7. **Click OK.**

   Your new outline style now appears in the list of Styles in the Styles window.

8. **Click the disclosure triangle next to your new style to view the different outline levels or click the Edit button to format them.**

   Choose an outline level to format.

   If you choose formatting options without clicking the Edit button first (where it changes to "Done"), you'll end up applying the formatting choices to the text around the cursor in your document and will not be modifying the style.

9. **Choose the settings for your new outline style from the menus, the ruler, or the button bar:**

   - *Selecting formatting:* While you're choosing formatting for the style, the pointer changes to an outline S with an arrow in the upper-left corner. Use this pointer to choose the formatting options for your new style. The choices you make appear in the Styles and Properties list at the top left of the Styles window.

   - *Easy selection:* You can select many formatting options with the Paragraph dialog box. To pull it up, choose Format⇨Paragraph.

   - *Mixing outline types:* Choose topic labels from the Label pop-up menu at the lower-left corner of the Paragraph dialog box. You can mix different topic label types in the same outline style. For example, use the Harvard format, but make all level four topics into checklists.

   - *Viewing a sample:* A sample displaying your current choices appears in the text box below the list of styles.

   - *Removing properties:* If you ever decide that you don't like a property, select it in the list and choose the Cut button in the Styles window. (Don't worry, it only cuts the one you select.)

   - *Copying properties:* After you set the look for one level, you can select the properties by clicking and dragging down the list or by pressing Option as you click each property you want. Then press the Copy button in the Styles window and click the next style level and press Paste.

10. **Click Done when you finish.**

For more information about styles and the Paragraph dialog box, see Chapter 5.

Part III
Working with Graphics and Graphics-Based Documents

The 5th Wave   By Rich Tennant

The new desktop publishing software not only lets Rags produce a professional looking greeting card quickly and inexpensively, but it also allows him to say it his way.

In this part . . .

Are you ready to flex your artistic muscle? Or, are you looking to create a professional-caliber flyer or a multipage newsletter that shines with charts and graphics as text flows across your pages? Either way, you're in the right place!

AppleWorks provides a full-fledged drawing program and one for painting as well. You can build graphics or create your own designs by using the shape tools provided, or you can create freehand paintings using the flexible brush and spray can. In case you're not inclined to create your own graphics, you can take advantage of clip art libraries. Use an entire graphic as-is or as a basis for your own personalization.

An AppleWorks drawing document also has amazing power as a page layout document. In a high-priced professional page layout program, you can place text and graphics, and maybe even a spreadsheet, and then move those components around until they look just right or link text to flow from one box to another, even from page to page. In AppleWorks, you can do the same things. In AppleWorks, though, your spreadsheet is still active and calculating at all times, and the charts you create from those spreadsheets are continually updated.

New in AppleWorks 6 is a dedicated Presentation document. With all your drawing, painting, charting, text, and table tools available to you and the addition of transitions, speaker's notes, and grouping you can create eye-popping digital presentations.

Time and time again, people are surprised by what they can create when using AppleWorks drawing or painting tools, and they're even more surprised by the intricate polished layouts they can create. Take a look. Try your hand. Be surprised.

Chapter 9

Drawing versus Painting

*I*f a picture is worth a thousand words, this chapter gives you a chance to save a hefty amount of typing. AppleWorks is a natural for creating pictures and other *graphics,* as the designer folks call them.

The AppleWorks paint environment and draw environments descend from the legendary personal computer programs: MacPaint and MacDraw. You don't have to be able to draw a cartoon turtle to use these graphics tools. Instead, you can do wonders in the drawing environment by simply creating a few shapes and moving them together. Even a rectangle in the right place on your letterhead creates a nice accent. If you are artistic, you can create something as complex as a stylized logo with special effects either in the paint environment or with drawing tools. Each graphic environment has its own special features and tricks — and with this book, you can master graphic manipulation magnificently.

When it comes to graphics, the main question for most people is, "Do I draw or do I paint?" The answer depends on the kind of graphic you want and how you want to manipulate it. In general, drawing enables you to manipulate the big picture — for example, when you want to create a layout with both text and graphics — and it gives you sharp printouts. Painting works on a smaller scale — for example, when you want to apply special effects to your graphics and do more detailed editing — and its images may look somewhat coarse when printed out. The rest of this chapter goes into more detail about each of the graphic environments and helps you decide which is right for your work.

When to Start with a Draw Document or Use Draw Tools

Draw documents are great when you need text and graphics on the same page. When printed, draw documents produce crisp graphics and razor-sharp text. These qualities make draw documents good for the following purposes:

- Diagrams
- Flowcharts
- Maps
- Line-drawing illustrations
- Envelopes
- Invitations and greeting cards
- Paper doll cutouts
- Pop-up paper geodesic domes that have your resume on the inside
- Page layouts for fliers and newsletters

That's right; you read that last item correctly. One of the most popular uses for a draw document is page layout — creating printed pages that contain some combination of graphics, text, charts, and spreadsheets on one page. Using a draw document gives you the most flexibility to position all those different types of information on a page.

Drawing tools are always available in word processing, too, so you can simply add a drawn element here and there anytime.

When to Start with a Paint Document or Add a Paint Frame

Use a paint document when you want to

- Create freehand art
- Make illustrations that you need to edit down to the individual pixel
- Create logos
- Apply special effects like free rotate and distort to text and graphics
- Edit scanned photos

On one level, painting gives you more flexibility to create finely detailed images because you edit paint images dot by dot (or *pixel by pixel* in computerese). But this detail comes at a price. First, you can't make changes as easily because you must apply changes pixel by pixel. Second, graphics and text created in the paint environment may look coarse or jaggy when printed. The trick is to match the document's resolution, or the number of dots per inch, to your printer's resolution. When the printer and document resolutions match, your document prints as clearly as possible.

Advantages and disadvantages

In order to help you decide which environment — draw or paint — is better for your graphic task, consider the advantages and disadvantages of each.

Advantages of the draw environment:

- ✔ You can always move, resize, or fill a draw shape with a different color.
- ✔ Each draw shape is an independent object and can be moved without disturbing other objects. (Take a look at Figure 9-1 for an example.)
- ✔ You can rotate text and graphics freely or by numeric increments, and the text or graphics remain editable.
- ✔ Draw graphics look great when you print them, even when you've resized them.

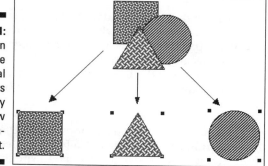

Figure 9-1:
You can move individual objects separately in the draw environment.

Advantages of the paint environment:

- ✔ AppleWorks painting works like ink or watercolors.
- ✔ You can make changes to any single dot in a paint image.
- ✔ You can create more detailed artwork in the paint environment than in the draw environment.

✔ You can rotate text and graphics freely or by numeric increments (as in the draw environment) but with an added bonus: You can stretch, shear, or distort them to create interesting effects.

✔ You can use a variety of special effects on a paint image that aren't available in the draw environment.

✔ You can add a gradient, fill, pattern, or texture to text.

After you put a shape or text on the page in the paint environment, it's no longer recognized as a specific shape or as text, just as a pattern of color. Therefore, you can't modify individual shapes like you can in the draw environment. Instead, you move chunks of your image. To edit the image or text, you must redraw it pixel by pixel. (See Figure 9-2 for an example.)

Figure 9-2:
Moving a
selection in
the paint
environ-
ment.

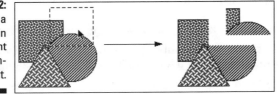

Combining Both Worlds

Paint and draw environments have their unique advantages. Fortunately, you don't have to choose one environment over the other. Thanks to the AppleWorks integration, you can paint and draw in the same document. Simply create one or more paint frames in a draw document. Using both environments in a single document gives you the flexibility to move objects and frames on the page and print high-quality text, while retaining the best features of the paint environment.

Frames are special draw-like objects that give you a window to another environment. As far as the draw environment is concerned, a frame is just another rectangle — until you start working inside the frame, thereby switching out of drawing and into the frame's environment. In that case, the frame is no longer an object to be moved, but a whole other tiny document all its own — until you click outside the frame and tell the draw environment that the frame is just another object to move around.

Are you wondering why we didn't say you can create a draw frame in a paint document? It's because you can't. Remember that the draw environment doesn't use a separate frame. Besides, all the graphics tools work in a paint-like way in the paint environment. You can select a draw tool and use it — but it turns "painted" when you click off of the object.

Actually, frames don't really exist in the paint environment. Everything you add is simply painted onto the page — even a spreadsheet. You can place a spreadsheet and even place information in it, but after you click outside of it, you can't go back to edit it with the spreadsheet tools.

When you use paint frames in a draw document, you typically use the draw tools for design elements, such as lines, solid shapes, diagrams, and maps. You use the paint frames for detailed graphics and graphics with special effects, such as company logos.

Make sure that you create your paint frame the exact size that you need it to be. You can't stretch or shrink an image in a paint frame in the draw, spreadsheet, or text environments. The painted image doesn't change. Stretching the frame adds white space around the image, and shrinking the frame crops the image.

You can make some really awesome-looking graphics when you use each environment for what it does best. Look at Figure 9-3 for an example of what you can do when you combine the two graphics environments.

Figure 9-3:
Party time!
Combining
paint and
draw
graphics
can make
you more
popular.

Chapter 10

Drawing and Painting Basics: AppleWorks Art 101

. . . .

In This Chapter

▶ Setting up your graphics document

▶ Shaping your world with the shape tools

▶ Experimenting with the freehand tools

▶ Setting graphics preferences

▶ Applying patterns, textures, or gradients as fills

▶ Creating lines and arrows

▶ Creating custom graphics styles

▶ Selecting, deleting, and copying your artwork

. . . .

*T*he drawing and painting environments enable you to create graphics. Both environments use the same tools to create shapes — with a few extra tools in the painting environment. When you *draw*, the shape you create remains an *independent object* that can be moved, resized, filled with color, deleted, and so on at any time. In the painting environment, objects become *painted in* or turned into individual pixels in the document. After you place a shape in the paint environment, you must manipulate it pixel by pixel.

You can create a paint document that is in itself a work of art, or you can create your painting and then copy it into another document such as a letter or a flier that you lay out in a drawing document. (Chapter 13 gives ou the lowdown on laying out complex documents such as fliers and newsletters.) Alternatively, you can use your palette frame tool to create a paint frame directly within any document and then create your artwork right there. Likewise, you can create a stand-alone drawing document, or you can create your drawing and then copy it into another document. You don't need to create a drawing frame to create your artwork directly within any document because drawing tools are available anywhere. (If you're new to environments and frames, check out Chapter 1.)

In this chapter, we give you a crash course in drawing and painting basics, from setting up a draw or paint document to spicing up your masterpiece with borders, lines, and fills. Think of this chapter as AppleWorks Art 101.

Setting Up a Graphics Document

When you open a new draw or paint document, you're greeted by a blank page, similar to the one in Figure 10-1. From there, you have a lot of control over how that page looks and acts. Graphics page setup is covered in more detail in Chapter 13, but you can find the short course here.

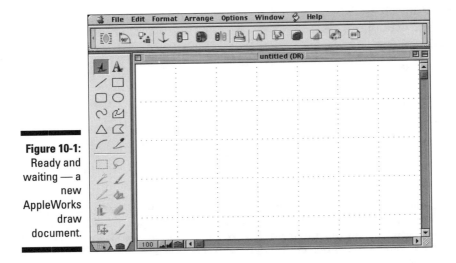

Figure 10-1:
Ready and waiting — a new AppleWorks draw document.

Using drawing and painting tools

For the most part, tools in AppleWorks work the same way in every environment, so when you know what a tool does in one environment, you know how to use it in the other environments, too. Here are a few general tips to keep in mind when using AppleWorks tools in the draw and paint environments:

- ✔ Before you can work with a tool, you must click it to select it.
- ✔ To bring a tool to your page, click the tool once to select it and then release your mouse button. Your cursor takes the shape of a crosshair. Move your mouse to the page, click at the location you want to begin creating your shape, and hold down the mouse button as you drag to define the shape. (Some tools require multiple clicks to define a shape. Such exceptions are noted in the details for each tool throughout this chapter.)

✔ In the paint environment, double-clicking some tools not only selects the tool but also displays a dialog box that controls how the tool works. Bringing up a dialog box by accident is okay, but you may not want to perform the extra step required to close the dialog box. (The tool controls in those dialog boxes are explained later in this chapter.)

✔ Normally, when you use a tool, the pointer switches back to the arrow pointer. To lock a tool so you can use it more than once without reselecting it, double-click the tool in the Tools panel of the Tools window. The tool turns dark to let you know that it's selected until you select another tool. The paint environment is the exception to this rule; tools there are automatically locked and remain in effect until the next tool is selected.

✔ Remember that in the paint environment, tools act differently than in any other environment. Although you can add text and draw objects any time, after they're placed in a painting, editing is trickier and can be tedious. Don't be afraid to try anything — just check your results right away so you have the option to undo your last change. If you realize that you want to undo something later, choose File⇨Revert to restore your entire document to the way it was when you last saved it. You may lose several changes, though, so revert works best when you save often.

Sometimes, when you want to draw or paint a graphic to an exact size, AppleWorks instead resizes the graphic in increments. The object jumps from one preset size to another, skipping intermediate sizes. The *autogrid* causes this phenomenon by constraining the sizing or moving of shapes to a preset interval (such as an eighth of an inch). The autogrid helps you line up objects or create consistent shapes, but it also limits you. To toggle the autogrid off or on, choose Options⇨Turn Autogrid Off/On or press ⌘-Y. You can also toggle the autogrid from your contextual menu when you Control-click the layout surface.

Draw and paint documents can be positioned either horizontally or vertically, as with most other documents. To change your page's orientation or size, choose File⇨Page Setup. You can find more information about this in Chapters 2 and 13. You can also add extra pages to your graphics documents (see Chapter 13).

Drawing documents have a bunch of dots called a *graphics grid* in the background to help you line up objects. The graphics grid appears only on-screen and never prints. Choosing Options⇨Hide Graphics Grid makes the grid invisible. (Painting documents don't have a visible grid.)

As you work, you may want to see how your document *really* looks. Choosing Window⇨Page View or clicking the optional Show Margins button enables you to see your margin area. Show Margins is on by default. If you haven't added it to your button bar, you can find a checkbox for it in the Format⇨Document dialog Displaying a ruler along the top and left sides of your document enables you to see the size of your document or image in inches or other units of measurement. Choose Format⇨Rulers⇨Show Rulers to display the rulers. For more information about rulers, see Chapter 13.

After you set up your page the way you like it, you might want to make that setup your default document so you won't have to go through the same setup over and over again for future documents. You can have one default document for your drawing documents and one for your painting documents. Save the document, choosing the Template option and saving it to the Templates folder, and name it "AppleWorks DR Options" or "AppleWorks PT Options."

Setting graphics preferences

The preferences that you set determine how some of the tools behave. To change the graphics preferences, choose Edit⇨Preferences⇨General. The Preferences dialog box appears (see the Figure 10-2). If you're in a graphics document when you open the Preferences dialog box, you're taken straight to the graphics choices. Otherwise, select Graphics from the Topic pop-up menu. Most of these preferences affect only drawing, not painting.

Here's how the graphics preferences break down:

- ✔ **Polygon Closing:** You can select Manual or Automatic closing. Manual enables you to draw open shapes; double-clicking finishes the shape wherever you double-click. To create a closed shape, you must finish by clicking back at the starting point. Otherwise, the shape remains open. Automatic closes any shape you create by automatically drawing a line from your ending point to the starting point. Any line that you select in the line palette appears around the part of the shape you define, but not around the part that is closed automatically.

    Paint shapes always close automatically regardless of this preference setting. Even lines drawn with the squiggle tool always close. The only effect this preference has on a painted shape is the outline: With automatic closing, your shapes always have full outlines (as defined by the line tool at the time of shape creation).

- ✔ **Object Selection:** You can choose to display four or eight handles when an object is selected. The four extra handles in the middle of each side let you move each side individually when you resize an object. Be careful, though: Dragging a side handle pulls the object, distorting it. Due to the nature of object selection in painted items (see "Selecting Graphics," later in this chapter) this preference doesn't have any effect in the paint environment.

- ✔ **Automatically Smooth Freehand:** Freehand smoothing only affects drawing. If this box is checked, the squiggle tool draws shapes made up of many small curves. If the box is not checked, the squiggle tool draws shapes made up of many tiny, straight lines. You can also add buttons to the button bar to smooth and unsmooth your creations.

✔ **Mouse Shift Constraint:** If you hold Shift while drawing a straight line and pivot the end of the line around the starting point, the line clicks into place at various places around the circle. The angle you type in this box determines the angle at which the line clicks into place. This setting also affects how regular polygons appear on-screen. This option applies to both paint and draw environments.

After you change the preferences, click OK to set these preferences for your current document. To make these the default settings in every new graphics document, click Make Default. If you wish to go back to the original AppleWorks defaults, click Restore Defaults. To restore the original settings of the dialog box, click Cancel.

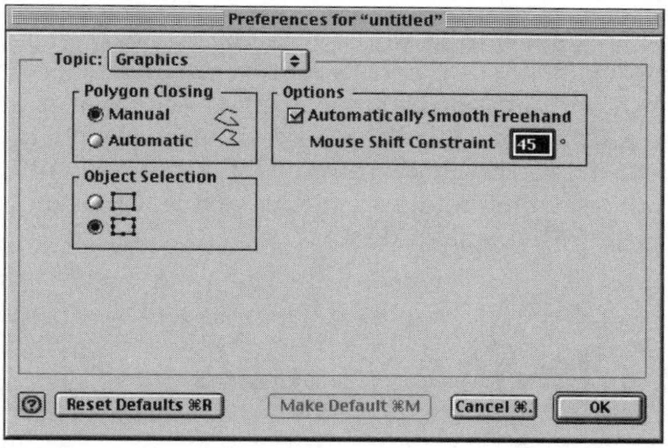

Figure 10-2:
Show your
artistic
preferences

Working with Text Boxes and Other Frames

One of the reasons AppleWorks is so versatile is the ease with which you can place and manipulate text, spreadsheets, and paint frames. The frame tools on the Frames panel of the Tools window enable you to create frames and edit the information inside them.

Within a frame, you have all the same capabilities as within that frame's environment. When you work inside a frame, you actually switch to that environment. For example, when you edit text inside a text frame, the menus change to the text environment's menus.

If you're working in a document and your menus seem messed up, you're probably in a frame rather than in the document's master environment, which is drawing for a drawing document. To return to the drawing environment, click the arrow pointer icon in the Tools panel.

To make simple captions, click the text tool to select it. Bring the I-beam cursor over to your document and then click and drag to create a free-floating text frame. Type your text and format it any way you want.

To do more fabulous, complex things with columns of text or to wrap text around graphics, check out Chapter 13. If you need help formatting text, check out Chapters 5 and 6.

Frames work differently in the paint environment than in any other AppleWorks environment. Here are the differences:

- The arrow pointer and the paintbrush don't have frame-related functions in the paint environment. Instead, they simply provide a pencil tool that places pixels individually.

- The text and spreadsheet tools work within the frames they create, but after you click outside those frames, your text or spreadsheet is painted onto the background, and you can't use the text or spreadsheet commands anymore. You can't use a painted spreadsheet to make a chart (although you can paste in a chart created elsewhere). The only exceptions are headers or footers, which retain all normal text features and editing capabilities even within a paint document.

Working with the Shape Tools

Do you scream for ice cream? With AppleWorks, you can have it in any cone you like. In this section, we help you choose the right shape tools for the job, whether you're creating something as simple as a wafer cone or something as complex as a waffle cone. Figure 10-3 shows the Tools window's nine shape tools in the draw and paint environments.

Figure 10-3:
Getting in shape is no sweat with the shape tools in the Draw palette (top) and the Paint palette (center).

The shape tools fall into two basic categories:

- **The regular shape tools** are the line, rectangle, round rectangle, oval, arc, and regular polygon tools.

  The regular shape tools let you create the basic building blocks of your artwork. For example, if you'd like your ice cream in a wafer cone, you can build your cone with a horizontal rectangle atop a vertical rectangle. For a sugar cone, you can use the regular polygon tool, set to three sides.

- **The freehand shape tools** (not to be confused with the freehand *paint* tools, discussed later in this chapter) are the squiggle, polygon, and bezigon tools.

  If you prefer a waffle cone, call upon one of the freehand shape tools to create it. The freehand shape tools provide much greater drawing flexibility and allow you to completely reshape your objects later.

In the following two sections, we describe the nine shape tools and tell you how to use them. When the way a tool works varies in drawing and painting, we point out the differences. The preferences you set for the graphics environment may also affect the shapes you create. See the section on setting graphics preferences for more information.

Using the regular shape tools

This section describes the regular shape tools and offers tips for using them.

Line: The line tool creates straight lines. Click the line tool to select it and then click the location on your page where you want the line to begin. Without releasing the mouse button, drag the mouse to the point where you want the line to end. If you want to constrain the line to a horizontal, vertical, or 45-degree line, hold down the Shift key as you drag the mouse. You can also add arrowheads to the beginning or end of a line or at both ends. Just set the desired arrow option in the Lines panel of the Accents window before creating the line, or — if you're in the drawing environment — set the option any time that line is selected.

You can change the angle to which a line is constrained by entering a new number in the Graphics section of the Preferences dialog box.

Rectangle: Rectangles and squares are easy to make with the rectangle tool. Select the rectangle tool by clicking it once, and then click at the location where you want a corner of the rectangle to appear. Holding down the mouse button, drag the mouse to the point where you want the opposite corner of the rectangle to be located. To draw a perfect square, press the Shift key as you drag the mouse.

Round rectangle: The round rectangle tool works the same way as the rectangle tool, except it makes kinder and gentler rectangles with rounded corners. In the drawing environment, create your round rectangle and then reshape it anytime later by double-clicking it to bring up the Corner Info dialog box. In the Painting environment, double-click the round rectangle tool to bring up the Corner Info dialog box and specify the settings before you draw your round rectangle.

The Radius option in the Corner Info dialog box determines the roundness of the rectangle's corners. You enter the radius of the curve for the corners (in points) in the box next to the Radius button. The larger the number, the rounder the corner. The Round Ends option creates a shape that looks like a rectangle with a semicircle stuck on each end. To create a square with rounded corners, press Shift as you draw with this tool. Applying the Round Ends option in addition to pressing Shift creates a square with rounded sides — you probably know this shape as a circle.

 Oval: Use the oval tool to create an oval or a perfect circle. As with the other tools, click the tool, click the point where you want the oval to begin, and drag in any direction to expand the shape to the size you want. To constrain your shape to a circle, hold Shift as you draw.

 Everyone calls it an oval, but it isn't really. What you get is an ellipse. An ellipse is an oval that is concentric around two axes and its center. An oval is an egg shape, in other words, it doesn't have to be mirrored through its center as well.

 Arc: Use the arc tool to make sections of circular shapes. The default arc is a quarter of an ellipse (90 degrees), but you can create anything from a line to a nearly complete circle. To create an arc, click the arc tool and then click the location where you want the arc to begin. While holding the mouse button down, drag in the direction you want the arc to curve. Release the mouse button at the edge of the arc. The direction in which you drag determines where the outer edge of the circle appears. Press the shift key as you drag to keep the inside sections equal.

In the drawing environment, you can reshape an arc after you draw it by double-clicking the arc to bring up the Arc Info dialog box (see Figure 10-4). In the painting environment, you must specify the settings before you paint the arc. Double-click the arc tool to bring up the Arc Info dialog box.

The arc angle setting lets you control how many degrees the arc covers; you can set it anywhere from 1 to 359 degrees. A full circle is 360 degrees, a half circle is 180 degrees, and a quarter circle is 90 degrees. The start angle is effective only in the drawing environment and determines where the arc starts. The outer perimeter of the arc is determined by the outline you select from the pen settings in the Line panel of the Accents window. To apply the outline to the inside cut of the arc as well, click Frame Edges.

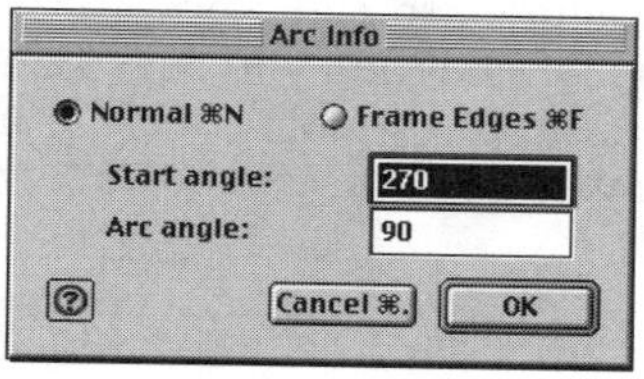

Figure 10-4:
When drawing, change the Start Angle and Arc Angle settings in the Arc Info dialog box to produce various arcs.

Regular polygon: The regular polygon tool draws multisided shapes with all sides equal in length — squares, pentagons, octagons, and so on. After you select the polygon tool, click the location where you want one corner of your polygon to appear. While pressing the mouse button, drag away from your starting point to expand the shape. The direction in which you drag the mouse determines the direction of the shape. The shape pivots around the starting point.

Your polygon can have anywhere from 3 to 40 sides. You must always set the number of sides prior to creating your regular polygon. In the drawing environment, click the tool once and then choose Edit⇨Polygon Sides. This opens the Number of Sides dialog box, where you enter the desired number of sides. In the paint environment, double-click the regular polygon tool in the Tools panel to open the Number of Sides dialog box, and then enter the number of sides. All polygons in the current document have that number of sides until you change the setting. (You can't change the number of sides after you draw the polygon.)

Using the freehand shape tools

This section describes the freehand shape tools (not to be confused with the freehand *paint* tools, discussed later in this chapter) common to both drawing and painting and offers tips for using them.

Freehand: The freehand tool enables you to paint a squiggly line. Click the freehand tool and then click at the location where you want to begin your line. Keep the mouse button pressed as you drag freehand-style in any direction you desire. Release the mouse button when you're done.

Polygon: Use the polygon (or edged shape) tool to make odd shapes with straight edges. Select the tool and then click at the starting point of your shape but immediately release the mouse button. You then drag in the direction you want the line to go. As you drag, the line follows. Click the mouse button again where you want that line segment to end. Repeat this process, dragging and clicking, to create line segments. When you get to the place where you want the last segment to end, simply double-click. If you want the shape to automatically close when you double-click, you can set that option in the Preferences dialog box.

Bezigon: For freehand shapes with curved "sides," call on the bezigon (or curved shape) tool. Some folks, and even AppleWorks, sometimes refer to this as the Bezier tool. Bezigon works like the polygon tool but makes curves rather than straight lines. Think of the line as a piece of flexible wire: Every time you click the mouse, you stake a *tack* that the wire curves around. As you bend the wire around a tack, the length behind it bows out as well.

 The polygon and bezigon tools are the two most powerful and overlooked tools in AppleWorks. The secret to using these tools is to draw shapes that combine curves and straight lines — with help from the Option key. If you're using the bezigon tool, just press the correct key and the next segment is a straight line. The polygon tool works in reverse, making the next segment of your shape a curve. Take a look at the examples in Figure 10-5.

Figure 10-5:
The U.S. Mail is brought to you by the polygon tool. The bone is brought to you by the bezigon.

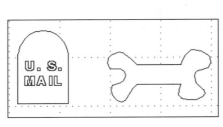

The shape on the left was drawn with the polygon tool. The shape on the right was drawn with the bezigon tool. To make a straight segment with the bezigon tool, hold down the Option key when you click both of the end points. If you hold down the Option key on only one end point, that endpoint becomes a counterpoint for two opposite curves. See Chapter 11 for more drawing specifics.

Working with the Freehand Paint Tools

You can use the three freehand tools — pencil, brush, and spray can — to paint over other shapes, create highlights and accents, or perform detailed editing. Figure 10-6 shows a sample of how each tool paints. All three tools paint based upon the current fill colors, textures, and gradients, so be sure to set those palette choices before you begin to paint. For added effect, you can also combine patterns with colors.

Figure 10-6:
The different strokes of the freehand paint tools.

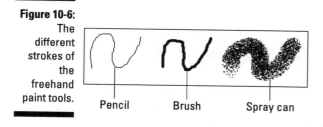

Pencil   Brush   Spray can

Pencil: This tool appears first when you open a new paint document or frame. It draws a one-pixel-wide line, assuming you haven't set the line width to a greater number. If the current fill color is black and you start by clicking a black dot that you previously drew, the pencil tool paints in white. If you're viewing a document with magnification set higher than 100 percent, double-clicking the pencil tool in the Tools panel zooms your document back to 100 percent. When viewing at 100 percent, double-clicking the pencil tool zooms you to 800 percent, enlarging the last location you clicked. Double-clicking again takes you back to 100 percent.

Paintbrush: This tool paints with various brush shapes, including patterns. You really can have fun with the paint brush. Here are a few ways to make the most of the brush tool:

- You can replace the standard round brush with any of several provided brushes, or even create your own. To edit your brush, double-click the paint brush tool or choose Options⇨Brush Shape. Doing this brings up the Edit Brush Shape dialog box shown in Figure 10-6.

- Simply click any of the brush shapes to put that brush shape into effect. If none of those brushes suits you, click Edit to open the Brush Editor dialog box (see the right side of Figure 10-7), where you can create your own brush shape. The pattern of dots represents the brush shape. Use the pointer to edit them (you can't paste into this area), and then click OK.

✔ After you apply a color to your document, the paint brush becomes a color-adjustment and blend tool. Double-click the paint brush tool or choose Options⇨Brush Shape. In the Brush Shape dialog box, select a brush size and choose an effect from the Effects pop-up menu. Your brush lightens, darkens, tints, or blends the colors you brush over, depending on the effect you choose. Continuous brushing increases the effect.

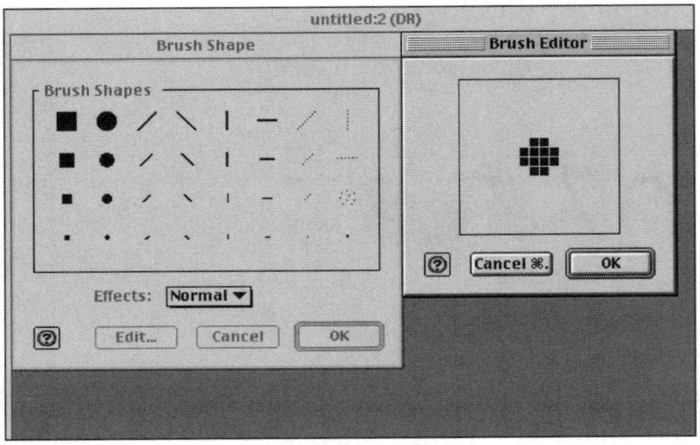

Figure 10-7:
Choose a brush shape, or create your own in the Brush Shape and Brush Editor dialog boxes.

✔ The brush can also behave like a stamp. Instead of dragging the brush in your document as you would drag a brush while painting, just position the brush pointer, hold it still, and click. Instead of a line or an area full of paint, you paint one focused area, as if you used a stamp and stamp pad. You can paint or stamp wallpaper, gradients, colors, and patterns.

 Spray can: This tool applies color, textures, and gradients with a spray-paint-like effect. The spray can is often used over a brick pattern for that graffiti-on-the-wall effect. Here are a couple of tips for using the spray can tool:

✔ As with real spray paint, you control the spray. Double-click the spray can tool or choose Options⇨Spray Can and change the options in the Edit Spray Can dialog box, shown in Figure 10-8.

These options let you control the size of the dot produced by the spray can and the speed at which the paint sprays. The dot size can be from 1 to 72, and the flow rate ranges from 1 to 100. As the flow rate increases, the spray effect is more blotchy, similar to what's shown in the Edit Spray Can dialog box's sample area in Figure 10-8. You can experiment with new settings in the sample area. Try a setting, use the Clear Sample Area button, and then try another. Ultimate convenience. Click OK when you're done.

> ✔ Like the brush tool, the spray can tool can also be used like a stamp, stamping its color, pattern, and so on as a rubber stamp would. Instead of dragging to spray within your document, keep the spray-can cursor still and press your mouse button to "spray" long enough for the texture, gradient, color, or pattern to fill in completely.

Figure 10-8:
I can't believe it's not spray paint: the Edit Spray Can dialog box.

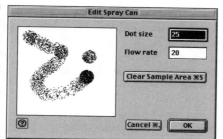

Jazzing Up Your Shapes with the Fill and Line Palettes

If all your shapes were solid black (the default), life would be pretty boring. Fortunately, you can save yourself from such a tedious fate. Any shape you create can have any color, fill, or border.

Each item you create, whether drawn or painted, comes into being with the attributes currently selected in the Accents window for fill and pen. In the drawing environment, or with objects and lines drawn in other environments, you can change any object's fill and border (pen) characteristics at any time. In the paint environment, you need to properly choose these characteristics *before* you make the shape because you can't always change them after the shape is placed on the page.

In this section, we introduce you to the various fill and line settings you can control. We discuss the specifics of changing these characteristics in drawn objects in Chapter 11, and we cover the details for changing painted items in Chapter 12.

Understanding fill settings

Fill settings apply to the inside of a shape. If a shape is open, AppleWorks draws an invisible line from the starting point to the ending point of the shape and fills any areas enclosed by that line. You can fill an object with a color, pattern, gradient (an area that fades from one color to another), or wallpaper. The patterns panel of Accents also includes a transparent option, which makes the inside of the object clear, so you can see whatever background is behind the object.

If your drawn object has a transparent fill, actually, there *is* no inside of the object — which means you have to click exactly on the object's outline to select it.

The fill choice in the Accents window provides several choices of fill types: solid colors, patterns, colors and patterns in tandem, gradient fills, and wallpaper. Each fill type can be edited, except the solid colors — but you can change those, too. Figure 10-9 shows the panels of the Accents window where fill can be set.

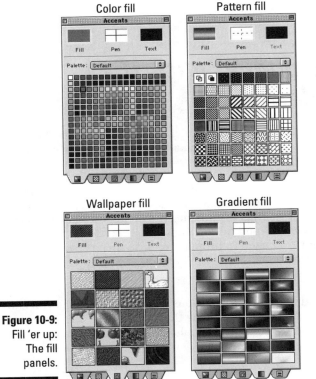

Figure 10-9:
Fill 'er up:
The fill
panels.

Understanding border and line settings

The pen settings control the borders and lines of the shapes and lines you create. Borders are preset to a thin black line around a solid black shape, so you may not even know that they're there, especially if your shape is black. You can change borders and lines to any color, thickness, or pattern you want. Straight lines can also have arrowheads. Figure 10-10 shows the panels where pen settings are available.

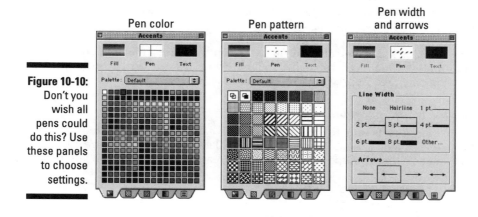

Figure 10-10: Don't you wish all pens could do this? Use these panels to choose settings.

Working with fill and line palettes

To select the fill and pen attributes of your new shape, click the icon for the panel you want to choose from and select the attribute you wish to set at the top of the panel. Just move the mouse to the color, pattern, wallpaper, gradient, or (for lines) width that you want and click. A black square surrounds any color or pattern you select. A check mark appears in front of the line width you choose and any arrowhead setting you choose.

The color, pattern, wallpaper, gradient, or width that you select also appears in the sample area above the setting for which you chose it. The sample area gives you an opportunity to preview your choices and experiment before making changes in your document.

The following sections describe the various fill and line palettes.

The fill and pen color choices

You can apply a color to both fills and lines. You can also combine a color with a pattern by selecting both a color and a pattern. Note that you can't apply a color and also apply a wallpaper or gradient. The last color, wallpaper, or gradient you select is the fill that's used.

Choose Fill on the color panel to create a fill and choose pen on the color panel to affect your lines. If you're sure that you changed a color but don't see your color, you may have chosen the wrong attribute at the top of the panel.

The fill and pen patterns panel

You can apply patterns to both fills and lines. Patterns work in conjunction with colors, so you can choose both a pattern and a color to create interesting fills and lines. If you apply a pattern to an object that already has a texture or gradient, the texture or gradient is replaced with the pattern and the color currently selected in your color panel goes into effect along with the pattern.

As with the color panel, choose Fill at the top to create a fill and Pen to affect your lines and borders. You can also create your own pattern by editing an existing one. (See Appendix B for instructions.)

The fill wallpaper panel

Wallpaper applies only to fills, not to lines. It can make a graphic look almost like a real object. The wallpaper panel has 20 selections. (See Figure 10-11.) You can edit these wallpapers, or you can create your own. We tell you how in Appendix B.

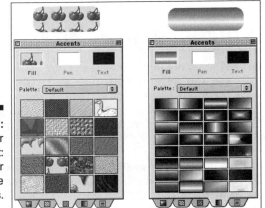

Figure 10-11:
Wallpaper
or gradient:
whatever
your palette
desires.

The fill gradients panel

Gradients are another fill option that lend reality to your graphics. A *gradient* is a pattern that fades from one color to the next. Take a look at the gradient panel in Figure 10-11. You select a gradient like you select any other fill attribute. However, like wallpaper, gradients apply only to fills and not to lines. The 32 gradients can also be edited. For the lowdown on editing them, check out Appendix B.

The pen width panel

The pen width panel enables you to determine the width of all lines — both regular lines and borders (outlines) or objects. You can use the pen width panel along with a color and pattern. In the drawing environment, you can set or change your line width at any time. However, if you paint, you must set the width before creating a line.

You can turn off a border by selecting None from the Line Width pop-up menu. You can also make a border or line as wide as you like by selecting Other from the Line Width pop-up menu and entering a width (in points). For an interesting effect, create a wide line and select a texture.

This panel is also where you select whether you want arrowheads at one, both, or neither end of lines you draw. Arrows are great for pointing out objects in presentations and manuals. The Arrows choices enable you to create straight-lined arrows (arrows are available only with the straight-line tool). You can use the arrows along with any of the other pen palette settings: color, pattern, and width. Arrowheads grow in proportion to line width. To set your arrow, simply choose an option from the Arrows section of the Width panel.

In the drawing environment, you can create a line and then apply arrow attributes, or you can select arrow attributes before you draw the line. You can also select the line at any time and change your arrow, just as you can change any line attribute in a drawing. In the paint environment as with any painted object, you must set your arrow option before you create your line.

Creating and Using Graphics Styles

You can really create graphics in style with AppleWorks. Use the Styles window to save a set of object properties, such as the fill's color, pattern, gradient, or wallpaper; and the border's width, color, and pattern. After you set up a custom style to reflect your format choices, you can apply that format to any object in that document with just one step.

Whether painting or drawing, styles may save you a lot of time and effort because they make it easy to create consistent-looking objects.

In the drawing environment, styles also allow you to make changes easily. You can change the format of all the objects that have a specific style simply by making changes to the style — the objects update automatically.

You create a style for graphics the same way you create a style for text in the word-processor environment, except that you choose graphics settings rather than text settings for your style. (To find out how to set up text styles, see Chapter 5.) Here are a few tips that are specifically related to making a graphics style:

✔ A graphics style can include settings for the fill color; the color and pattern combination; the gradient or wallpaper; and the pen's thickness, color, or color-and-pattern combination.

✔ Select Basic as the style type in the New Style dialog box. Graphics styles are always Basic styles, not Paragraph, Outline, SS-Table or Table styles.

✔ When editing the style, you can select a new color, pattern, wallpaper, and so on by clicking the attribute you want to change and selecting the new properties from the Accents window. Just bring the style editor's S pointer over to the panel(s) you want after selecting the attributes you want to change.

Selecting Graphics

Nobody's perfect (well, except for your authors), and your graphics probably aren't, either. No matter how exquisite today's masterpiece is, you may want to tweak it a little later when inspiration strikes. Before you can cut, copy, or move any part of your artistic creation, though, you must select it so that AppleWorks knows which item or items to affect. Selection methods differ in the drawing and painting environments. The following sections explain how to select objects in these two environments.

You can tell when an object is selected because you see its handles at its corners and possibly midpoint on its sides.

Selecting graphics in the drawing environment

To select drawing objects, use any of the methods in the following list (Figure 10-12 illustrates the methods).

Click   Shift-click   Drag a box

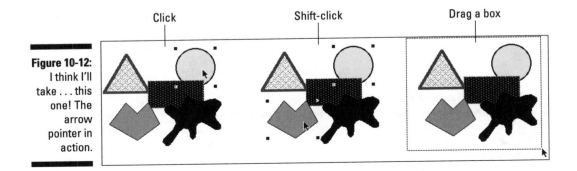

Figure 10-12:
I think I'll take . . . this one! The arrow pointer in action.

- **Click:** Click any object to select that object.

- **Shift-click:** To select several objects at once, press Shift as you click each object. You don't have to keep the Shift key pressed. You can release it, and then press it again before clicking to add another object to the selection.

- **Drag a box:** You can also select a group of objects by using the arrow pointer to drag a box (marquee) around the objects; only objects that are completely inside the box are selected, unless you press the ⌘ key while dragging. In that case, any object your arrow pointer touches is selected.

You can deselect one object in any group of selected objects without deselecting the entire group: Simply press Shift and click the object you want to deselect.

Selecting graphics in the painting environment

In the paint environment, individual objects don't exist, so selection techniques are different from those in the drawing environment. Rather than using the arrow pointer to make your selection, you use one or more of the following paint-specific selection tools. Figure 10-13 shows examples of how each tool works, and the following list gives you more details.

If you accidentally miss selecting part of the artwork and leave it behind when you move or copy the selection, use the Undo command, deselect the area, and try again. Undo to the rescue again!

Figure 10-13:
Selection antics: how each selection tool does its job.

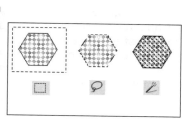

- **The selection rectangle or marquee tool:** This tool selects rectangular areas. It's known as the marquee tool because after something is selected, a rectangle flashes around it, like a theater marquee. Everything inside the rectangle moves or is copied, including the white space, which *whites out* anything you move it over. Double-clicking the selection rectangle selects the whole document.

✔ **The Lasso:** Yee-haw! You can rope any odd shape you can draw a line around. The Lasso selects only colored pixels — not white ones — so you can leave a wide space around your art and be sure that you get it all. When you move something that's selected with this tool, it doesn't *white out* your other work. Therefore, unlike the marquee tool, this tool doesn't leave obnoxious white space around your art when you move or copy it to another document. The Lasso tool automatically closes an open loop by drawing a straight line from the point where you release the mouse button to the point where you started the loop. Consequently, you should try to complete your loops to avoid having parts of your shape cut off by the straight line that the Lasso tool inserts to complete an open loop. Double-clicking the Lasso tool lassoes all colored pixels in the document.

Perhaps the easiest selection method is to use the selection rectangle while pressing the ⌘ key. With this modifier, the selection rectangle looks like a rectangle and is as easy to use, but it works like the Lasso by selecting only the colored pixels within the rectangle. The best of both tools!

✔ **The magic wand:** A true magician's tool, the magic wand is used to select any area that is all one color. For example, suppose you have a map of the United States that shows each of the states in a different color, and you want to select only Kentucky. Because all the states are different colors, clicking anywhere inside Kentucky with the magic wand selects the entire state.

If you hold down the option key when dragging the selection created with any of these tools, you drag a copy of the selection.

Removing Parts of Your Graphic

You can remove any element or elements of your artwork several ways. The method you choose depends upon the final result you desire. Regardless of which removal method you choose, you must first select any element or elements of your artwork before you can remove it (see the previous section, "Selecting Graphics," for help). Figure 10-14 demonstrates how each of the three deleting techniques works in the paint environment.

Figure 10-14:
Cut it out: tools for deletion.

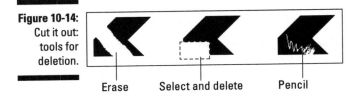

Erase Select and delete Pencil

Try one of these methods to remove part of your graphic:

- To remove a selected object that you don't want to Paste into another location, choose Edit➪Clear or Edit➪Cut or press Delete. Remember that the Clear and Delete commands totally remove the item, so it can't be placed elsewhere. The commands don't keep that item in the Clipboard the way the Cut option does, so we suggest that you cut an object to the Clipboard (unless you already have something on the Clipboard that you don't want to lose).

- To remove a selected object and place it elsewhere, choose Edit➪Cut The cut object moves to the Clipboard and is held there until you cut something else.

- When painting (not drawing), you also have the option of using the eraser tool. Simply select the eraser and then drag it over any colored area to erase everything under it, turning the area white. Be careful with the eraser, though! Double-clicking it deletes everything in your paint document or the active paint frame. Use the Undo command to get everything back.

When you're painting, you may not have to actually delete your errors. Instead, you can try using the pencil tool to correct tiny flaws. Zoom in to edit individual pixels.

Copying Graphics

One of the most efficient things you can do is copy an existing item or section of your artwork and reuse it in another part of your document, or even in a separate document.

Before you can copy anything, you have to tell AppleWorks what to copy, so first select the item or area to be copied (see "Selecting Graphics," earlier in this chapter, for tips on selecting).

You can choose from two methods of copying:

- **Copy and Paste:** Use this option when you want to copy an object to another document or to another part of the document you're in, or to copy the object directly on top of the original. Choose Edit➪Copy or press ⌘-C. Then, to paste what you copied, either choose Edit➪Paste or press ⌘-V.

Here are the secrets of pasting:

- *Pasting to a different page:* If you're pasting to a page other than the one you copied from, click the location in the document where you want the object to end up. If you don't click before using the Paste command, AppleWorks pastes the object into the center of your screen.

- *Pasting to the same page:* If you're pasting to the same page that you copied from, click the location where you want the object to end up, and then paste. You can make the copied object paste directly on the original by using the Paste command without clicking anywhere in the document prior to pasting. This is a great trick for creating drop shadows. You can use the arrow keys to nudge the pasted art just a tad.

✔ **Duplicate:** A faster way to create a copy in the same spot as the original is to use the Duplicate command. Just choose Edit⇨Duplicate or press ⌘-D. AppleWorks places the duplicate copy over the original, but slightly offset. Use Duplicate several times to create a stack of objects. Duplicate doesn't leave a copy of the object on the Clipboard, which comes in handy if you have other plans for the Clipboard soon, or if you don't want to displace something currently on the Clipboard.

Chapter 11
Drawing Details

- -

In This Chapter

▶ Changing colors, fills, and outlines

▶ Resizing, reshaping, and rotating objects

▶ Moving objects

▶ Placing objects in front of or behind one another

▶ Aligning objects

▶ Grouping and ungrouping objects

▶ Joining objects to create new shapes

- -

*T*he object of drawing is to draw objects. Oops! The preceding sentence is a circular reference. We'd better reshape it. And speaking of reshaping. . . .

One of the main reasons for choosing the draw environment over the paint environment is the ability to rearrange your graphics easily. You can choose among plenty of arrangement tools and options. You can move or change each object individually at any time, or you can compile objects (shapes) to create intricate graphics.

Due to the differences in the natures of drawing and painting, we dedicate this chapter specifically to drawing. Chapter 12 addresses the manipulation of painted graphics. Skip back to Chapter 9 for a comparison of drawing and painting if you're unsure of which to use in a particular situation.

Drawn objects are rather deceptive. They seem simple — and indeed *are* quite simple to create and work with. But they actually contain a lot of hidden power. With the help of this chapter, you can unleash this power.

Changing Fill and Line Attributes

In the drawing environment, you can easily change the fill or border of an object. All you need to do is select the object or objects and then choose a new attribute or combination from the Accents window.

When you select a new color, pattern, wallpaper, or gradient, any selected object takes on that new attribute. If you've grouped several objects, they all take on the new fill or border. If you want to change only one object (or a few) within a group, you must ungroup the objects first and then select only the one(s) you want to change. You can regroup them later. (See "Grouping and Ungrouping Objects," later in this chapter.)

An *object* is any selectable item on your draw layout. This includes rectangles, lines, frames, ovals, and all the other cool things you can select with the arrow pointer.

Changing fill attributes

Any color, pattern, wallpaper, or gradient *within the shape* is considered a fill. To select a fill, select any of these panel(s) of the Accents window and click Fill at the top. Move your mouse until the desired color, pattern, wallpaper, or gradient is bordered by a square. You see the results of your selection in any objects that are selected.

Wallpapers and gradients take over a shape completely, but solid colors and patterns can be used in combination. If you fill a shape with a gradient or wallpaper and then choose a pattern, the shape's color reverts to the last color selected for that shape's fill and uses that color in combination with the pattern.

Changing pen attributes

Any color or color and pattern combination *surrounding the shape* is considered a pen attribute. Pen attributes are also selected from the panels of the Accents window in the same way as fills. Pen attributes include color, pattern, and line width. Each of these attributes, alone or in combination, can be applied to any line, whether it is the outline of a shape or just a plain line. The arrows on the Width panel only apply to straight lines.

Picking up fill and pen attributes

After you set up any object with a fill and outline, you can go back and pick up the same qualities again to use as you create new objects or to change existing objects. The tool you use to do this is called the eyedropper. The eyedropper creates different effects within the paint and draw environments. Here, we tell you how to use the eyedropper in the draw environment. See Chapter 12 to find out how the eyedropper works in the paint environment.

To pick up an existing shape's fill and pen attributes, click the eyedropper once to select it, and then click the shape. If the object is transparent, click its border (there's nothing to click inside the shape). If you miss the desired shape, just move the eyedropper and click again.

After you pick up the attributes and they appear in the sample areas, any new shapes you create have these qualities. But what if you want to apply these attributes to existing shapes? In that case, after you pick up the desired qualities, click the eyedropper again and then press the ⌘ key as you click the shape or shapes that you want to change.

The eyedropper only works within the environment you're in when you select the eyedropper. You can't select the eyedropper while on a main drawing page and then click inside a paint frame to pick up a color.

The very tip of the eyedropper is the *hot spot*. For example, to catch the attributes of a thin line, you have to land the tip exactly on that line. You can zoom in on the page, enlarging the object on-screen, to make selection easier and that's a pretty good idea if you have lots of small objects close together.

Resizing Objects

You just spent an hour meticulously drawing a map to your home for a very important party invitation — only to run out of room before the road actually leads to your home. Everyone runs into situations like this in which they need to adjust a graphic a bit. Fortunately, in the AppleWorks drawing environment, resizing graphics is easy. You can resize any draw object to your heart's content.

You can resize an object in three ways: by dragging, by using the Scale Selection dialog box, and by using the size palette. (Just for the record, scaling also works the same for painted objects, which are discussed in detail in Chapter 12.)

Dragging objects

Use the arrow pointer to select the object, and then drag any of the handles to enlarge or reduce the object's size. If you select several objects at the same time, they're all affected when you resize, even though you only select and drag one handle. The other handles tag along proportionally. Figure 11-1 shows the resize process. You can easily distort an object this way.

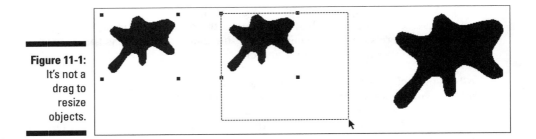

Figure 11-1:
It's not a drag to resize objects.

To maintain the object's proportions, hold down the Shift key as you drag.

Scaling objects

Scaling enables you to reduce or enlarge an object to a specific percentage of its current size. Here's what you do:

1. **Use the arrow pointer to select the object(s) you want to resize.**

   Be careful not to select extra objects, or they'll also be scaled.

2. **Choose Arrange⇨Scale By Percent.**

   This action opens the Scale By Percent dialog box, shown in Figure 11-2.

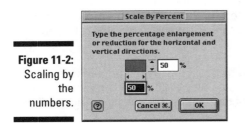

Figure 11-2:
Scaling by the numbers.

3. **Enter the percentage by which you want to resize the object.**

   You can resize horizontally (sideways), vertically (up and down), or both. To maintain the object's current proportions, type the same number in both boxes.

4. **Click OK to resize the object.**

   Remember that if you aren't happy with how the resized object turns out, you can use the Undo command and try again.

Just for the record, scaling works the same for painted objects, too. (See Chapter 12 to find out more about working in the painting environment.)

Using the Size palette

If you want an object to be a precise size, use the Object Size palette to reduce or enlarge the object:

1. **Select the object with the arrow pointer.**

2. **Choose Options⇨Object Size to call up the Object Size palette.**

3. **In the boxes with the double-headed arrows, enter your choice of horizontal and vertical measurements, as shown in Figure 11-3.**

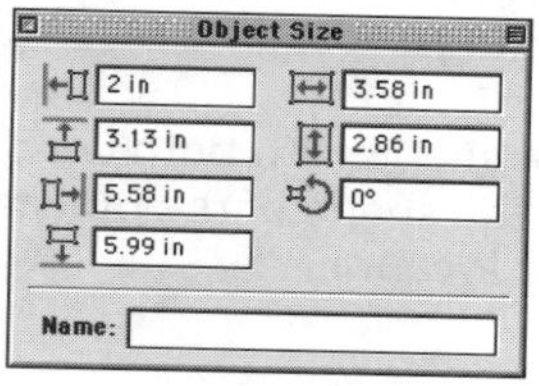

Figure 11-3:
If you need an object to have exact dimensions, use the Object Size palette.

Object Size

2 in	3.58 in
3.13 in	2.86 in
5.58 in	0°
5.99 in	

Name:

4. **Click the arrow next to the measurement, or press Return to make the change.**

You can also use the Object Size palette to position an object at a precise location on the page. The left four boxes are used to set how far you want the object to be placed from the left, top, right, or bottom margin. The bottom right box lets you specify the angle by which you wish to rotate the object. You can also give the object a name.

Reshaping Objects

Bend it, shape it . . . any way you want it. The most powerful graphics feature in AppleWorks is the capability to reshape draw objects. Reshaping lets you change any object by manipulating the points and lines that define its shape.

You can reshape only freehand shapes, regular polygons, arcs, and round rectangles. Reshaping doesn't work on regular rectangles, ovals, and straight lines. (See Chapter 10 to find out more about the various shape types.)

Reshaping freehand objects

To reshape an object, either add the optional Reshape button to your button bar (see Appendix A) and click it, or choose Arrange⇨Reshape or press ⌘-R. This command puts the selected object in reshape mode. The pointer changes to a crosshair with a box in the middle, and all the anchor points that make up your shape are visible. AppleWorks features two kinds of anchor points:

> ✔ **Corner anchor points:** These points are marked by squares. Corner anchor points appear at the ends of straight-line segments and at the corners where two straight lines meet.

> ✔ **Curve anchor points:** These anchor points are marked by circles and control where the bend of the curve changes.

Figure 11-4 shows the reshape pointer and a shape with both corner anchor points and curve anchor points. To change the shape of the object, just click an anchor point and drag the point to a new location.

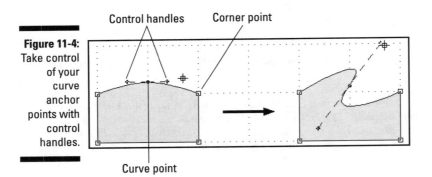

Control handles   Corner point

Figure 11-4:
Take control
of your
curve
anchor
points with
control
handles.

Curve point

You also can change the way a line bends around a curve anchor point by using the control handles that appear when you click a curve anchor point, as shown in Figure 11-4. Drag either handle to change how the line bends around the anchor point. Experiment by pivoting and stretching the control handle. Figure 11-4 shows the same object before and after adjusting a control handle.

You also can reshape objects in the following ways:

> ✔ **Add anchor points:** Click anywhere along the object's border with the reshape pointer to add an anchor point. This process lets you add sides to your shape.

✔ **Delete anchor points:** Click an anchor point with the reshape pointer and press Delete. This method smoothes curves because fewer controls affect the curve. Use the other control handles to reshape your line. Using fewer anchor points creates a smoother line; your printer also has one less piece of information to clog its memory, which leads to speedier printing.

✔ **Smooth out the sharpness of a polygon or a bezigon:** Click the anchor point with the reshape pointer to select it, and then either add the optional Smooth button to your button bar (see Appendix A) and click it, or choose Edit➪Smooth or press ⌘-(— the open parenthesis key. This method actually changes the corner anchor point to a curve anchor point. To make the control handles appear on these curves so you can work with them, press Option. You can also smooth multiple anchor points or the whole object by selecting them before you use the Smooth command.

✔ **Sharpen the smoothness of a bezigon or make a polygon even sharper:** This method the anchor point with the reshape pointer to select it, and then either add the optional Unsmooth button to your button bar (see Appendix A) and click it, or choose Edit➪Unsmooth or press ⌘-). (That keyboard command is the close parenthesis.) You also can sharpen the smoothness of multiple anchor points or the whole object.

Figure 11-5 shows you how a blob becomes a Valentine heart when we change two curve anchor points to straight-line anchor points.

Figure 11-5:
We love changing anchor points.

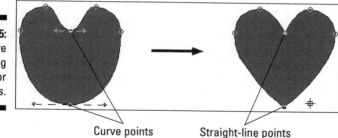

Curve points   Straight-line points

Reshaping round rectangles and arcs

In the drawing environment, you can reshape round rectangles and arcs at any time after you create them. This ability contrasts with the paint environment in which you must specify the settings first and can't edit the shape after it's made. Simply double-click the object to bring up the Corner Info or Arc Info dialog box and then enter the desired numbers to change your shape. We covered this procedure in detail in Chapter 10.

Rotating Objects

AppleWorks can rotate any object or frame to any angle from 0 to 360 degrees — and even create a mirror image by flipping the object or frame.

✔ **Flip Horizontally:** You can flip any draw object or frame. To flip an object horizontally, either add the Flip Horizontal button to the button bar (see Appendix A) and click it, or choose Arrange➪Flip Horizontally. Flipping in the draw environment works the same way as in the paint environment, so take a look at Chapter 12 for examples of how the flipping commands work.

✔ **Flip Vertically:** To flip your draw objects or frames vertically, either add the Flip Vertical button to the button bar (see Appendix A) and click it, or choose Arrange➪Flip Vertically. We cover this in the paint environment, so take a look at Chapter 12 for examples of how the flipping commands work.

✔ **Rotate 90 Degrees:** You can use the Rotate 90 Degrees command to rotate a draw object or frame clockwise in 90-degree increments. The Rotate 90 Degrees command is a button on your Button bar, so you have easy access to it. Click the button twice to rotate 180 degrees or three times to rotate 270 degrees.

✔ **Free Rotate:** You can *free rotate* any frame or object — that is, rotate it in one-degree increments from 0 to 360. You can do this in either of two ways: by dragging or by designating a specific angle:

  • *To rotate by dragging:* Either choose Arrange➪Free Rotate or press Shift-⌘-R to turn on Free Rotate mode, which changes your arrow pointer to an *X,* as shown in Figure 11-6. Click any shape or frame, and then drag the handles at the corners to rotate it. You see an outline of the shape as it moves. Free Rotate mode stays on until you select another tool. You can turn off Free Rotate mode the same way you turn it on. Try rotating some text for effect. Then try editing it. (Wait until you see how your text pops into line to edit and then rotates itself again!)

  • *To rotate to a specific angle:* Choose Options➪Object Size to show the Object Size palette. Click the object or frame that you want to rotate, type the angle in the box at the bottom of the three on the right on the palette, and then click the arrow next to the box or press Return.

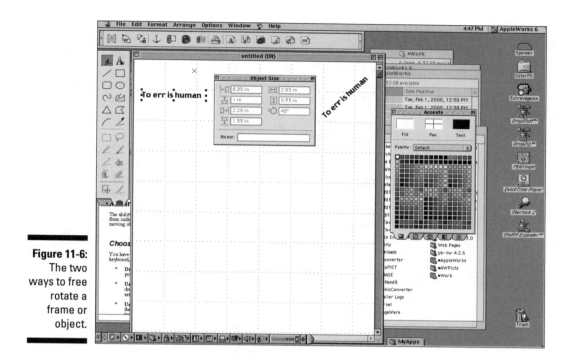

Figure 11-6:
The two
ways to free
rotate a
frame or
object.

Moving Objects

The ability to move your objects around easily makes it a cinch to create intricate graphics from individual objects. Here, we tell you everything you always wanted to know about moving objects but were afraid to ask.

Choosing a moving method

You have three ways to move objects in the draw environment: by dragging, by using the keyboard, or by using the size palette.

- ✔ **Dragging:** The most obvious way to move objects around the screen is to use the arrow pointer to drag them to a new location. Nothing tricky here.

- ✔ **Using the keyboard:** If you need to move your object more precisely than you can by dragging it, you can select the object and use the arrow keys on the keyboard. The arrow keys move the object one pixel at a time or one unit on the autogrid at a time.

✔ **Using the size palette:** Moving objects with a palette works the same way as resizing them with this palette: Just type how far you want the object to be located from the left, top, right, or bottom margin of your document. To bring up the size palette, choose Options⇨Object Size. Moving objects this way lets you specify a precise position on the page.

Using the autogrid

The autogrid affects dragging and keyboard navigation. Autogrid may sound like an L.A. freeway at rush hour, but it's actually an invisible grid that makes your objects move across the screen in set increments. The autogrid is useful for drawing consistent shapes and for lining up objects evenly, but it also prevents you from drawing a shape whose size isn't a grid increment multiple or moving an object just one or two pixels at a time. Here are some tips for using the autogrid:

✔ **To toggle the autogrid off or on:** Choose Options⇨Turn Autogrid Off/On or press ⌘-Y.

✔ **To set the autogrid increments:** Choose Format⇨Rulers⇨Ruler Settings to open the Ruler Settings dialog box. The autogrid is based on ruler settings, so to change the autogrid increments, type a new number in the Divisions box and then click OK. The greater the number of divisions, the smaller the autogrid's increments.

✔ **To snap-align existing objects:** If you want objects that were drawn with the autogrid off to snap to the nearest grid point, select the object, and then either choose Arrange⇨Align To Grid or press ⌘-K.

Manipulating layers

You may notice that objects can overlap one other. Each draw object or text block exists in its own layer. Each new object is added in front (on top) of any existing layers. When one object covers another, you may need to shuffle the layers. Four commands enable you to move objects in front or in back of others. These are optional buttons that you can add (see Appendix A). You can also find commands for all four options in the Arrange menu. They are

✔ **Move Forward:** Moves the currently selected object one layer toward the front. The keyboard shortcuts are Shift-⌘-+ (that's a plus sign).

✔ **Move to Front:** Moves the selected object in front of all other layers.

✔ **Move Backward:** Moves the currently selected object one layer toward the back. The keyboard shortcut is Shift-⌘-– (that's a minus sign).

✔ **Move To Back:** Moves the currently selected object behind all other layers. This is an optional button.

For example, say you're creating a logo. You begin with text for your company name. Then you add a big oval. Next a small graphic. Your text is in back and you need it in front, so you can either click the Move Forward button twice or click the Move To Front button once for faster action. If you can't see the text, select the oval and click the Move Backward button a couple of times or click the Move To Back button once.

You also can use these commands to hide objects behind other objects. For example, you may have a logo that you don't want to show. Just send it behind something. (Or create a shape to put over it.) This is the AppleWorks equivalent of sweeping the dust under the rug, except there's no bump to trip over.

Aligning Objects

If you want your objects to line up perfectly, the alignment tools have you covered. You have six commands, all buttons on the default palette. If you prefer, you can use the Align Objects dialog box instead. Whichever method you use, first select the objects you want to align. Then click the button or buttons to do the alignment or choose Arrange⇨Align Objects to summon the Align Objects dialog box. The following list explains the eight commands that all have button equivalents:

- ✔ **Align Top:** Aligns all selected objects along their top-most edges.

- ✔ **Align Bottom:** Aligns all selected objects along their bottom-most edges.

- ✔ **Align Left:** Aligns all selected objects along their left edges.

- ✔ **Align Right:** Aligns all selected objects along their right edges.

- ✔ **Align Centers Horizontally:** Aligns all selected objects along an imaginary horizontal line that goes through each object's center.

- ✔ **Align Centers Vertically:** Aligns all selected objects along an imaginary vertical line that goes through each object's center.

- ✔ **Distribute Horiz:** Spaces the objects so that there are equal amounts of space between them horizontally.

- ✔ **Distribute Vert:** Redistributes the objects vertically so they are spaced equidistantly from each other.

Grouping and Ungrouping Objects

Grouping lets you link several objects together to be treated as one object. This option comes in handy when you're making any kind of graphic that's a composite of several objects. Grouping ensures that objects stay together relative to one another during resizes and moves.

Grouping has another benefit: In a document with many objects, selecting specific items can be difficult. Grouping can help limit the number of elements that can be selected inadvertently. This section tells you what you need to know to group and ungroup objects. We also tell you how to join and lock objects.

Grouping objects

To group objects, just follow these steps:

1. **Select the objects you want to group together.**

   You can either drag a selection box around the objects with the arrow pointer or click each object as you hold down the Shift key.

2. **Either place the optional Group button on your button bar (see Appendix A) and click it, or choose Arrange⇨Group or ⌘-G.**

   Your objects are now grouped. You may notice that all the individual selection handles have been replaced by selection handles for the group as a single object, as shown by the image in Figure 11-7.

Free rotate cursor

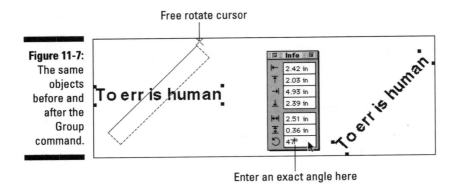

Figure 11-7:
The same objects before and after the Group command.

To err is human

Enter an exact angle here

Ungrouping objects

To bust up this cozy situation and work on one of the objects individually, select the group and then choose Arrange⇨Ungroup.

AppleWorks clip art can be ungrouped, allowing you to work with each element separately or even discard unwanted parts of a graphic. For example, if you need a single balloon, you can place the AppleWorks balloons graphic on your page, ungroup it, and delete all but one balloon. You can even further ungroup that single balloon and change the flow of its string. Any clip art that is *layered* can be ungrouped and edited.

Joining objects

Joining lets you link together two freehand objects to make one single object. This option is different from the Group command because the two objects can't be "unjoined." Joining takes place with Reshape mode on.

To turn on Reshape mode, either add the optional Object button to your button bar (see Appendix A) and click it, or choose Arrange⇨Reshape or press ⌘-R. The pointer changes to a crosshair with a box in the middle, and all the anchor points that make up your shape are visible.

Here's how you join two objects:

1. **Select the first object.**

2. **Either place the optional Reshape button on your button bar (see Appendix A) and click it or choose Arrange⇨Reshape or press ⌘-R.**

3. **Cut or copy the object to the Clipboard.**

4. **Select the second object.**

   Normally, the Join command attaches the starting point of the object on the Clipboard to the ending point of the object you just selected. If you want to connect the starting points of both objects, click the starting point of the object you just selected. Both of these options are shown in Figure 11-8.

5. **Either choose Edit⇨Paste or press ⌘-V.**

   Notice in Figure 11-8 that the object that was pasted assumes the fill and line settings of the other object.

6. **Either choose Arrange⇨Reshape or press ⌘-R to turn off Reshape mode when you finish. (Or click the Reshape button if you've added it.)**

You can use this process to join several copies of the same object together to form a border or a pattern.

Figure 11-8:
The objects
at the top
are going to
be joined.
On the left,
they are
joined end
point to
starting
point, and
on the right,
starting
point to
starting
point.

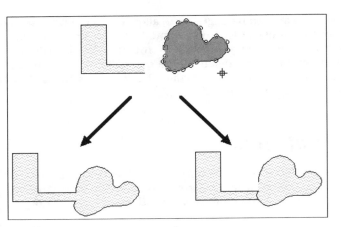

Locking objects

Locking is like nailing down the object on your page, because a locked object can't change or move — that is, until you use the Unlock command. In an intricate image, locking an object that you don't want affected makes it easier to select and change the objects around it.

To make an object or frame stay put, select it and choose Arrange⇨Lock. You know something is locked if its handles appear grayed out when the item is selected. You can copy a locked object, but you can't delete it.

Note, however, that frames work a bit differently: You can't move or resize a locked frame, but you *can* change its contents, which is very handy.

Many Templates and Assistant documents have locked frames and objects. If you see gray handles when you select an object or frame, use the Unlock command to move or resize it.

Chapter 12

Special Effects with Paint

*R*emember being a kid and creating all those great works of art for your parents to hang proudly on the fridge? Working with the paint environment brings back those fond memories. The paint environment lets you play around, experiment, explore new ways to make your pictures look cool, and feel like a kid again without all the hassle and mess: You don't get stains on your clothes, you never run out of paper, and the teacher doesn't scold you for eating the paint!

This chapter is for those of you who aren't satisfied with average graphics. You want to create something really eye-popping, different . . . unusual. You want to push your pixels around and make your text and graphics look like they've been put through a taffy-puller. The special effects commands in the paint environment's Transform menu give you powers that fall loosely into four categories: color manipulation, resizing, warping, and rotating.

Coloring Your World

One of the first things a person notices about any document or image is its color. Color adds dimension and emotion to any document. When you paint, you usually choose your colors as you create your work. However, you're bound to want to change the color of an area at one time or another.

Unlike the drawing environment, where you can change lines or shapes in their entirety just by choosing a new fill or pen attribute, in the painting environment, a line or fill is simply a bunch of unrelated dots (or pixels). Therefore, to change the color of a line, you usually must change each pixel that comprises the line. However, there are some times when you can change entire areas at once.

We strongly recommend that you always keep the Accents window open when you're in the paint environment. It's a good idea when in the drawing environment, too, but you really can't do anything exciting without it when painting.

Choosing new colors

One way to change a line, fill, or area is with the pencil tool. After you choose your new color, select the pencil tool and click on each pixel you want to recolor. This technique is most helpful for fine detailing.

The paint bucket tool allows you to change entire areas (or several pixels) at once. After you create your shape, you can use the paint bucket tool to pour a new color into (or onto) it. Select the desired fill, select the paint bucket, and then click in the area to which you want to apply the new color.

You can alter any solid colors or white areas (even those within patterns). For example, if you draw a rectangle while the fill color is set to white or another solid color, you can easily change the color later. You also can fill the rectangle with a pattern, gradient, or texture. However, after you fill it with a pattern, gradient, or wallpaper, only the white spaces or solid colored areas within that design can have the new fill applied. All patterns, gradients, and wallpapers are actually composed of solid colors — they just happen to all be mixed together. Therefore, you can point your paint bucket at any one area of color, and that area changes — whether it's one lone pixel or a large area.

For an interesting effect, fill an area with a wallpaper or gradient and then apply a solid color or gradient to the background or the solid areas within the pattern. Simply select the fill you want, select the paint bucket tool, and then click inside the area you want to fill.

The very tip of the paint, spilling out of the bucket, is the _hot spot,_ which is the part of the paint bucket that has to be inside the area you're filling. If you are working with a small shape, it is helpful to zoom in on the shape.

Only closed shapes can be filled with the paint bucket tool. If you create your shapes by hand and even one pixel is missing from your object's outline, paint "leaks out" to fill the entire background on which the object is placed. Along the same line, a line cannot be filled with the paint bucket tool. Instead, your entire background will be filled. In these cases, remember the trusty Undo command. Undo your work, zoom in, plug the leak, and then try again. You can set your shapes to close automatically with the Edit➪Preferences command, if you want to avoid such problems.

Adopting existing colors

At times, you may find that you want to use a color that you used someplace within your paint document or in your paint frame. You can match a previously used color exactly by picking up that same color — with the help of the eyedropper tool.

 To pick up a color, click the eyedropper to select it and then move the eyedropper into your document until its tip is on the color you want to use. (The very tip of the eyedropper is the *hot spot.* The color the tip is on when you click the tool is the color that's adopted.) Click this color to pick it up as your new fill color. This newly selected color appears in the fill sample area in the Accents window. If you picked up the wrong color, just move the eyedropper back into your document and click again.

You can also use the eyedropper to pick up a pen color. Just press the Option key as you click your desired color. Only the color is adopted, not the line width or arrowheads.

The eyedropper only works within the environment you're in when you select the eyedropper. If you're in a painting frame in another main document, you can't select the eyedropper while you're on a main drawing page and click it inside a paint frame to pick up a color for application in the main page.

Choosing a paint mode

Paint modes affect what happens when you draw or paste one shape or line on top of another. You can choose from three different modes to designate how new paint interacts with existing patterns underneath it. You can add buttons for each of these modes to your button bar (see Appendix A).

 ✔ **Opaque:** This is the normal setting. In opaque mode, new paint covers anything underneath it. It's like working with oil paints.

 ✔ **Transparent:** In this mode, any white space in your new shape is transparent. Whatever color, wallpaper, or pattern is underneath the shape shows through in the white space. The rest of the colors work as they do in opaque mode.

✔ **Tint:** This mode mixes the new paint with any existing pattern under it. For example, if you paint a blue square over a red circle, the overlapping area is purple. Tint mode works like watercolors.

If you would rather not use buttons, you can change the paint mode by choosing Options⇨Paint Mode to access the Painting Mode dialog box.

Transforming colors

The following color tricks appear in the Transform menu. Some of these are in the default button bar; the rest can be added (see Appendix A).

✔ **Fill:** Works kind of like the paint bucket tool. The major difference is that this command fills in the entire current selection without the limitations of the paint bucket. Absolutely any area you select is filled when you use this command.

Use the magic wand tool to obtain control, and then use this command to easily change colors, patterns, textures, and gradients in your images. This button can be added.

✔ **Pick Up:** Breaks the ice at a singles event. Actually, this is a really cool command that lets you transfer the colors and patterns of an image to a selection that's placed on top of it — kind of like lifting up newsprint with Silly Putty. Select the image or area you want to apply the effect to. Move that selected image on top of the part of the paint image that you want to pick up. Click the Pick Up button or choose the command. Your image/selection picks up the same painted image that it's on top of. Of course, you don't want to keep your selected image on top of that other image. You just want to borrow (copy) the other image's pattern or color. While the original image is still selected, you can move it back where you want to use it. This button is on the default painting button bar.

✔ **Invert:** Changes black to white and white to black. Invert also transforms colors into their opposites. In an image with lots of colors, using this command is kind of like looking at the negative of a color photo. (Use this command selectively: If white is included, it turns black.) Just select the image and click the Invert button. This button is on the default painting button bar.

✔ **Blend:** Makes the selected area look out of focus by blending colors into the neighboring dots, which can soften sharp edges in an image. It's the AppleWorks version of smearing petroleum jelly on a camera lens. Just select the area to blend and click the Blend button or choose the command. This button is on the default painting button bar.

✔ **Tint:** Want to look at your artwork through rose-colored glasses? This is the way to do it. The Tint command tints a selected area with whatever color is selected in the fill sample area. Click the Tint button several times to increase the effect. This effect doesn't apply when working in black and white. This button is on the default painting button bar and should not be confused with the Tint Mode button.

✔ **Lighter/Darker:** These two commands work like the Tint command. They lighten or darken a selected image by adding more white or more black. Just select an area and click the Lighter or Darker button or choose the command. Click the button several times to increase the effect. This effect doesn't apply when working in black and white. These buttons are on the default painting button bar.

Resizing Graphics

You can resize your artwork two ways: by hand or by dialog box. The manual method enables you to resize your graphic any way you like. The Scale Selection dialog box lets you type in the percentage by which you want to scale your artwork.

Resizing graphics manually

To resize artwork manually — the quickest way to fit your artwork to a specific area — follow these steps:

1. **Select the part of your painting you want to resize.**

2. **Choose Transform⇨Resize.**

   Hollow handles appear at the corners of your selection.

3. **Drag a handle to reduce or enlarge the size of your selection.**

Hold down the Shift key as you drag to resize proportionally. That way, you don't squash or stretch the image.

Resizing graphics precisely by using the Scale By Percent dialog box

To precisely resize something, follow these steps:

1. **Select the part of your document that you want to resize.**

   You can use any of the three AppleWorks selection tools.

2. **Choose Transform⇨Scale By Percent.**

   This command brings up the Scale By Percent dialog box shown in Figure 12-1.

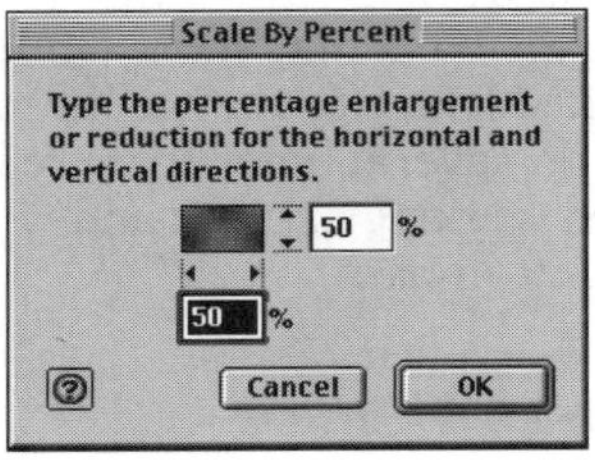

Figure 12-1: Scaling graphics is easier than scaling walls, as you can see by the simplicity of this dialog box.

3. **Enter the percentage by which you want to scale your selection in the boxes next to the horizontal and vertical axes.**

   A number less than 100 reduces the graphic's size; a number greater than 100 increases the graphic's size.

   Enter the same number in both percentage boxes to maintain the selection's proportions.

4. **Click OK to accept the change or Cancel to call off this resize thing.**

Warping Graphics

You designed your company logo, but it still doesn't look quite right to you. Maybe if the whole thing leaned to the right a little to make it more dynamic. . . . Or maybe you want the design to stretch out toward the horizon. The commands in this section are all about twisting your artwork.

Stretching graphics

The Stretch command lets you pull the corners of a selected area in any direction you want. To use this command, follow these steps:

1. **Using any of the selection tools, select what you want to distort.**

2. **Choose Transform⇨Stretch.**

   Hollow handles, or white squares, appear at the corners of your selection. Click and drag them to stretch your selection.

3. **Drag the corner handles to reshape the selection.**

   Click once outside the selected area to make the distort handles go away. The graphic is still selected. If you decide that you liked the graphic better before, now's the time to use the Undo command.

Remember how you could pick up pictures from the newspaper with Silly Putty and stretch them out to make them look really strange? That's sort of what the Stretch command does. We stretched out a sample newspaper column in Figure 12-2.

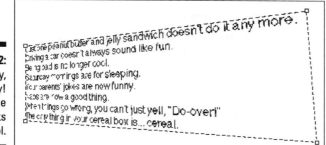

Figure 12-2:
It's not putty, you silly! It's the AppleWorks Stretch tool.

Putting things into perspective

The Add Perspective command lets you extend your art toward the horizon. It works much like the Stretch command:

1. **Select any part of your painted area.**

2. **Choose Transform⇨Add Perspective.**

   The hollow handles appear at the corners.

3. **Drag the handles to create the perspective effect.**

   The direction in which you first drag the handle determines how the perspective effect looks. Drag sideways to work with the top or bottom edge; drag up or down to work with the side. You can see examples of both in Figure 12-3.

Figure 12-3:
Perspective is all in how you look at it.

Slanting graphics

You know what happens if you open both the top and the bottom of an empty cereal box? If you look through it from end to end and smoosh the sides a bit, the rectangle turns into a parallelogram — that's kind of what you do with the Slant command.

1. **Select whatever you want to shear.**

2. **Choose Transform⇨Slant.**

   Hollow handles appear at the corners.

3. **Drag the handles in the direction you want your graphic to slant.**

   Moving side to side slants the sides. Moving up and down slants the top and bottom. Keep dragging the handles until you're happy with the result.

You can make your artwork look like it's caught in a heavy wind, speeding along, or sliding down a hill in San Francisco, as shown in Figure 12-4.

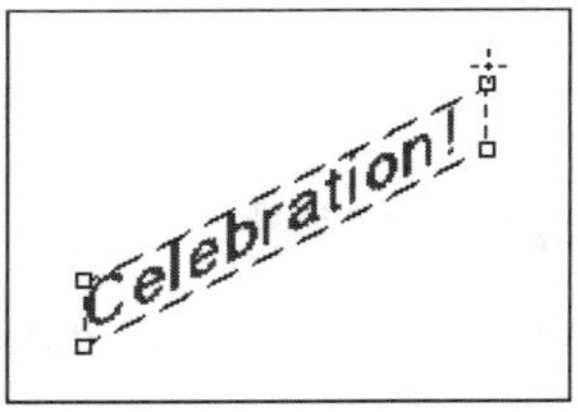

Figure 12-4:
Celebrate
the Slant
command.

Flipping and Rotating Graphics

Flipping and rotating are really cool and sometimes very handy operations. You can flip, rotate, or free rotate your artwork.

Flipping graphics

Flipping a graphic makes it a mirror image of itself. An image can flip sideways or up and down. Flipping is different from rotating a graphic. When you flip an image, it's actually reversed, as if in a mirror.

Keep the following two tips in mind as you flip images:

- Flipping an object once horizontally and once vertically does the same thing as rotating the image 180 degrees.

- Flipping twice in the same direction brings the image back to its original position.

Flipping graphics horizontally

To flip your graphic horizontally, follow these steps:

1. **Select the area you want to flip.**

2. **Choose Transform⇨Flip Horizontally or click the Flip Horizontally button.**

   The image flips from side to side, as shown in the third image in Figure 12-5.

   If you decide you liked the image better before the flip, or you chose the wrong direction, click Undo right away, before you deselect the image.

Figure 12-5: Eggs over easy — with the flip commands.

Flipping graphics vertically

To flip your graphic vertically, follow these steps:

1. **Select the area you want to flip.**

2. **Choose Transform⇨Flip Vertically or click the Flip Vertically button.**

   Flip Vertically flips the image up and down, as shown in the second image in Figure 12-5.

Rotating graphics

Rotating literally turns the image around, rather than mirroring it. You can rotate images via the Rotate dialog box or via the Free Rotate command.

Rotating graphics via the Rotate dialog box

The Rotate dialog box allows you to precisely control the angle of rotation. This control is extremely helpful when you need to match several objects (such as text blocks). Using the Rotate dialog box also ensures you can rotate to exactly 45, 90, or 180 degrees. Keep in mind that at an angle larger than 180 degrees, the image is turned upside-down.

1. **Select the image you want to rotate.**

2. **Choose Transform⇨Rotate.**

   In the Rotate dialog box, enter a number for the angle at which you want to rotate the selected image. You can type any number from –1 to 360.

3. **Click OK to rotate the image or Cancel to call it off.**

The Rotate 90 Degrees button is the fastest way to rotate a selected image. Click the button once to rotate your image 90 degrees, twice for 180 degrees, or three times for 270 degrees.

Rotating graphics via the Free Rotate command

The Free Rotate command lets you rotate an image manually to any angle.

1. **Select the image you want to rotate.**

2. **Choose Transform⇨Free Rotate.**

   Hollow handles appear at the corners of your selection.

3. **Drag any handle in the direction in which you want the image to rotate.**

   The image pivots around its center, as shown in Figure 12-6.

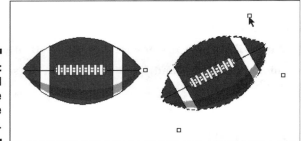

Figure 12-6:
Have a ball with the Free Rotate command.

To line up several images in Paint mode: Draw a straight line using the pencil tool (or line tool) while holding down the Shift key. Use this line as a visual guide to align your images, but be sure to leave a little space between the line and your images. Erase the line when you finish.

Chapter 13

The Lowdown on Page Layout

*P*age layout is where AppleWorks really struts its stuff. An AppleWorks drawing document is a natural for page layout because it lets you combine different frames and graphics and has the tools you need to make everything look the way you want it to.

One reason the draw environment is so versatile is the ease with which you can place and manipulate text, tables, spreadsheets, and paint frames. The frame tools in the top of the Tools window enable you to create frames and edit the information inside. Within a frame, you have all the same capabilities that you have in that type of document. When you work inside a frame, you actually switch to that environment. For example, when you edit text inside a text frame, the menus change to the menus available in the text environment.

In this chapter, we show you everything you need to build a newsletter, flier, certificate, envelope, or other intricate document. The truth is that you may never have to build these documents from scratch because the AppleWorks Assistant builds them for you to spec based on your responses to simple interviews. However, we want you to be able to do anything! We also want to show off how incredibly, unexpectedly powerful AppleWorks can be in yet another way.

Setting Up a Document

Before you can do anything, you need to set up a document on which to do your layout. The foundation for all page layout is a drawing document, the most flexible environment.

 To begin a new blank document, click the AppleWorks Draw button or choose File⇨New⇨Drawing.

To tell AppleWorks what size and orientation you want for your document, choose File⇨Page Setup. This command brings up the Page Setup dialog box. Figure 13-1 shows the Page Setup dialog box. Your document setup dialog box may look different depending on the printer you are using and what version printer software you have.

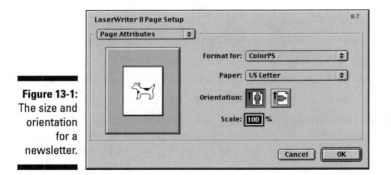

Figure 13-1:
The size and orientation for a newsletter.

The following list recommends page setups for common documents:

- ✔ **Creating a standard-page-sized newsletter:** Set the page size to US Letter (or A4, if appropriate). US Letter sometimes comes in two variations — choose the larger in most cases. Choose the standard portrait (vertical) orientation. Click OK after you set these specifications. You should see on-screen a single, standard-sized, vertically positioned page.

- ✔ **Creating a certificate:** Use the standard page size, set the orientation to landscape (horizontal), and click OK. Your document appears horizontally distributed on-screen.

- ✔ **Creating an envelope:** Set the page size for Comm 10 Envelope (standard business size) or Monarch Monarch (personal letter size). Set the orientation to landscape (horizontal). Click OK. Your document appears true to envelope size and orientation on-screen.

Changing Document Margins

You should set your margins when you first begin your document. You can change them later, but that can throw off your layout.

To set or change the margins, choose Format⇨Document.

You can individually set the top, bottom, right, and left margins; they can each be different sizes. Some printers are capable of handling margins as small as ¼ inch. However, set your margins to 0.5 inches to make your newsletter flexible. The Document dialog box is shown in Figure 13-2.

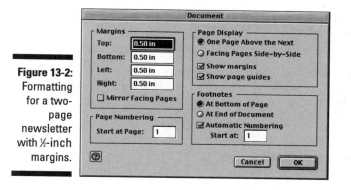

Figure 13-2:
Formatting
for a two-
page
newsletter
with ½-inch
margins.

For an envelope, try setting the margins at 0.25 inches to place your return address way up out of the way, in the corner. If the return address is cut off *(clipped)* when you print, increase the margins to 0.5 inches each.

If you already have objects on your page, you may find that making the margins wider (larger) pushes some objects into the margin area — off the working area of the page. If you can still see part of an object, select it and pull it into the active area. If you do not see the object that landed in the margin, you have these options:

✔ Temporarily make the margins narrower again, pull the objects into the center of the page, and reset the margins.

✔ Determine where on the page your objects are and follow the appropriate directions:

   • If all the objects are on one side of the page and you can't see them, choose Select All and use the arrow keys to move the objects back into the active page area.

- If objects are on both sides of the page and those in the margin are on only one side, lock the items on the other side prior to selecting all objects and using the arrow keys. (See Chapter 11 if you're not sure how to lock objects.)

- If objects off the active area on both sides of the page, see the next section on adding pages and then perform the Select All trick previously described.

Adding Pages to Your Document

To lay out longer documents, such as a double-sided flier or a newsletter, you need to add pages to your draw document. You can always add or delete pages in the Document dialog box. Choose Format⇨Document to bring up this dialog box.

You can have your document pages travel across your screen horizontally, vertically, or both. If your document is more than one page across, use the scroll bar along the bottom of the page to move between pages. For a document that's more than one page down, use the scroll bar along the side of the page instead.

In the Document dialog box, type the number of pages across and down for your document; the pages are added when you click OK. Figure 13-2 shows a newsletter format that scrolls two pages going down.

When adding pages, keep in mind the following tips.

- Some people like to enter 1 for Pages Across and additional Pages Down so they can scroll downward to the next page as in a word-processing document. Others prefer to have the pages move across the screen. You can also set your newsletter to have two pages flow across like a newspaper does, and then have subsequent sets of pages flow downward.

- If you have two or more pages across and several down as well, the page numbering proceeds from left to right until the rightmost page is reached and then moves down to the next row continuing sequentially from the leftmost side.

- If your monitor is large enough to display two pages at once, you may want to make your document two pages across when you're working on a newsletter or other document that has double-sided or facing pages. If you can't fit two pages on the screen, try zooming out to 75 percent.

Viewing Your Document

AppleWorks provides many visual aids and tools to help you see how your document is shaping up. You can turn these features on or off at any time without affecting your document. The following sections tell you how to change view options and how to display the rulers.

Changing view options

Some people find it easier to work on a document when the screen closely represents the way the document will print. The way you view a document doesn't actually affect how it prints, so you can change the view options at any time without hassle.

- ✔ To see the whole page on-screen, including the margin area, choose Window➪Page View or press Shift-⌘-P.

- ✔ If you prefer to use buttons, remain in the current view, add the Show/Hide Margins button (top) to your button bar, and click it.

  Show/Hide Margins is only available if Page View is selected. The margin area shows up as white. Clicking the Show/Hide Page Guide button (bottom), which is also optional, adds a hard line view of the margins. With these buttons, or with page view on, you can see a document as it looks when printed. This view helps you get the best feel for the balance of a newsletter or envision how an envelope looks.

The graphics grid does not print; it's there only to help you place objects on the page. You can turn it off anytime. See Chapter 10 for more information about the graphics grid.

Using the graphics and text rulers

Rulers help you work with objects and frames. AppleWorks features two kinds of rulers: graphics and text. A *graphics ruler* runs along the left and top sides of your page, showing you where objects and frames are located on the page. The *text ruler* appears only along the top of the page, but it allows you to format text inside the text frames on your page. The text ruler is the same in the draw environment as it is in the text environment; it lets you change line spacing, set tab stops, and control alignment. Check out Chapter 5 for more information about formatting text.

To show and select your desired rulers at any time, choose Format➪Rulers➪ Show Rulers (Shift-⌘-U). Show Rulers changes to Hide Rulers when the rulers are on-screen. You can also change the unit of measurement or the ruler's divisions by choosing Format⇨Rulers⇨Ruler Settings to bring up the Ruler Settings dialog box. AppleWorks rulers can reflect inches, centimeters, millimeters, picas, or points (see Figure 13-3).

You can also change rulers by changing environments, hiding the rulers, and then showing them again.

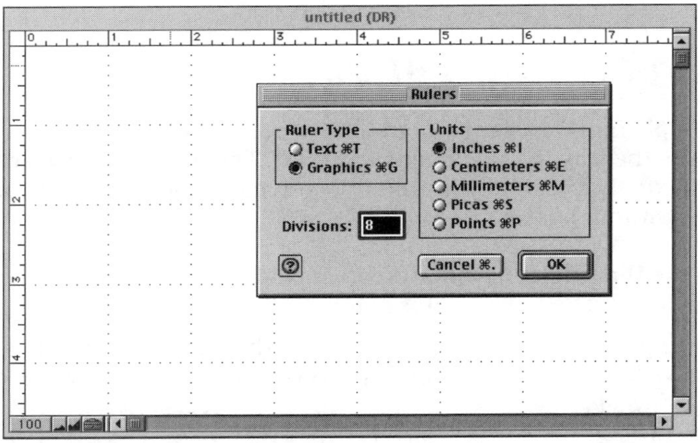

Figure 13-3:
Rulers rule.
The Ruler
Settings
dialog box in
front of a
draw docu-
ment with
graphics
rulers
visible.

Using Headers and Footers

Headers and *footers* let you put in one place all the information that needs to appear on every page of your document. There are lots of reasons to use headers and footers when laying out a document. People commonly place page numbers on each page of a newsletter, for example. In a book-like document, people usually place the name of the book and chapter in the top margin. You know these things. What you need to know from us is *how* to create the headers and footers.

You add a header or footer to your draw document just as in a text document. To add a header (or footer), choose Format⇨Insert Header (or Insert Footer). The header appears at the top of your page with the cursor flashing and ready to enter centered text; the footer, at the bottom.

Technically, you can put a page-number placeholder in any text frame in a draw document — but that's not practical. For a five-page document, you would have to create five text frames, one per page, and make sure that they all lined up to get those page numbers in the same place on every page.

Instead, use a header or footer, which lets you add the page number once and displays on every page. Because headers and footers are actually text frames, you can put anything in them that you can put in other text frames — text, placeholders for page numbers, time, date, or graphics. You can even insert a spreadsheet frame if that's your idea of the perfect header or footer. Take a look at Chapter 5 for a complete rundown on headers and footers.

The most impressive page numbering includes the total page count so that your page says something like "page 1 of 3." With AppleWorks, your page count can automatically update. Follow these steps to create this count:

1. **In the header or footer, type the word** page **followed by a space.**

2. **Choose Edit⇨Insert Page #.**

   The Insert Page Number dialog box appears.

3. **Click the Page Number option and then click OK.**

   You're back in the header or footer.

4. **Type another space, the word** of, **and another space.**

5. **Choose Edit⇨Insert Page #.**

   The Insert Page Number dialog box appears.

6. **Click the Document Page Count option and then click OK.**

Page numbering is the same in a drawing text frame, header, or footer as it is in a word-processing document; see Chapter 5 for more details.

Adding Visual Elements

One old saying says that a picture is worth a thousand words. Images can, indeed, add a lot to a document. This picture can be art that you (or an associate) create in another AppleWorks draw or paint document; purchased clip art; clip art that AppleWorks provides in Clippings form; tables; spreadsheets; or charts generated from your spreadsheets. You can add the text or graphics after you set up the framework for your document.

Adding images

Whether the image you want to add to your document is drawn or painted in AppleWorks, created in a high-end graphics program, or purchased as clip art, you can add it to your layout by using one of the following methods. (You also can use these techniques to insert charts or tables copied from other documents.)

✔ **The copy-and-paste method:** Open the clip art document you want to use and copy the image by choosing Edit⇨Copy. Return to your layout document. To insert the clip art image as a free-floating object, make sure that the arrow pointer is selected and then paste the image from the Clipboard into your layout document. If you click the arrow pointer in a specific location on your page, the image lands at that location.

✔ **The Insert method:** Click the Insert button on your button bar (you need to have added it — see Appendix A to learn how to add buttons) or choose File⇨Insert to bring up the Open dialog box. Navigate to the image you want. When you select a document and click Insert, the image is placed on your layout page.

✔ **The drag-and-drop method:** You can drag any object from one open document right into another open document, even from other drag-aware applications. You can also drag a closed AppleWorks document onto an open document's page, which places the contents of the AppleWorks document right into your document. This approach also works with some other documents created by other programs. Screen shots, which are SimpleText PICT documents, can be dragged unopened into place. You can also drag GIFs, JPEGs, and PICT files.

You can use the Create Preview button in the Open/Save dialog box to preview the image before you place it into your document. Be aware that not all images will have previews.

After inserting a draw or paint object in your document, you can move it and resize it just like any other object. (See Chapter 11 for more about moving and resizing objects.) The art may appear in a paint frame, depending on the document format. (See "Inserting paintings" later in this chapter.) If the art is composed of several objects grouped together, you can even ungroup these objects and modify the image — or just use certain pieces. (See Chapter 11.)

Checking out AppleWorks Clippings

AppleWorks comes with libraries of ready-to-use clip art images, stored in AppleWorks Clippings files. AppleWorks *Clippings files* are organized into groups and stored in folders within your AppleWorks folder's Clippings sub-folder. You access Clippings files through the Clippings window (File⇨Show Clippings, ⌘-2). The Clippings window has a tab for each of the supplied clippings groups as well as a Search tab. From the Search tab, you can search all the groups based upon descriptive keywords or can search AppleWorks Web site and its extensive collection of additional clippings. You can also add your own groups and clippings.

To open an existing clippings collection, such as the one in Figure 13-4, choose File⇨Show Clippings (⌘-2) and select the tab for the collection you wish to view. You use contextual menus to manage the contents of each tab:

✔ Use the contextual menu's Clippings Settings command to set the size of the clippings. Click the Show Details disclosure triangle to see the file's name and size and, if it is on the Internet, its URL.

✔ Search your clippings by name or keyword, type the word(s) you seek in the Search field at the top of the Search tab, and click Search. If you are connected to the Internet and wish to search the thousands of images there, check the Search Web Content box.

TIP

You need to have a live Internet connection for this to work. Sometimes AppleWorks doesn't believe that your connection is active. Opening your Web browser and going to just about any Web page usually triggers AppleWorks to know that your connection is active, and then the search will work.

✔ Alphabetize your tab by choosing Sort⇨By Name from the contextual menu.

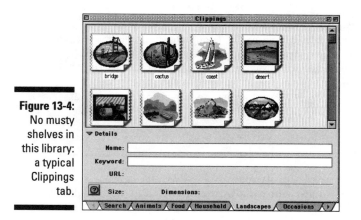

Figure 13-4:
No musty shelves in this library: a typical Clippings tab.

To use a clipping, just drag it into your document. If you're connected to the Internet and the clipping is Web-based, AppleWorks will download it for you.

Inserting paintings

To add a painting to your document, you can either create a paint frame and paint directly within the document, or you can create your painting separately and then paste it into the layout. As with all frames in a drawing document, you can reposition a paint frame at any time. Later you can set your text to wrap around the painting, or mingle it with other frames as desired. Figure 13-5 shows a paint frame in a drawing document.

 To place a paint environment within your document, click the artist's paint palette to select it, move your mouse onto your document, dragging and

Creating your own image collections

You can create your own collections to hold frequently used images, such as company logos, borders, or stock images. You can even store text and spreadsheet frames. Here's how:

1. **Click the plus (+) tab on the Clippings window and enter a name for the new collection.**

   If the collection is all the images on a Web page, choose Internet Based from the pop-up menu and provide the Web page's full URL.

2. **Select an image from any open document and either drag it into the Clippings window. Alternatively, you can Control-click the item you wish to add and choose Add To Clippings, selecting the destination tab from the submenu.**

   This step adds the image to the tab. You can also drag an image onto a tab from another drag-aware application.

3. **AppleWorks gives it a name, such as Clipping 1 if it is an unnamed object; however, the clipping receives the name of the file or the object, if one exists. You can click Show Details to rename the object and provide Search keywords.**

4. **Repeat Steps 2 and 3 to add images.**

5. **You can save collections anywhere, but to have them show up in the Add To Clippings submenu or in the Clippings window, save to the Clippings folder (in the AppleWorks folder).**

Use the Group command on images that are made up of several objects before you try to add the image to a collection. Otherwise, all objects in the image are added separately. For tips on personalizing AppleWorks clip art, check out Chapter 11.

---

releasing to create a default-sized paint frame or clicking and dragging within the document to define the painting area. The paint tools immediately enable in your Tools panel on the Tools window. You can move back and forth between the drawing and painting environments by clicking outside the frame or back inside it.

If you already have a painting in its own document and use the File⇔Insert command to place your painting, the entire document is inserted. To an extent, you can reduce the frame so it shows only the desired area. However, if you only want to insert the part that contains your painting, select and copy the desired portion within the original and then paste that selection into the layout document.

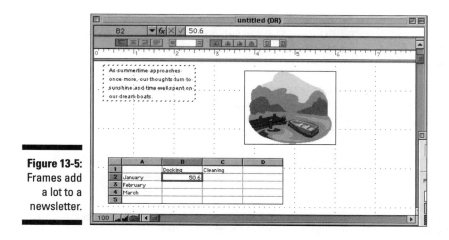

Figure 13-5:
Frames add
a lot to a
newsletter.

Inserting tables

You can create tables on your layout, just as you do in a word-processing document.

To add a table frame to your document, either select the table frame tool and drag it to your layout or click the table frame tool and drag an outline for it on your layout.

You can also drag tables you've already created from other documents; alternatively, you can select the table, copy it to the Clipboard, and then paste it into your new document.

You can even convert spreadsheet selections into tables in a rather round-about way. First, select the cells you want to use for your table and copy them to the Clipboard. Select the text tool, and click the draw layout, and paste. The data is now pasted into a text frame, and you can select it and choose Table⇨Convert to Table. This command gives you a table frame that is inline with your text, so you can copy or cut it, select the pointer (drawing), and paste again. Somehow, it seems like this task hould be easier, but it works.

Inserting spreadsheets

You can place spreadsheets in your layout to create tables, charts, or graphs, or to reflect calculations. They definitely add interest and diversity to your newsletters and fliers. Figure 13-5 shows a spreadsheet frame in action.

To add a spreadsheet frame to a document, click the spreadsheet tool to select it, move — don't drag — your cursor onto your document, and click and drag within the document to define your spreadsheet. If you drag the spreadsheet tool, you receive a small (8 row, 2 column) frame.

What if you already created your spreadsheet in its own spreadsheet document? Select and copy the cells to be transferred. Start a new empty spreadsheet in the drawing document, click in the first cell of the empty spreadsheet, and then choose Edit⇨Paste.

A spreadsheet frame from one document can be selected as an object (the handles show when you select it), copied as an object, and pasted into another drawing document. It remains a fully functioning, floating spreadsheet.

You can control how much information a spreadsheet reveals by resizing the frame to show only the desired columns and rows. You can reveal a lot, enter the data, and then reduce the size of the frame so it prints or shows only what you want your audience to see; or, instead of making it larger, you can open the frame to work on the entire spreadsheet. (See the "Opening frames" sidebar below.)

Opening frames

Spreadsheet and paint frames are actually like windows; they can reveal entire spreadsheets and paintings, or just a part of them. In order to see and edit the whole image or spreadsheet, AppleWorks lets you open a frame into its own, separate, full-sized document window. Follow these steps to open a frame:

1. **Click once on the paint or spreadsheet frame.**

2. **Choose Window⇨Open Frame.**

You can now view and edit whatever's in the frame as if it were a separate document. After you click the Close box on this new window, any changes you made show up in the frame. Easy as pie.

When you use the open frame tool to add information to a spreadsheet, the frame in the layout document may expand to reveal the new addition. Just drag the handles to reduce the frame again if you don't want the new data to show. To show a chart inside a spreadsheet frame instead of in a separate frame, as you usually would, open the spreadsheet frame first, and then create the chart. Either way, the chart updates if you change the numbers in the spreadsheet.

When you open a paint frame, you see a document that's the same size as the frame you opened. If several frames are linked together, the window shows a document that's as tall as all the frames stacked on top of one another and as wide as the widest frame. You can change the size of the paint area by choosing Format⇨Document. See Chapter 10 for more information on resizing paint documents.

If you're working in a draw document that has many different kinds of frames and your menus seem messed up, you're probably inside one of the frames. To return to the drawing environment, click the arrow pointer in the Tools window.

Adding and Working with Text

You probably want to add text to your newsletter, flier, certificate, or envelope. No problem for AppleWorks! You can type text directly into the document or paste text from elsewhere.

Entering new text into the document

Want to add text to your layout document? Follow along:

1. **Click the Text tool.**

2. **Click the area of the page where you want the text block to begin.**

3. **Here's the secret — to define the size of the text block keep the mouse button pressed as you drag the cursor.**

   This way, the text you type starts at the left edge of your defined text area, gets to the right boundary, and wraps to the next line. You don't have to define the area perfectly. You can resize it to make it longer, shorter, wider, or narrower. You can also move a text block around the page at any time.

You *could* also just select the Text tool, click your page to place the cursor, and begin typing. However, because you didn't define a boundary, your text continues to expand the text area — and keeps going right off the page! Later, you'll have to resize the text block (by dragging its handles) to fit it on the page; this can take several steps. It's a real time-waster.

Pasting text into the document

Follow these steps to paste text from elsewhere:

1. **Open the document that contains the text you want to copy.**

2. **Select the desired text and choose Edit⇨Copy.**

   You can also copy and paste an entire floating text frame instead.

3. **Return to your new drawing document.**

- **Adding the text as a new text block:** Select the arrow pointer tool, click the location where you want the text to land, and paste.

- **Adding the text to an existing line of text:** Select the text tool, click the I-beam to place the cursor, and paste.

The new text comes in where the cursor was flashing.

Text frames come in very handy for creating captions and labels. You can move the frame close to its graphic and then group it. If the frame must be farther from its target graphic, you can use the line tool to create an arrow that points from the text label to the target graphic. After you have them positioned, you probably want to group them so that they move together if you decide to place them elsewhere or duplicate them.

Working in a text frame

To work with text in a drawing document, click the text tool inside a text frame or double-click in a text frame. This switches you to word-processing mode. The menus change to the menus available in the text environment, and you have all the same capabilities of a text document.

Moving and resizing text blocks

One of the reasons the draw environment is so versatile is the ease with which you can place and manipulate text. With the arrow pointer tool selected, clicking a text block selects the block as an object — and allows it to be moved around and resized as an object.

- **Moving the text block:** Click once (don't double-click) in the text area and then drag the text.

- **Resizing the text block:** Click once on the block (don't double-click) to select it. Then click and drag one of the object's handles.

You can't make the text block smaller than is necessary to fully contain the text within it. Instead, the block automatically grows long enough to do its job — even if that means extending the block out of the page's boundaries.

Adding Borders to Text and Graphics

Sometimes a border around a block of text, a graphic, or a grouping of text and graphics adds a nice touch or helps set that text apart from the rest of the page. Here are a few tricks for creating borders:

✔ **Adding a border around a single text frame:** Click once on the text to select it as an object; choose a line width from the Accents window, Lines pane, with Pen selected. (By default, there is no line around a text frame.) If this line is too close to your text, try the rectangle tool method described in the next paragraph instead. (Remember to first set your line width back to None.)

✔ **Adding a border around several objects at once or creating a custom-sized border:** Use the rectangle tool (or any other shape tool). Set the fill pattern to transparent first so you can see the area you want to encompass; then choose a line width. Next, draw your rectangle. Adjust the rectangle and the inner objects; fine-tune the line's width, color, and pattern if desired; and then group the contents for easier layout. The newsletter in Figure 13-5 has a wide, gray-striped border around a single text block.

✔ **To add a single line on one side, the top, or the bottom to set something apart:** Use the line tool to create that line. Duplicate the line and make one wider, then align them and place them next to each other to create a *scotch rule*.

You can take advantage of the various pen traits to help set your document's mood and border. By adding a pattern in conjunction with line thickness, your line becomes dashes. Using gray instead of black may make the box less distracting.

You can also shade within the box; just choose a fill using the Accents window. If the border is made with a shape, the fill obscures your text and graphics when you fill the shape. Use the Arrange options to move it behind the frame's objects. (See Chapter 11.)

Wrapping Text around Graphics

Isn't it cool when text flows around a graphic and the margins take on the shape of the graphic? You can do that! It's easy, and it definitely adds flair to a flier and savvy to a certificate.

You can have one or more text frames surround one or more objects by wrapping the frame's text around the objects. Regular text frames just lie there over or under your objects. The trick to wrapping the text around the graphic is setting up the text as a frame link:

1. **Click once on the text frame to select it and then choose Options⇨ Frame Links.**

   This lets AppleWorks know that you want to set up the text as a frame link.

You can have more than one block of text wrap — even around the same object. Just set the other text frame to Frame Links as well.

2. **Select the graphic that the text will wrap around and then choose Options➪Text Wrap.**

   The Text Wrap dialog box opens.

   You can also click one of the text wrap buttons instead of choosing the menu command. A button for text wrap — it's the irregular one, the most exciting type of text wrap — is on the default button bar; you can add optional buttons for regular text wrap and unwrap. (You can find more information about text wrap in Chapter 7.)

   You can wrap the text around more than one graphic. Just set the other graphic(s) to Text Wrap as well.

3. **Choose the type of wrap you desire. When you're done, click Done.**

Now, as you move the text block and graphic around, the text flows and reflows to surround any sides of the graphic that touch the text block. The graphic may cut between sentences and make the text hard to read. Use the arrow keys on your keyboard to nudge the text until it wraps nicely. You may also want to adjust the *gutter* (space between the text and the graphic). You can do so in the Text Wrap dialog box. (Choose Options➪Text Wrap to open this dialog box.)

Oh . . . but you want even more, right? You want your text to be in two separate parts of the page, too? Guess what . . . you can do that and it still wraps around your graphics. Read the next section to find out more.

Linking Frames

Linking text frames enables you to automatically flow text from one frame into another. This capability lets you create columns of text that continue across several columns, even to another page. You can also use frame links to show several different views of a spreadsheet or paint frame in the same document. By linking frames, you can also recycle a paint graphic or spreadsheet data without using several copies of the same frame and making your document a huge file.

You can create as many groups of linked frames in a document as you like. And, of course, you can mix linked and unlinked frames within your document.

Linking text frames

Linked frames are special text frames that form a chain. When the first frame fills up, any extra text flows into the next frame in the chain or waits until you create one. This way, you can move and resize graphics and text until they feel just right — the text reflows to accommodate your moves. You can link as many frames as you want by adding to the end of the chain. Sorry, you can't add frames in the middle or at the beginning. However, you *can* delete from the beginning or middle — the text just reflows.

You can turn an existing frame into a linked frame or create an empty linked frame. Existing frames or chains can't be linked to each other, though. Instead, paste all the text into the first existing frame of one chain and create new frames from there. With this stuff in mind, we show you two ways to create these magic linking things.

Linking an existing text frame

To link an existing frame, fly through these steps:

1. **Select the existing text frame and then choose Options⇨Frame Links.**

2. **Click once on the Continue indicator at the bottom of the frame.**

   Now AppleWorks knows to flow the text, linking to the next frame you create. Your arrow pointer becomes a special I-beam.

3. **Use the I-beam to create another frame by clicking and dragging to define the area.**

   The outline of your first frame becomes invisible, but because text is there, you know where the first frame is. You can see the frame when you click the text.

4. **Repeat Steps 2 and 3 to add more frames to the chain.**

   You always click the last Continue indicator to create a new link.

5. **Choose Options⇨Frame Links to turn off frame links when done.**

   Your pointer returns to the normal arrow.

Creating a new linked text frame

To create a new empty frame as your first linked frame is no more difficult:

1. **Choose Options⇨Frame Links.**

   This lets AppleWorks know you're creating linked frames.

2. **Select the text frame tool from the Tools window, Frames panel. Click the mouse and drag to create a new text frame.**

3. **Type any text in this frame as a placeholder.**

   The frame becomes invisible while you create the new frame it links to.

4. **Click outside the frame.**

   You're back in the draw environment, leaving the frame selected, as shown in Figure 13-6.

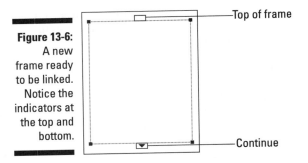

Top of frame

Continue

Figure 13-6:
A new frame ready to be linked. Notice the indicators at the top and bottom.

5. **Click once on the Continue indicator at the bottom of the frame.**

   Now AppleWorks knows to flow the text, linking to the next frame you create. Your arrow pointer becomes a special I-beam.

6. **Use the I-beam to create another frame by clicking and dragging to define the area as usual.**

   Your first frame becomes invisible, but your placeholder helps you see where it is.

7. **Repeat Steps 5 and 6 to add more frames to the chain.**

   Always click the last Continue indicator to create a new link.

8. **Choose Options⇨Frame Links to turn off frame links when done.**

   Your pointer becomes an arrow again.

To align your text fields, select them and use the Align Object buttons or commands. (See Chapter 11 for more information.) You can also use the rulers and the graphics grid to help with positioning. (See "Using the graphics and text rulers," earlier in this chapter.) You have two options when selecting the frames you want to work with:

  ✔ **Shift-clicking:** Hold down the Shift key and click once on each frame.

  ✔ **The marquee technique:** Drag the arrow pointer to surround the entire area. Notice that frames are only visible when they're selected.

You can add text to the linked frames by typing, pasting, or using the File⇨Insert command, just as for regular text frames. When there's more text than fits in the chain, the last frame shows a text overflow indicator like the one in Figure 13-7.

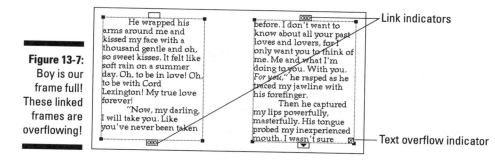

Link indicators

Text overflow indicator

Figure 13-7: Boy is our frame full! These linked frames are overflowing!

When you see the overflow indicator, you have four choices. You can

- ✔ Add another linked frame to the chain for the excess text.
- ✔ Make the existing frames bigger to display more text.
- ✔ Make the text a smaller point size so more words fit in the same space.
- ✔ Decrease the spacing between lines in the Paragraph dialog box. (Use points instead of lines.)

After you create a layout you like — even with empty linked frames — you may want to save it as a template. See Chapter 2 for more on templates.

Linking spreadsheet and paint frames

Linked spreadsheet frames and linked paint frames work a bit differently from linked text frames. Instead of making the information flow from one frame to another, *linked spreadsheet* or *paint frames* let several frames use the same information or image. It's like having more than one window looking at the same information. Suppose you want to use a paint image that takes up 25K of hard disk space. Using five copies of the image adds 125K to the document's size, whereas sharing one copy of the same image among five linked paint frames adds only 25K.

Another advantage to linking paint or spreadsheet frames is that any change you make in one frame shows up in the rest of the frames in the chain. For example, suppose you're using linked frames to show a small spreadsheet at several places in your document. If you need to change a number, all you have to do is make the change in one frame. The change shows up in all the linked frames that show the same cells. If the frames weren't linked, you would have to manually change the same number every time you used that spreadsheet in your document.

Follow these steps to add linked frames to an existing paint or spreadsheet frame:

1. **Select the frame with the arrow pointer.**

2. **Choose Options⇨Frame Links to turn on frame links mode.**

   This step lets AppleWorks know that you are going to add a linked frame. You should see a Continue indicator at the bottom of the frame.

3. **Click once on the Continue indicator.**

   Refer to Figure 13-6 to refresh your memory as to what the indicator looks like.

   Your arrow pointer is now a crosshair.

4. **Click and drag to create a new frame linked to the first.**

   If you want to add more linked frames, click the Continue indicator on the frame that you want to link to and drag another frame.

After you have all the linked frames you need for that spreadsheet or paint frame, you can resize and arrange them on the page.

The top of each new paint or spreadsheet frame starts where the last linked frame leaves off. Take a look at Figure 13-8 to see what we mean.

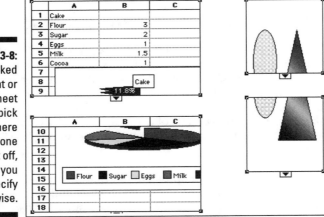

Figure 13-8:
Linked
paint or
spreadsheet
frames pick
up where
the last one
left off,
unless you
specify
otherwise.

If you want to have a different part of the paint image or spreadsheet displayed in a linked frame, you can specify what part of the document appears in the upper-left corner of the frame, which is known as the *origin*. You set the origin as an intersection of pixels for paint frames or as a specific cell for a spreadsheet frame. You type this information into the dialog box brought up by choosing Edit⇨Frame Info.

Chapter 14

Presenting Presentations

• •

• •

*R*emember when your presentations were considered *professional* just because you drew a *visual* to add dimension? These days, kids are using computer presentation software to create their "what I did on my summer vacation" reports.

An AppleWorks presentation is an electronic slide show — except you don't have to take photos. Instead, you get to make your slides because the slides are actually pages of your AppleWorks documents displayed on your computer screen. You can even run your show on automatic — if you want. But that's not all. You can also use movies and, for added effect, you can print your slides or subsets of them as overhead transparencies or as handouts.

AppleWorks enables you to create presentations that look every bit as professional as the expensive productions dished up by corporate highbrows at annual marketing meetings — only yours will be a lot easier to put together. It's the presentation that counts — not the cost of the software that creates it.

Laying Out a Presentation

Draw documents might be a natural choice for presentations, thanks to their layout flexibility. Word-processing documents are okay for presentations, too. In fact, you can use any type of document for presentations. In earlier versions, AppleWorks (also known as ClarisWorks) forced you to use your other environments for presentations. AppleWorks 6, however, gives you a dedicated Presentations document type. In this area, a bright new day has dawned and the bad old days are a thing of the past. If you're a little masochistic or curious how things were done in days of yore, pick up a copy of the previous edition of this book — *AppleWorks 5 For Dummies.*

Perhaps more important than the power of the presentation software is the look and feel of your slides. As you design your slides, keep these suggestions in mind:

- Slide dimensions are always 640 x 480 pixels. You should usually set your screen resolution higher so that your Tools and Controls windows don't overlap your slides. Don't worry, though, because when you play the slide show, AppleWorks changes your screen resolution to 640 x 480 and then back to whatever resolution you were using.

- Keep it simple. Don't overwhelm and confuse your audience with zillions of colors, backgrounds, and words.

- Create *master slides* for a consistent format and background, keeping attention focused on the information. (Read "Creating and Editing Master Slides" later in this chapter for details.)

- Use a clean, readable font and keep the wording simple and brief.

- Light text on a dark background shows up well. A good color combination is white or yellow text on a blue background. You might want to reverse this color scheme if your presentation is going to be handed out on paper and not shown on-screen.

- Align design elements and text well. If misaligned, they look sloppy. Take advantage of the rulers, the graphics grid, and the alignment button commands in AppleWorks.

- Let your speech provide the details; the slides are merely your outline. You can attach notes to your slides that don't display during a slide show, but are printable.

- Reveal your points one by one, building on each. You probably don't want transition effects between these slides.

- Create your handout's contents as you create your show and then hide the handouts by using Hide Slide during your presentation. Put each handout next to the slide it goes with to help you remember which handout goes with which slide.

You can customize plenty of style choices by using the draw tools and techniques we explain in Chapters 12 and 13 and add great *transition effects*, as we describe later in this chapter.

The presentation Controls window has four tabs, as shown in Figure 14-1. They are Master, Slide, Group, and Show. You can use the Controls window in conjunction with the Tools window and the Accents window to create your raise-earning presentations.

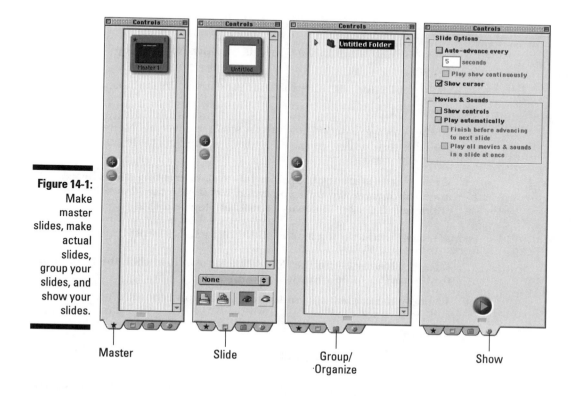

Figure 14-1:
Make master slides, make actual slides, group your slides, and show your slides.

Master   Slide   Group/Organize   Show

Creating and Editing Master Slides

A *master slide* is not a novice slide that's been promoted, but the slide full of all the elements common to each slide in your presentation. Master slides are an option only from within presentation documents, although there is something similar, called Master Pages, in draw documents — this is only really needed so that presentations created in earlier versions of AppleWorks can still be used. A draw document limited you to one master page, but a presentation document allows you to have many master slides.

Most often, you use a master slide to add a colored background and other stuff such as a company or school logo, a theme, a title, page numbering, and dates. You use a master slide for any element that you want to appear on every slide or group of slides. You can have multiple master slides and base different slides upon each. AppleWorks provides you with the first one when you create the document.

To create a master slide, follow these steps:

1. **Click the Master tab in the Controls window. Now, click plus (+) button.**

   You're presented with a new master slide in the Presentations window.

2. **Edit away!**

   All the drawing, painting, and layout stuff we cover in Chapters 10–13 is available to you here, as are Clippings and the text, table, and spreadsheet capabilities.

3. **When you finish, click the Slides tab to start creating slides based upon this master slide. Or you could just stay in the Master tab and create more master slides by repeating Steps 1 and 2.**

To add elements to or edit a master slide, follow these steps:

1. **Click the Master tab in the Controls window. Now, click the thumbnail for the master slide you wish to modify.**

   The page indicator at the bottom of the window reports which master slide you've selected.

2. **Edit away!**

   All the drawing, painting, and layout stuff we cover in Chapters 10–13 comes into play here.

3. **When you finish, click the Slides tab to return to your other slides. Or click the Show tab to play your slide show with the modified master slide(s).**

To create a slide based upon a particular master slide, select the master slide, click the Slides tab, and click the plus (+) button. You may want to name the master slide something other than the default Untitled; if so, click the thumbnail in the Controls window, click the default name to highlight it, and then type your new master slide's name.

That little minus (-) button is there for when you decide that you no longer want a master slide. Just click the slide and then click the button — bye-bye button.

On some pages, your master slide elements may not be appropriate. For example, on your title page, a page number may seem silly, or the header may be redundant. You can mask the offensive element by using your drawing tools on that particular slide to create a shape that covers it up; then set the shape's color to match the background color. Alternatively — and this is our preference — you can just duplicate your master slide, remove the offending items, and then base the title page on the new master slide while leaving the other slides based upon the original.

Opaque elements on the slide cover the graphics grid when you edit slides. Choose Window⇨Notes View so that you can see the grid with the slide reduced on a draw layout. If you prefer to see the background graphics, hold down the Shift key while using the line tool to draw temporary guidelines, either on the individual page or the master page. (Holding down the Shift key as you draw with the line tool lets you draw perfect horizontal or vertical lines with no slant to them.) Just remember to delete the lines when you're finished.

Creating, Editing, and Ordering Slides

As we describe earlier, after you've selected the master slide on which you wish to base one or more slides, just switch to the Slide tab and click the plus (+) button. This creates a new, untitled, slide that looks just like the master slide. Now you just use any or all the drawing, painting, text, table, and spreadsheet techniques already covered in this book to create your slide. When you finish it, just click the plus again to get another copy of the master slide on which to work your magic.

You can name the slides as described in the preceding section, "Creating and Editing Master Slides." You might notice a number in the upper-right corner of the thumbnail. This number tells you the order the slide has in your slide show.

When you want to select a particular slide for editing, just click it. A blue border replaces the gray border to indicate that it is the current slide. If you want to move it earlier or later in the slide show, just drag it until a line appears at the point where you want it inserted and then release the mouse button.

Four buttons lie below the thumbnails on the Slide tab. These are used to control whether slides show up in your slide show and print in your handouts.

Sometimes you may want to show only a subset of your slide show. By default, all the slides in your presentation are shown; you can, however, specify that certain slides not be shown. Select the slide and click the Hide Slide button (top). When a slide is hidden from the slide show, its thumbnail has an almost lowered venetian blind appearance. If you want to put the slide back in the show, click the Show Slide button (bottom).

When you prepare a slide with multiple bullet points on it, it's considered good form to have multiple slides, each adding one bullet point to the previous slide, until the slide is complete. Of course, when you prepare the handouts of your slides, you don't want to print all those intermediate slides, but all slides print by default. Select the slides that you don't want to print and click the Don't Print Slide button (top). This puts a little red circle with a diagonal line through it in the upper-left corner of the slide (center). If you decide that you want to print that slide, click the Print Slide button (bottom) and the circle disappears.

AppleWorks documentation refers to the third tab as the Organize tab, but the contextual menus call it the Group tab — we're gonna stick with the one-syllable name. You can use this tab to group your slides into pseudo-folders. This organization is not apparent anywhere except on this tab and is strictly a bookkeeping convenience so that you can group portions of the presentation for varying audiences and/or delete grouped slides.

Moving from One Slide to the Next

You can have slides advance from one to the next, but sometimes your audience won't notice it happening. Okay, sometimes that is a good thing — for example, when you're building a bullet list from one slide to the next. However, you sometimes want to wake them up that something new (although possibly similar) is now being displayed. Transitions give you that capability. AppleWorks provides 26 transitions (27, if you include None as a transition), as shown in the pop-up menu displayed in Figure 14-2. Click a slide and choose the transition you want to introduce to your audience.

Figure 14-2: Not everything in life is transitory. Special effects keep your audience aware.

Adding Movies

How would you like to transform your slide show into a state-of-the-art digital sound and video spectacle? It's a cinch with QuickTime or QuickTime VR. Movies can have video, audio, or both. Just drop in a couple of clips, and your audience will think that you're the presentation queen or king. Remember, though, that only the first frame will be present on any printout and the sound will not be present at all.

Add movies just like you would any other image. You can copy and paste them from another document, or use the File⇨Insert command. You can also drag the clip right onto the slide. See Chapters 10–13 for more about working with images.

Movies and sounds can use up a lot of memory. You might want to increase the AppleWorks memory allotment before you start working with these audiovisual enhancements. To increase the AppleWorks memory, perform the following steps:

1. **Quit from AppleWorks if it is currently running.**

2. **In the Mac Finder, select the AppleWorks file icon.**

3. **Choose File⇨Get Info⇨Memory.**

4. **Enter a larger number in the Preferred Size box and, possibly, in the Minimum Size box — this last is the smallest amount of memory in which AppleWorks will open and should be at least as large as the Suggested Size.**

You can move, align, and resize movies, just like any other draw objects. QuickTime movies have a small film icon, or in the lower-left corner. Clicking the control badge displays a VCR-style control bar for full video control. Double-clicking the movie also plays the clip. Figure 14-3 shows both states of the control badge and controls. You can control whether these badges show during your presentation on the Control window's Show tab.

There is a hidden way to control a video's speed and direction. Press and hold the Ctrl key and click and hold the Forward or Backward step button. A Speed slider appears. Drag the slider to adjust the video's direction and speed. Placing the slider near the center mark plays the video in slow motion. Moving the slider toward the outside plays the video faster in that direction.

If the QuickTime movie is pasted inline with text, the control badge has no effect. Instead, double-click the movie to play it. In order for the QuickTime controls to work, cut the movie and paste it back as a floating object.

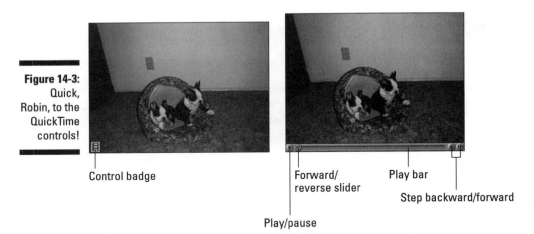

Figure 14-3:
Quick,
Robin, to the
QuickTime
controls!

Control badge

Forward/
reverse slider

Play bar

Step backward/forward

Play/pause

TIP

To add sound or music to your AppleWorks presentation, place a QuickTime movie that has no image, just a soundtrack. To get that soundtrack, you can create your own or convert a track from an audio CD (honoring royalties and rights).

WARNING!

Most music is copyrighted. You may come across two kinds of copyrights: one for the music and lyrics and one for the performance. Even classical music recorded by some unknown Slavic orchestra can have a performance copyright. Music on CDs that have no copyright notice on the CD or liner notes may still be copyrighted. To be safe, check with the music publisher before you use any music in a presentation.

If you put the QuickTime movie on your master slide, it stays present on all slides based on that master. Unfortunately, it starts over again as each new slide appears on the screen. In most cases, you do not want this.

Controlling the Show

And now, the moment you've been waiting for: seeing your slide show. After you get a few slides ready, test the presentation and see how it runs. Just choose the play button on the Controls window's Show tab, click the Show Slides button, or choose Window➪Slide Show.

Using the Show tab

The Show tab enables you to control how your slides and movies behave. The tab features two main sections and a button that starts the show playing.

You can quit the show and return to editing by pressing the Q key on your keyboard, or you can press ⌘-. (period) or the Esc key.

Slide Options

The Slide Options section enables you to put your slide show on autopilot, determine whether the cursor is visible, and choose whether to have the show play continuously (loop).

Slide options give you control over how your slide show looks and runs:

✔ **Show Cursor:** Keeps the cursor visible while the slide show is running. Some people like to use the cursor as an on-screen pointer; others find it distracting.

✔ **Auto-Advance Every:** Sets your presentation to run by itself. This feature is handy for timed presentations or self-running slide shows.

✔ **Play Show Continuously:** Shows your presentation over and over until the audience finally gets the point. This option is only available if you have Auto-advance set. After all, how can it loop automatically if autopilot isn't on?

Movies & Sounds

The Movies & Sounds section is where you tell AppleWorks how you want QuickTime movies to play back during the slide show. Of course, you have to have installed QuickTime. (QuickTime is part of the MacOS installation and is available for both Mac and Windows, along with tutorials and samples, at `http://www.apple.com/ quicktime`.) Fortunately, AppleWorks installs QuickTime for you if you don't already have it. Nevertheless, you should check out the QuickTime URL, above, for newer versions.

The choices in the QuickTime Options section are

✔ **Show Controls:** This option determines whether you see the badge or QuickTime controls on-screen.

✔ **Play Automatically:** Makes all QuickTime movies start playing as soon as the slide appears on-screen.

✔ **Finish Before Advancing To Next Slide:** Makes each QuickTime movie play to the end before advancing to the next slide. If you're advancing your slides automatically, your viewers won't be impressed to see the slide change in mid-movie. This choice is available only if Auto Play is checked.

✔ **Play All Movies & Sounds In A Slide At Once:** Plays all movies on a slide at once, when the slide appears on-screen. This option is available only if Play Automatically is checked.

To have a sound-only QuickTime movie play while another video QuickTime movie plays, be sure to check the Simultaneous box. Also make sure that the movie's volume is turned all the way down so you don't have problems with the sound playback.

Moving through the slide show

 After you've set your options, you can click the Play button to begin the presentation or you can return to the document.

 You can go right into the presentation by clicking the Start Show button, which is on your default Presentation button bar. Or, if you like to do things the hard way, choose Window⇨Slide Show. This method isn't as fast as clicking the Start Show button, but it beats trying to remember which button is which for the icon-weary.

After you start the slide show, you have lots of options for controlling it. Table 14-1 spells them out for you.

Table 14-1	How to Make Things Happen in a Slide Show
To Make This Happen	**Do This**
Move forward to the next slide	Click the mouse button or press →, ↓, Page Down, Return, Enter, Tab, or the spacebar.
Move backward to the previous slide	Press ←, ↑, Page Up, Shift-Return, Shift-Enter, Shift-Tab, or Shift-spacebar.
Play a QuickTime Movie	Click the movie once. You need to have the cursor showing.
Pause or resume a QuickTime movie	⌘-click or Option-click the movie. You need to have the cursor showing.
Stop a QuickTime movie	Click the movie once. You need to have the cursor showing.
Move to the beginning of the slide show	Press the Home key.
Move to the end of the slide show	Press the End key, if you have one.
Stop the slide show	Press Q, Esc, ⌘-. (period), or ⌘-Q.

Whew! Armed with all that information, you should be able to put together a presentation with little ol' AppleWorks that'll knock the socks off your audience.

Part IV
Working with Numbers: It All Adds Up!

The 5th Wave   By Rich Tennant

"MY GIRLFRIEND RAN A SPREADSHEET OF MY LIFE, AND GENERATED THIS CHART. MY BEST HOPE IS THAT SHE'LL CHANGE HER MAJOR FROM 'COMPUTER SCIENCES' TO 'REHABILITATIVE SERVICES.'"

In this part . . .

Remember when spreadsheets were long white scrolls of paper that ran to the floor as a half-blind, near-sighted, bespectacled man sat hunched over, eyes glazed, quill pen in hand? Okay, maybe we've gone back too far.

Remember when spreadsheets were long, perforated pages of hard-to-read numbers?

For us in-the-mode computer owners, those stacks are a thing of the past. Spreadsheets make numbers much easier to deal with. They back up onto a tiny disk instead of taking up shelves of cabinet space. They can be sorted and moved around — handled any which way we want — just to make them easier to see. Then there's the ultimate: turning them into charts so they're really easy to understand! Not the kind of chart it takes posterboard and a whole pack of markers to slave over. This is the kind where you drag your mouse once, click one button, and voilà — there it is!

Numbers are still numbers, and that's not very exciting to most of us. But they're certainly easier and more fun these days with things like AppleWorks around to help us.

If you're not into numbers right now, don't worry about this part. But when the time comes, we're here for you, ready to bring you into the groove of the spreadsheet.

Chapter 15

Spreadsheets 101

· ·

· ·

Spreadsheets are hopelessly tied to the geeky image of the corporate beancounter who plays with numbers all day and has a big coffee stain in the middle of a rumpled tie. The truth is, spreadsheets are cool! Maybe we could start a bring-a-friend-a-spreadsheet campaign to spread the word on spreadsheets. Or maybe we're being overzealous. Hmmm. . . .

Deciding When to Use a Spreadsheet

Visions of dreary bookkeeping duties, such as balancing your checkbook or setting up a company's financial statements, are probably dancing in your head (or, more likely, lurking). Actually, many people also get a lot of mileage out of spreadsheets as calendars and schedules. We've even seen spreadsheets used to create games like Yahtzee, StarTrek, and 21.

Spreadsheets are really good for working with numbers. You can use them to keep financial information and statistics, to record tax information, or to record and chart data for a chemistry experiment. Hey, speaking of charts, AppleWorks can create any kind of spiffy-looking chart or graph you want based on numbers in your spreadsheet. You don't even have to type any complicated formulas to create your chart; just click a button.

Working with Cells, Rows, and Columns

Spreadsheets consist of rectangular containers called *cells*. The cells are stacked on top of and next to each other to form a grid. A horizontal line of cells is a *row*. A vertical stack of cells is a *column*. Rows are labeled with numbers, starting with 1. Columns are labeled with letters, starting with A. Each cell's name is based on the intersection of the row and column where the cell is located. The cell at the upper-left corner of the spreadsheet is A1. Figure 15-1 points these things out to you. You can also assign cells friendlier names. We show you how in Chapter 18.

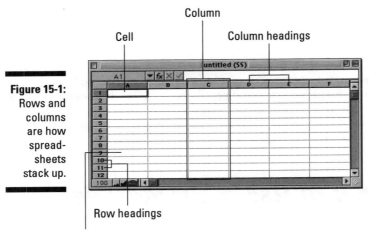

Cell

Column

Column headings

Figure 15-1:
Rows and columns are how spread-sheets stack up.

Row headings

Row

Selecting a single cell

As always on the computer, you have to select something before you can do anything to it.

To select a single cell, you need a microscope and very tiny tweezers — if you're in a biology lab. In an AppleWorks spreadsheet, you just click a cell to select it.

When you select a cell, a border — called the *selection box* — appears around it. For example, B3 is selected in Figure 15-2.

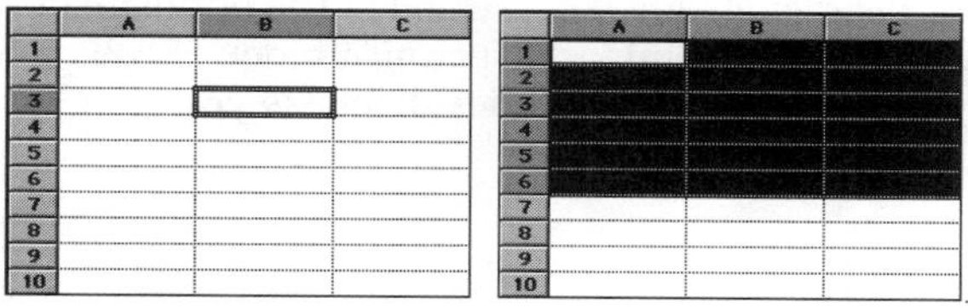

Figure 15-2:
Don't let
those
spaces get
you down.
Slide right
over 'em.

When you first open a new spreadsheet, cell A1, the cell in the upper-left corner, is selected. In the spreadsheet environment, you can move to your next selection by pressing keys. Table 15-1 lists the keys that move the selection box and in which direction they move it.

Table 15-1	Moving the Selection Box with the Keyboard
Press This Key	**To Move in This Direction**
Tab	Right one cell
Return	Down one cell
Shift+Tab	Left one cell
Shift+Return	Up one cell
→, ←, ↑, ↓	One cell in the direction of the arrow (If the cursor is visible in the entry bar, press Option and the arrow.)

Selecting a range of cells

You can only select cells that are next to each other in a rectangular block, so a selected block is always in a rectangular shape, even if it's only one row high or one column wide. You never see a T-shaped group of selected cells.

You can select a block of cells two ways:

✔ **Dragging:** Just position the plus-sign pointer in one corner of the block you want to select; then click and hold down the mouse button while dragging to the opposite corner. The block of cells highlights, like those back in Figure 15-2.

✔ **Shift-clicking:** Click once in one corner of the block you want to select; then press Shift and click once on the cell in the opposite corner diagonally. This is especially useful for selecting a block of cells that is larger than your screen or for any large block, because you avoid dragging long distances.

Selecting columns and rows

To select an entire column or row all the way out to the uncharted nether regions of the spreadsheet edge, just click the row or column heading. That's a lot of cells for just one click.

Selecting the whole spreadsheet

Do you wanna select the whole thing? If you really, really, really want to select every row and every column, here's how: Click the little box in the very top-left corner, where the row and column headings meet.

Many people get extremely frustrated when they try to select a block of cells because they can't get that one silly cell in the corner to select. Or at least they think they can't. Truth is, they did. It just doesn't change highlighting. So don't worry about that one silly cell; you got it.

Entering Data

Entering information into a spreadsheet is different from entering information into any other AppleWorks environment. Instead of typing directly into a cell, you type in the entry bar at the top of the window, as shown in Figure 15-3.

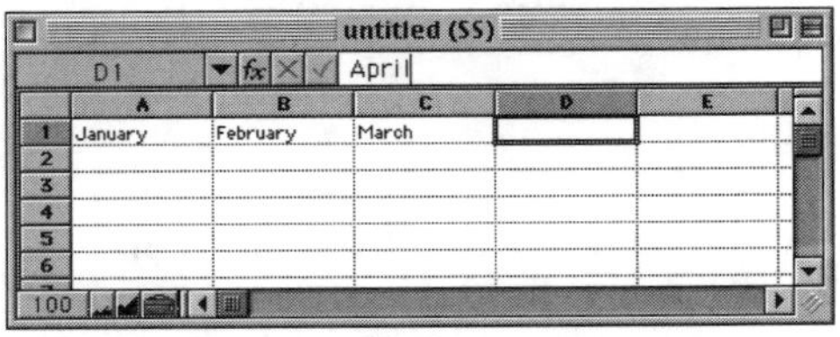

Figure 15-3:
All characters enter at the entry bar on the top, please.

	A	B	C	D	E
1	January	February	March		
2					
3					
4					
5					
6					

untitled (SS)   D1   April

After you type in your information, click the Accept button — the one with the check mark on it — to enter the information into the selected cell. To delete the information in the entry bar, click the Cancel button — the one with the *X* on it. You can save time by pressing Enter, Tab, or Return — or by selecting another cell. (Each has a different effect after entering your data. More on that subject soon.)

If you've used a spreadsheet before, you've probably been frustrated by having to manually select the cell at the top of the next column when you get to the bottom of the one you're in. The same thing applies to rows. Here's the $100 tip: When you reach the bottom of the first column, select the group of cells with which you're working. Then, when you press the Return button at the bottom of the first column, the selection box moves back to the top of the next column for you. If you're working in rows, when you press the Tab key at the end of a row, the selection box pops to the beginning of the next row. In either case, when you tab or return out of the last cell in the group, AppleWorks takes you back to the first cell in the group.

Setting Preferences

We all have our preferences. Movies, soft drinks . . . and now you have a spreadsheet action preference, too.

The spreadsheet section of the AppleWorks Preferences dialog box enables you to set how the Enter and arrow keys behave when you type information into a cell or move the selection box around. (That's the Enter key on the number pad.) Take a look at your options, as shown in Figure 15-4.

The preferences are for that spreadsheet document or frame that you have open, as shown in Figure 15-4. To set global spreadsheet preferences, make sure that no spreadsheet document or frame is active.

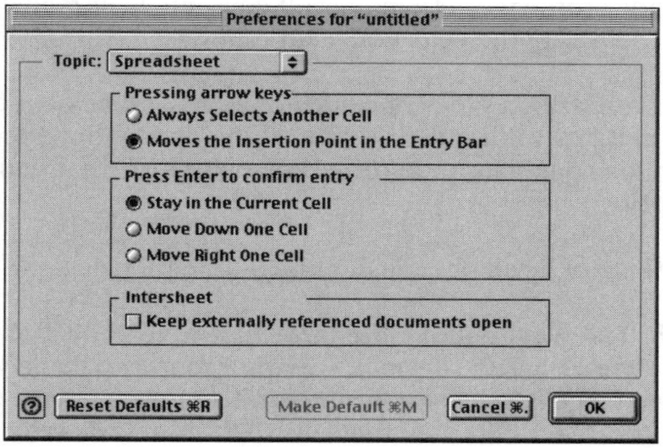

Figure 15-4:
The Enter key can take you any- where or nowhere; whatever you prefer.

Preferences for "untitled"

Topic: Spreadsheet

Pressing arrow keys
○ Always Selects Another Cell
● Moves the Insertion Point in the Entry Bar

Press Enter to confirm entry
● Stay in the Current Cell
○ Move Down One Cell
○ Move Right One Cell

Intersheet
☐ Keep externally referenced documents open

[Reset Defaults ⌘R]   [Make Default ⌘M]   [Cancel ⌘.]   [OK]

Choose Edit⇨Preferences⇨General to arrive in this window. If you don't land at spreadsheet options, use the pop-up menu to get here. The options here are pretty self-explanatory. Changing them helps if you're used to another spreadsheet. Most people change the arrow keys so that they move to the next cell. AppleWorks is preset to have the arrow keys move the cursor within the entry bar when the cursor is there, and to move from cell to cell when it's not. To have the arrow keys always move between cells, select Always Selects Another Cell and use the mouse to move your cursor through the text within the entry bar. If you always want to see the data your spreadsheet is referencing in another spreadsheet, check the final box.

Editing Data

You may find some errors after you look at the big picture. Use the entry bar to edit a cell's contents, just as when you entered the information. You can select, delete, copy, and paste in the entry bar, just like in a text frame. Remember to use one of these methods to enter your changes:

- ✔ Click the check mark.
- ✔ Press Enter on the number pad.
- ✔ Select another cell with the keyboard.

If you're working on a spreadsheet that someone else made and you click a cell, the entry bar may contain a bunch of gobbledygook that starts with an equals sign. Don't panic — that's a formula, which you can find out more about in Chapter 18.

Moving Data

AppleWorks provides three ways to move cell contents in spreadsheets. Each way involves first selecting the cells you want to move.

If you move the contents of a block of cells into another block of cells that already has stuff in it, the information that is at the destination is replaced. If you don't want to lose destination information, make sure that your destination cells are empty.

To move the contents of a cell or cells, do one of the following:

- ✔ **What's the fastest way to move the information to cells that are within your current view?** Select the cells you want to move. Place your mouse over the selected cells so that your cursor becomes a hollow arrow with a box at the end. Click and drag the cells to their new destination.

✔ **What's the fastest way to move the information across a large distance?** Select the cells you want to move, hold down ⌘-Option, and click in the cell where you want the upper-left corner of the selected block of cells to appear.

✔ **Copy and paste is the only method that places the cell data in the Clipboard.** Select a cell or group of cells and use the old copy (or cut) and paste routine. Just cut or copy the selection and click the upper-left corner cell where you want the just-cut or just-copied block of cells to appear; paste.

✔ **If you like dialog boxes, try this.** After selecting the cells to move, choose Calculate⇨Move. In the dialog box that appears, type the name of the cell where you want the upper-left corner of the selected block of cells to appear. Click OK or cancel the move with the Cancel button.

Filling Cells

Filling cells is a shortcut for typing the same thing over and over in a series of cells. It's also faster than copying and pasting, pasting, pasting. . . .

Fill Down and Fill Right

Suppose you're working on the spreadsheet shown in Figure 15-5 and you know the next ten entries are all the same:

1. **Enter the text to be copied in the first cell.**

2. **Select the cell you just entered text in, along with the cells you need to copy it to.**

3. **Choose Calculate⇨Fill Down.**

Want to fill the next nine cells to the right instead? The Fill Right command has you covered. When you have to enter the same information repeatedly, fill it instead!

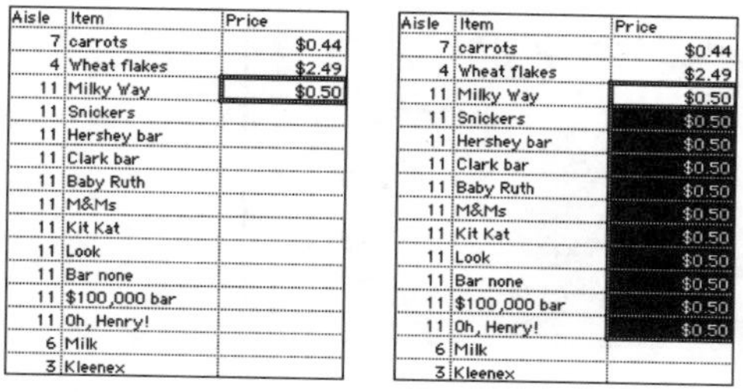

Figure 15-5:
Yo Phil!
It's easier
with Fill.

Aisle	Item	Price
7	carrots	$0.44
4	Wheat flakes	$2.49
11	Milky Way	$0.50
11	Snickers	
11	Hershey bar	
11	Clark bar	
11	Baby Ruth	
11	M&Ms	
11	Kit Kat	
11	Look	
11	Bar none	
11	$100,000 bar	
11	Oh, Henry!	
6	Milk	
3	Kleenex	

Aisle	Item	Price
7	carrots	$0.44
4	Wheat flakes	$2.49
11	Milky Way	$0.50
11	Snickers	$0.50
11	Hershey bar	$0.50
11	Clark bar	$0.50
11	Baby Ruth	$0.50
11	M&Ms	$0.50
11	Kit Kat	$0.50
11	Look	$0.50
11	Bar none	$0.50
11	$100,000 bar	$0.50
11	Oh, Henry!	$0.50
6	Milk	
3	Kleenex	

Fill Special

Fill Special is a smart fill. It auto-fills a selected group of cells with sequential information, such as times, days of the week, or month names. Simply complete one or two entries of the sequence; Fill Special guesses the pattern for the rest of the selected cells.

For example, suppose that you're a student creating a schedule of your classes for each day of the week. As Figures 15-6 and 15-7 show, Fill Special creates a schedule for you.

The spreadsheet in Figure 15-6 shows the seeds of a schedule. The first row, where the days of the week go, is selected. Calculate⇨Fill Special brings up the Fill Special dialog box below the selected cells. After the days are filled in, it's time to move on to the times. As Figure 15-7 shows, the times in the first column are selected, along with the next 35 or 40 cells down, and Fill Special works its magic again, knowing to complete the times in 15-minute intervals. Use Fill Special to complete any row or column of information that advances in regular increments.

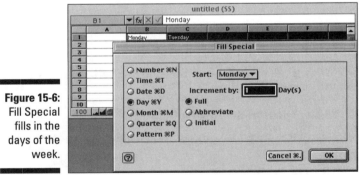

Figure 15-6:
Fill Special
fills in the
days of the
week.

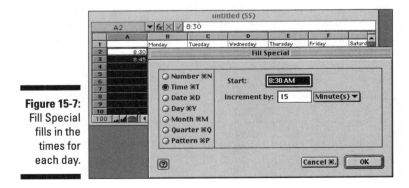

Figure 15-7:
Fill Special
fills in the
times for
each day.

Chapter 16

Formatting Spreadsheets

- -

In This Chapter

▶ Formatting numbers

▶ Formatting text

▶ Sorting stuff in spreadsheets

▶ Changing rows and columns

▶ Changing display options

- -

Do you remember spreadsheets as vast expanses of numbers, repeating endlessly with the mind-numbing sameness of a test pattern? Spreadsheets don't have to be like that. They can be as lively as a daytime talk show. You can use lots of clever formatting tricks to help people see that those numbers are actually important.

Formatting Numbers

What better place to start than with how you get your numbers to look the way you want? While we're at it, we tell you how to format dates and times, too — because they're all affected by the same dialog box, shown in Figure 16-1. Open the Format dialog box by choosing Format⇨Number or Shift-⌘-N, but don't go there until you select the numbers you want to format. (Actually, thanks to buttons and contextual menus, you may never go there anyway.) Actually, the easiest way to get to this dialog is to double-click the cell you want to format.

Number formats

The first radio button in the Format Number, Date, and Time dialog box is for numbers of any kind. With these options, you get to decide how the numbers in the selected cells look. Explaining the details of this side of the dialog box is much easier with a table, so here ya' go. Table 16-1 explains the various number formats.

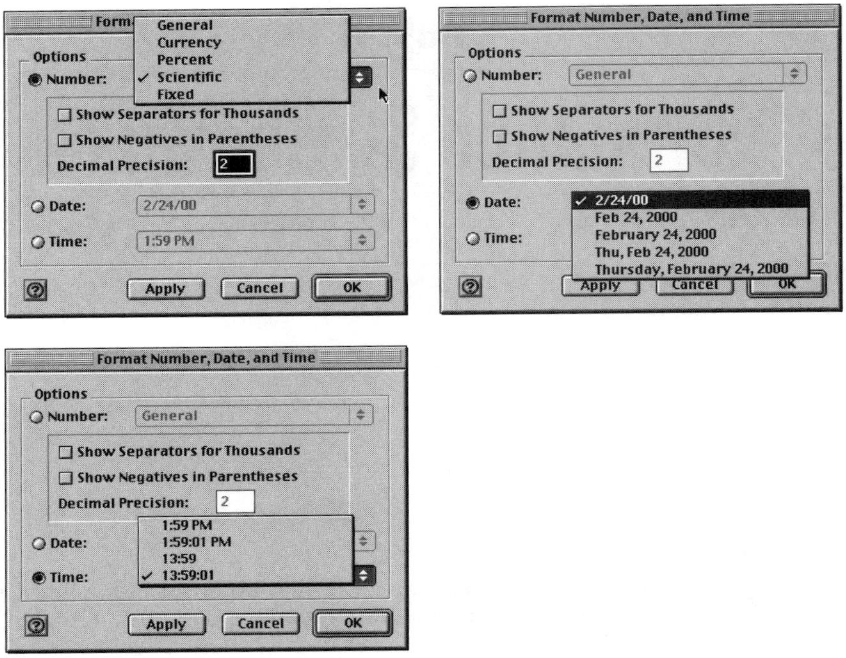

Figure 16-1:
Numbers
can be in
fine form
thanks to
this dialog
box.

Table 16-1		**Various Number Formats and What They Do**
Button	*Format*	*What It Does*
No button	General	The standard number format — for example, 25.1415. This format displays as many decimal places (up to 11 digits of precision) as you enter — as long as they fit in the cell. If more than 11 digits appear to the left of the decimal, AppleWorks converts the number to scientific notation. AppleWorks rounds decimal fractions greater than 11 digits in length.
$¥€	Currency	Automatically puts the currency sign (from ⇨ Control Panels ⇨ Numbers) in front of the number and inserts decimal points, as in $25.14.
%	Percent	Automatically multiplies your number by 100 and adds the percent sign to the number.
e+	Scientific	Displays the number with one digit to the left of the decimal point and as many digits to the right as you specify in the Precision box — for example, $2.51e+1$ would be the representation of 25.1.
No button	Fixed	Rounds numbers to however many decimal places are set in the Precision box, as in 25.14.

The following three options appear below the number formats in the Number section of the dialog box:

- ✔ **Show Separators for Thousands:** This option inserts commas (or whatever you have set in the Numbers control panel) after every three digits to show thousands, millions, and so on. Check this box to turn on the option, or click the optional button. The button turns on the formatting, but it doesn't turn off the formatting. To turn off comma formatting, you must uncheck the option in the Format Number, Date, and Time dialog box.

- ✔ **Show Negatives in Parentheses:** This option puts parentheses [( )] around negative numbers — as bookkeepers do. If this checkbox is unchecked, negative numbers appear with a minus sign. The button for this is optional, so you can put it on your button bar if you tend to use it. You can use the button to turn on this formatting but not to turn it off. To turn it off, use the Format Number dialog box.

- ✔ **Decimal Precision:** This option dictates how many digits appear to the right of the decimal point. It affects all number formats except General. The default is 2, so if you don't change it, all numbers with more than two decimal spaces are rounded to hundredths, as in 25.14. The top button reduces the number of digits displayed to the right of the decimal, and the bottom button increases the number of digits displayed.

Date formats

You have five formatting options for showing dates, which are shown in the Date pop-up menu in Figure 16-1. Your choices range from showing dates in numbers only (as in 2/24/00), to showing the day and month completely spelled out (as in Thursday, Feburuary 24, 2000). The button for this cycles through the five formatting choices. There is no button for this option, so you have to use the dialog Format Number, Date, and Time dialog box. However, after you have formatted it as a date, you can use the Next Date button to cycle through the formats. The longest date formats don't fit in a standard-sized cell. The upcoming section "Inserting and Resizing Rows and Columns" explains how to make room for the longer date formats.

If you convert a number in a cell to a date, the date returned is that number of days after January 1, 1904. For example, 10,000 is converted to May 19, 1931. AppleWorks ignores anything to the right of the decimal. Conversely, if a date is converted to a number, the number changes to the number of days since January 1, 1904.

Time formats

As the Time section of Figure 16-1 shows, you can choose from four formatting options for displaying the time: regular or military time formats and with or without seconds. Like with dates, there is no button for this, but the Next Time button cycles through these time format options after you've made it a Time format. Add it to your button bar if you like, or you can use the Format dialog box.

If you convert a number in a cell to a time, the decimal fraction is converted to that portion of 24 hours — for instance, 13.5 becomes 12 p.m. (half a day). Conversely, 3 a.m. converts to the number 0.125 (one-eighth of a day).

Formatting Cells

Here's where you get to change the font, style, and other formatting options for your cells. Formatting lets you make important totals or labels stand out in your spreadsheet.

Text styles

Spreadsheets have almost all the text-formatting options that are available in the text environment. One limitation is that you can only have one font, size, and style per cell. However, these options take a back seat to number functions in spreadsheets, and therefore are found in submenus of the Format menu, as are the text color and alignment options. To apply a different font or style, first select the cells you want to change, and then choose the new font, style, size, color, or alignment. You don't have to go to the Format menu for these things — they can all be added to the button bar (see Appendix A).

What's *your* environment?

It's bound to get you one of these days — you go to a menu to choose an option or function with your mouse, only to find that the option isn't there. After all these years of using AppleWorks and its predecessor, ClarisWorks, we still forget where we are and think we've lost our minds. If you get discombobulated, by an option you could swear *should* be there but isn't, remember to take a look at the shape of your pointer or at which frame tool is selected. Then, switch environments if you need to, or check the other menus.

Default font

Let's face it: Geneva isn't the most exciting typeface in the world. But it's destined to fill every cell in your spreadsheet unless you tell AppleWorks otherwise. Spreadsheet documents can have a default font that is different from the default set for Text Preferences. Changing the default spreadsheet font is so easy that we aren't even going to bore you with a picture. To set your font to something you actually want to look at, follow these steps:

1. **Choose Options⇨Default Font.**

2. **Choose a new font from the scrolling list.**

3. **Type a new point size in the Size box.**

4. **Click OK (or click Cancel to call it off).**

When you change the font, any text for which you haven't explicitly specified a font and size changes. Any custom formatting you apply overrides the new default settings.

Text wrap

What happens when you enter more text into a cell than it can hold? Normally, one of two things happens:

✔ If the cell to the right is empty, the text stomps right over it.

✔ If the cell to the right has something in it, any text you type that doesn't fit in the cell gets cut from view.

Because neither of those options is too pretty, set up the cell so that, when it's full from left to right, the text wraps around to a new line. To turn on text wrap for a cell, just select the cell and click the Text Align Wrap button (top) — you'll need to add it to your button bar, or choose Format⇨Alignment⇨ Wrap. After wrapping a cell, adjust the row height so that all the text is visible. An optional button makes this adjustment a breeze — see the upcoming section "Inserting and Resizing Rows and Columns." If you want to reverse the process, press the Text Align General button (bottom).

Figure 16-2 shows the same cell with text unwrapped and wrapped.

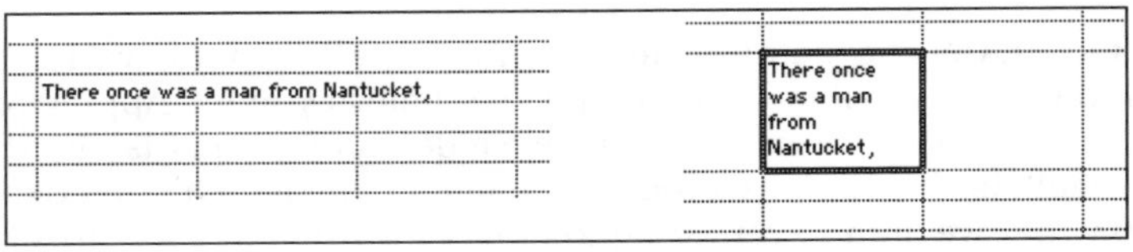

Figure 16-2:
Wrapping
text in a cell
is like
coloring
inside the
lines.

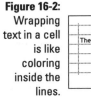

Cell color

A nice, colorful background spices up even the most mind-numbing financial statement. AppleWorks comes with table styles that format your whole spreadsheet and add uniform color quickly. These styles are available in the stylesheet palette. Follow these steps to manually add color and patterns to your cells:

1. **If the Accents window is not showing, choose Window➪Show Accents (⌘-K).**

2. **Select the cells you want to colorize.**

   (Just like they did to those old movies!)

3. **Use the Color and Pattern tabs to set the fill and border colors and patterns.**

   In case you're wondering, gradients and wallpaper don't work in spreadsheets. For more about cell borders, see "Adding Borders, Gridlines, and Headings," later in this chapter. See Chapter 10 for more information on using the Accents window.

Spreadsheet styles

After you format your spreadsheet cells the way you want them, you can save your formatting as a style that you later can apply to other areas of your spreadsheet. You use the Styles window (Format➪Show Styles, Shift-⌘-W) to do this. You can find the details of how to create a style in Chapter 5, but here's a tip on making styles for spreadsheets.

You use the SS-table style type to create a new spreadsheet style. A SS-table style has many substyles that can have separate formatting for odd and even rows or columns, top and bottom rows, and the outside columns. Set up an example of the formatting you want in your style, and then use the Inherit Document Selection checkbox in the New Style dialog box to copy your formatting into the new style.

Sorting

Suppose that you just put together a spreadsheet to track how many boxes of cookies each Girl Scout in your troop has sold. Besides the total number of boxes sold, you need two other lists from the spreadsheet: an alphabetical list the girls can check to make sure you have the correct number of boxes they sold, and a list that shows the top ten sellers for number of boxes sold. You can get both of these lists from the same spreadsheet by using the spreadsheet environment's built-in sorting feature:

1. **Select all the data in the spreadsheet that you want to sort.**

   In the Girl Scout example, make sure that you select all cells that contain data. If you select only the names of the girls and not the number of boxes they sold, only the names are sorted, and you scramble the information about which girl sold how many boxes.

2. **Choose Calculate⇨Sort (⌘-J).**

   This command brings up the Sort dialog box, shown in Figure 16-3.

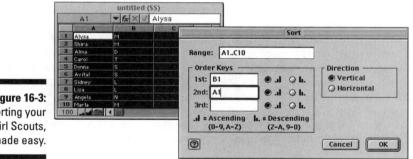

Figure 16-3:
Sorting your
Girl Scouts,
made easy.

3. **Choose the range, order keys, and direction, and then click OK to sort:**

   - *Range:* Range lets you verify and change the selected range of cells. The number to the left of the two dots is the cell in the upper-left corner of the range. The number to the right of the two dots is the cell in the lower-right corner. If the range doesn't reflect what you want to sort, select again in the spreadsheet or enter the correct cell names in Range.

   - *Order Keys:* The order keys tell AppleWorks what to sort, and how to sort it. In the Girl Scout example, to sort alphabetically by last initial, the first cell to contain a girl's last name is in the 1st order key box. The Ascending button to the order key's right tells AppleWorks to sort A to Z. If Descending is selected instead, the names sort from Z to A. The 2nd order key box creates a subsort.

For example, after the list sorts the Girl Scouts by their last initial, if two of the girls happen to have the same last initial, the subsort then sorts those two girls' first names in alphabetical order. By having three sort levels, a spreadsheet can cover the whole district, sorting first by troop, then by last name, and then by first name.

To sort by the number of boxes sold, starting with the most boxes, enter C1 for the 1st order key in descending order and leave the other two order keys blank. If two or more girls sell the same amount of cookies, you can subsort by last name, and even use the first name as the third level sort.

- *Direction:* If you have the spreadsheet set up so that each row contains one set of information, such as a Girl Scout's first name, last name, and boxes sold, select Vertical. If each column is one set of information — as in the daily schedule shown in Figure 15-7 in Chapter 15 — select Horizontal.

Inserting and Resizing Rows and Columns

Have you ever realized partway through a spreadsheet project that you really, really need to add another set of information? AppleWorks figures this will happen to somebody sooner or later, so it makes it easy to sneak those extra rows or columns into your spreadsheet. (Do it when no one is looking, and they'll never know.) We show you how to add those afterthoughts to your spreadsheet (before you get in trouble with the boss for leaving them out). While we're at it, we show you how to resize cells, because you're bound to find that the standard cell sizes don't cut it for your project.

Inserting

Okay, it happened. You just found that vital piece of information that *needs* to be in the middle of your spreadsheet. Cool . . . you get to insert a column.

To show you how, we use the Girl Scout cookie example from the previous section. Say you forgot to include the troop number for each girl and need to add it between the last name and the number of boxes sold. To perform this trick, follow these steps:

1. **New column cells are inserted to the left, so select the column to the right of where you want to insert the new column. In this case, select column C by clicking the letter *C* at the top of the column (refer to Figure 16-3).**

2. Click the Insert Cells button (it is not on the default button bar). Or, either choose Format⇨Insert Cells or press Shift-⌘-I.

Here's the trick: If you selected the entire column by clicking the column head (as we did in Step 1), the column pops in. But, if instead you only selected some cells in the column — by dragging through the cells — a little Insert Cells dialog box pops up, asking whether you want to shift the selected cells to the right or down. Make your choice, which for this example is to the right. Of course, you need to click OK, too.

New rows are inserted above the row(s) you select. Inserting a new row works the same except, if asked, you select Shift Cells Down.

The number of rows or columns that you select is the number of rows or columns that are inserted. To add two rows, select two rows.

Resizing

You can resize rows and columns in three ways. Regardless of which method you choose, to resize several columns or rows at once, making them exactly the same size, first select all the rows or columns you want to resize.

Resizing with the mouse

To resize visually, use the mouse. Move the plus-sign pointer over the row number or column letter area and then over the line between the rows or columns to be adjusted. The pointer changes to a line with two arrows, as shown in Figure 16-4. After the pointer changes, drag the gridline to make the row or column larger or smaller.

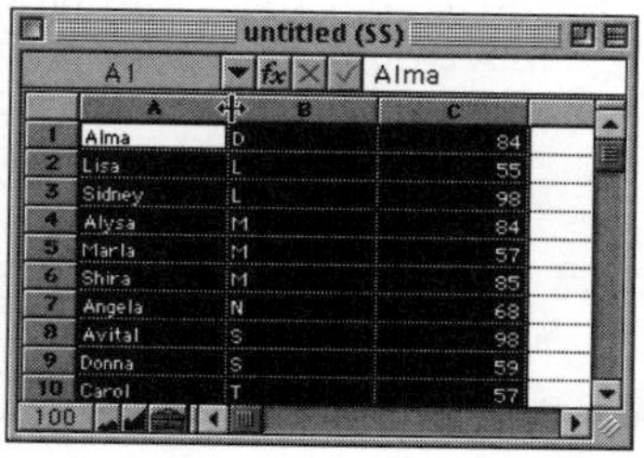

Figure 16-4:
The double-arrow pointer (between column A and column B) resizes rows and columns.

Resizing with buttons

To quickly make cells fit the text that is inside them, you can use either of the two resizing buttons on your button bar:

 ✔ You can automatically resize a single selected cell to the correct height to fit its contents. If you select several cells, this button makes them all the height of the tallest cell in the group.

 ✔ As you can with height, you can automatically resize widths. If one cell is selected, automatic resizing makes the cell wide enough to fit that cell's contents. If you select several cells, automatic resizing sets the width of all of them to that needed by the widest cell.

Resizing with the dialog box

If your column and row headers are hidden so that the numbers and letters don't show, you can't use the mouse method. In that case, or if you need exact control over your heights and widths, the dialog box option gives you control in points, as font sizes are measured (one inch = 72 points):

1. **Select the row or column to resize, or just select one cell in that row or column.**

2. **Choose Format⇨Column Width or Row Height or Control-click the cell and choose Column Width or Row Height from the contextual menu.**

3. **In the dialog box that appears, enter a measurement in points, and then click OK.**

Adding Borders, Gridlines, and Headings

One good way to call attention to or categorize a number is to put a border around it. You probably also want a line above your totals or below your column titles. Speaking of headings, you may not want the column and row headings to appear in your spreadsheet, or the cell grid for that matter.

Borders

 A border is only a click away. Just select the cells around which you want to put a border, and then click a button. A button for each option is located on the default button bar, making selection very easy. Each button clearly illustrates its effect, so you can easily find the buttons you need. One button puts a border around the whole perimeter of the selected cells. (That's the one shown here as an example.) The rest of the buttons let you place a border only on the left side of each selected cell, on the right, on the top, or on the bottom. To place a border on the top and bottom, click both of those buttons — more than one is okay. These are toggle buttons, so if a border is on, clicking the button again turns it off.

If you prefer, you can choose Format⇨Borders or choose Borders from the contextual menu and use the Borders dialog box to check off your options, but that requires extra steps.

Gridlines

Gridlines can be effective — or distracting. Whether you love 'em or hate 'em, you're in control with optional push-button action ('cause the button isn't on the default button bar), or the Options⇨Display dialog box. The grid does appear on printed copies, by the way. Unlike borders, gridlines affect the entire spreadsheet.

Here's the inside scoop on grids:

✔ To remove gridlines from view, either take advantage of the optional button shown here, or uncheck Cell Grid in the Display dialog box.

✔ For solid gridlines, add the button shown here to your button bar and click it. Cell Grid must be turned on for the lines to appear as solid, so this button has no effect when you turn off the gridlines. In the Display dialog box, Cell Grid has to be checked for this to be an option.

✔ To get back to normal dotted lines, turn on the grid (by clicking the button or checking the option), and then, if solid lines are turned on, click the Solid Lines button to turn them off (or uncheck Solid Lines in the dialog box).

If you use solid gridlines, you won't be able to see any black borders around cells. Colors will show, though.

Headings and other display settings

Column and row headings are a big help while working in a spreadsheet, but you probably don't want them in a presented document, on a table, or as a part of such items. (Headings are the A B C . . . and 1 2 3 . . . at the top and side of your spreadsheet.)

You can turn off both top and side headings with the optional Display Headings button shown here, or you can control them individually with the Display dialog box shown in Figure 16-5 by unchecking the Column Headings or Row Headings box or both boxes.

You can use column and row headings on the screen but keep them from printing out. Three checkboxes appear in the Print dialog box when you print a spreadsheet: Print Column Headings, Print Row Headings, and Print Cell Grid. All three boxes are normally checked. Uncheck the appropriate box to keep the headings or cell grid from printing. Depending on your printer, you might need to select AppleWorks from the pop-up menu below your printer's name to get to this set of options.

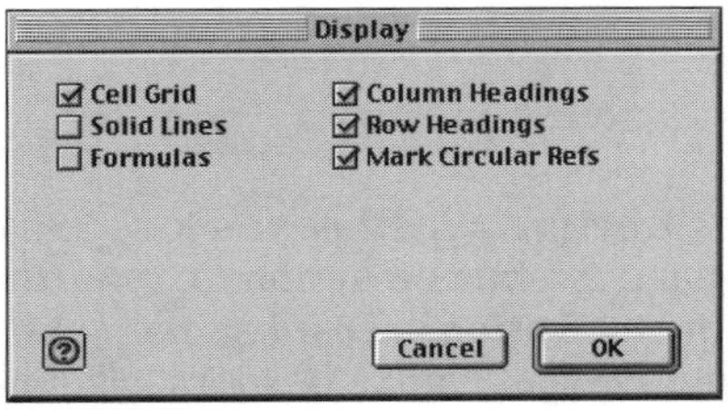

Figure 16-5:
The Display
dialog box.

If you explore the Display dialog box, you may notice two checkboxes. They deal with spreadsheet formulas. The Formulas checkbox is checked if you want a cell to display the actual formula rather than the result of the formula. Normally, it's unchecked. The Mark Circular Refs checkbox helps you track down problems in your formulas. If two or more cells refer to each other, which causes an error, these cells are marked to call your attention to the problem. By default, the Mark Circular Refs checkbox is checked.

Using Titles, Page Breaks, and Print Ranges

What do titles, page breaks, and print ranges have in common? They all determine how your spreadsheet pages look on-screen and in print.

Locking titles

Have you ever had your column titles scroll out of sight while you're working on a long spreadsheet, leaving you with no idea of what kind of information is in each column unless you continuously scroll up and down to see the titles? Not fun? Then you'll love Lock Title Position. It prevents your column titles from scrolling out of sight. To lock column titles in place:

1. **Select the cells that contain the column or row titles.**

2. Choose Options⇨Lock Title Position.

A check mark appears next to this command when the titles are locked.

Now when you scroll, the row containing your titles is always at the top of the window. The same applies for scrolling sideways when you have locked row titles. The locked titles also print out as the first row or column on every page — excellent for multipage spreadsheets, so you don't have to shuffle through the pages to find the top page every time you forget what information a particular column contains.

Locked titles have two drawbacks, though. One is that you can't have both a column heading and a row heading locked. You must choose one or the other. The other drawback occurs when your titles aren't in the top row or left-most column. In that case, locking the titles also locks the rows or columns above or to the left of them as well. You can avoid this problem simply by splitting the window with the pane controls. See Chapter 2 for more information about splitting a window.

Unchecking Lock Title Position unlocks the titles, whether they are selected or not.

If you want information to appear on every page of a printout of your spreadsheet, such as your name, the date, or a title for the spreadsheet, just insert a header or footer. Choose Format⇨Insert Header or Format⇨Insert Footer. (These commands change to Remove Header and Remove Footer after you add a header or footer.) Choosing one of these commands switches your spreadsheet to page view, where you can edit the contents of the header or footer. See Chapter 5 for more information on headers and footers.

Page breaks and new pages

AppleWorks puts in an automatic page break when you fill up enough cells to run into a margin. If you want to insert a page break before the automatic break, here's what you do:

1. Select the cell to appear in the lower-right corner of your old page, the row to appear at the bottom of the page, or the column to appear at the right edge of the page.

2. Choose Options⇨Add Page Break.

This command puts a page break at the right of the selected cell and below it, below the row, or to the right of the column. Page breaks show up as dashed lines that intersect at your corner cell.

To remove a page break, select the same cell (at the intersection of the dashed lines) and choose Options⇨Remove Page Break.

You don't actually add new pages to a spreadsheet. Instead, you add columns and rows. Spreadsheet documents are normally 40 columns by 500 rows. To add more, choose Format⇨Document and type new numbers into the Size area of the Document dialog box. Spreadsheet frames default to 20 columns by 50 rows. To increase the size of a frame, you first have to open it as a separate window by choosing Window⇨Open Frame. Then choose Format⇨ Document and enter your new numbers into the Size area of the Document dialog box.

If your document is printing more pages than you planned, try choosing Options⇨Remove All Breaks. This command deletes all manual page breaks; it does not remove automatic page breaks inserted by AppleWorks. Also try resetting the print range, which we describe next.

Print range

The Print Range dialog box limits the printing of large spreadsheets to just the parts you want. This dialog box lists two options: Print All Cells with Data and Print Cell Range (just a specified range of cells). Bring up this dialog box by choosing Options⇨Set Print Range.

To print a range of cells, you can either select the cells you want to print before calling up the Print Range dialog box, or enter the cell range into the box. If you want to enter your range, type the name of the cell that's in the upper-left corner of the range, followed by two periods and the name of the cell at the lower-right corner of the range.

To print all cells containing *any* information, select Print All Cells With Data. This, however, is a bit of a misnomer. If the only cell with data in it is Z30, you get a printout of 30 rows and 26 columns — 779 empty cells and the one with data at the bottom-right.

Following are a few more tips for printing spreadsheets:

- ✔ You can set a print range to include blank cells. This setting is handy if you want to print a list or schedule and leave blanks to be filled in later by hand.

- ✔ If your document prints out on too many pages, try selecting just the cells that you want to print, and then set the print range to those cells.

- ✔ To print spreadsheet cells that include a locked title, select the lower-right cell that you want to print, such as AA55. Choose Options⇨Set Print Range to open the Print Range dialog box, and then in the Print Cell Range text box, replace the first cell name with A1. In this example, the print range would be A1–AA55.

Chapter 17

Charting: Pictures from Numbers

● ●

In This Chapter

▶ Introducing chart types

▶ Creating a chart

▶ Customizing a chart

▶ Resizing, moving, or deleting your chart

▶ Making charts from spreadsheet frames

● ●

Charts are fun — or at least a lot more fun than looking at spreadsheets, in our humble opinion. Charts enable you to represent sterile numbers in a lively, visual way to which people can relate. You may stare at columns of numbers for ages before spotting a trend that you would spot in an instant with a chart. Most people think better in pictures than in numbers.

AppleWorks charts are especially fun because they're tied to your spreadsheet, which means they change automatically whenever you change your data!

Getting to Know Chart Types

You can choose from 12 AppleWorks chart types. Each type has at least three variations. Using these variations separately or together, you can make hundreds of different-looking charts. On top of that, you can make other modifications to further customize a chart. The trick to choosing a chart is finding one that displays your data the way you want it and helps people notice what you want them to see. The Chart Options dialog box, shown in Figure 17-1, presents the different chart types for you to select from.

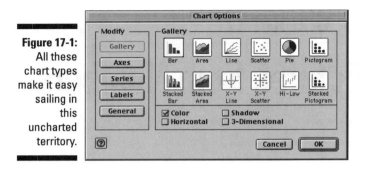

Here's a quick breakdown of each chart type and its possible uses:

✔ **Bar/Stacked Bar:** Bar charts have one bar grouping for each category of data and are usually used for comparing rankings. The number of bars in the group depends on how many figures you have for each category. A variation of the bar chart is the stacked bar chart. Instead of showing a group of bars, this chart stacks the bars on top of one another. For example, you can include bars for three companies showing each company's total earnings over three years; each bar could be broken down into three different colors or patterns to show earnings for each year.

✔ **Area/Stacked Area:** An area chart is good for emphasizing how quantities change over time. An area chart shows the quantity data as the area under a line — one line for each category. The stacked area chart stacks the series of data on top of one another so that you get a total amount for each category, broken down by series.

✔ **Line/X-Y Line:** Line charts are made up of points and lines. Each line is created by connecting points. These points begin at the intersection of the chart's X-axis (horizontal) and Y-axis (vertical). Usually, the X-axis is a time interval, and the Y-axis is the variable that the chart illustrates (interest rates, temperature, and so on). You see this kind of chart on the news all the time when there's talk about falling interest rates or skyrocketing inflation over a particular time period. Line charts make it very easy to see a trend in a series of data.

An X-Y Line chart takes a line chart one step farther by allowing for negative numbers. The 0 point is in the middle of the chart in order to show the negative numbers. This chart is usually used to compare pairs of values.

✔ **Scatter/X-Y Scatter:** A scatter chart is a lot like a line chart, except no line connects the points on the chart. The X-Y scatter chart works the same as the X-Y line chart, without the lines. A scatter chart helps emphasize data points rather than an overall trend.

✔ **Pie:** A pie chart is as American as apple pie. Pie charts graphically display data percentages in relation to 100 percent of a whole pie. This type of chart is useful for showing, for example, how much of your income you blow on different expenses. You don't want negative numbers, because a pie chart works only with absolute values.

✔ **Hi–Low:** This chart uses two sets of numbers for each data point to show high and low points. It's good for tracking stocks or commodities.

✔ **Pictogram/Stacked Pictogram:** This is like bar and stacked bar charts, but with a twist: You get to add a picture inside the bars. For example, this is the kind of chart *USA Today* and *Newsweek* use to show weapons buildups, with little tanks stacked on top of each other.

Making a Chart

You build a chart from the data in your spreadsheet, so the first step in making a chart is to select a block of spreadsheet cells. Most chart types use whatever you enter in the upper-left cell as a title. The labels along the left side and across the bottom (the axis labels) come from the first row and the first column. Figure 17-2 shows a block of selected cells and the rows and columns that become labels on the chart.

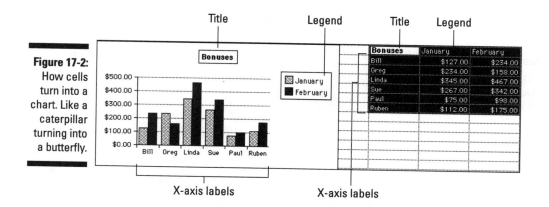

Figure 17-2: How cells turn into a chart. Like a caterpillar turning into a butterfly.

After you select the cells that contain the data you want in your chart, the quickest way to make a chart is to click one of the chart buttons, shown in Figure 17-3. Every type of chart described in the preceding section has a corresponding button. If you want to use these buttons, you need to add them to your button bar.

From left to right we have

- ✔ Bar
- ✔ Stacked bar
- ✔ Line
- ✔ X-Y
- ✔ Scatter
- ✔ X-Y scatter
- ✔ Area
- ✔ Stacked area
- ✔ Pie
- ✔ Hi-low
- ✔ Pictogram
- ✔ Stacked pictogram

To find out how to add optional buttons to your button bar or make your own custom button bar, see Appendix A.

In previous versions, the buttons were identical to the dialog representations. Although these are similar, they are no longer identical, so you're going to have to remember two representations for most of the chart types.

Figure 17-3:
Buttons are the fastest way to make charts.

If you select a chart for which you don't have enough data, AppleWorks warns you or you get a chart that says `Not enough chart data`. If this happens, delete the selection and try another, or look more closely at your selection or data.

If you prefer to use the menus or the keyboard to make your chart, select your cells and then either choose Options⇨Make Chart or press ⌘-M. This takes you to the Gallery section of the Chart Options dialog box, shown back in Figure 17-1. Click the type of chart you want and then click OK to create the chart.

Modifying a Chart

After you see your chart on-screen, you may want to change it. To modify a chart, you get to bring up the Chart Options dialog box, but you get to do it a whole new way — by double-clicking the chart. Of course, you can always choose Edit⇨Chart Options.

Chart type and variations

Flip back to Figure 17-1 for a look at the Chart Options dialog box. Notice the check boxes at the bottom of the Gallery section. Depending on the type of chart you're working with, you should see three to five checkboxes with different options for your chart. You can use these options alone or in combination to give each type of chart tons of different looks. Here's what the options do:

- **Color:** This option turns the color on and off in your chart. It substitutes black-and-white patterns for colors in bars, pie pieces, and other filled areas.

- **Horizontal:** This preference changes the orientation of the chart to horizontal. For example, with this option turned on, bar chart bars grow from left to right rather than bottom to top.

- **Shadow:** This choice adds a drop shadow behind the chart elements for a 3-D effect.

- **Square grid:** This option is for X-Y line and X-Y scatter graphs only. It uses a grid that shows both negative X and Y values, so the origin, or center point, is in the middle.

- **Scale multiple:** This option applies only to pie charts. Pie charts make a new pie for each series of data in a category. This shrinks pies so that they all fit in the chart window.

- **3-dimensional:** This choice adds depth to chart types, when available. This option actually draws a representation of a 3-D object. For example, if you check the 3-dimensional box for a bar chart, the bars are actually drawn as 3-D boxes rather than flat bars. This option is only available for bar/stacked bar and pictogram/stacked pictogram charts.

- **Tilt:** This option applies only to pie charts. It tilts the pie instead of showing the normal top-down view. Try it along with shadow for a 3-D look.

Other chart options

You may notice the five buttons on the left side of the Chart Options dialog box. Each button takes you to an area of that dialog box. Table 17-1 describes what each area does for your chart. You can access certain areas of the dialog box directly by double-clicking the related part of your chart; these double-click shortcuts are included in Table 17-1.

Table 17-1	The Five Areas of the Chart Options Dialog Box
This Area	*Does This*
Gallery	Lets you choose a chart type and variations. Double-click the chart background to get here.
Axes	Lets you modify the axis labels, set intervals, set tick marks, and more. You can go directly to this area by double-clicking either axis.
Series	Lets you modify how some or all of the data series are displayed. You can add a label to the data. Most important, this area lets you change a series to a different type.
Labels	Lets you set up how and where you want the title and legend to appear — or not to appear. Also lets you add a drop shadow to the title and legend boxes or have them print sideways to sneak them in on the side. Double-click the title or legend box to come directly to this area.
General	Controls which cells are used for the chart, and whether the data series are in rows or columns — that is, do the numbers in your spreadsheet progress left to right (rows) or top to bottom (columns)? Also lets you use numbers in the first row or column as labels.

Changing colors and line width

How would you like to change the colors AppleWorks picks out for your chart? You can change the fill color and pattern of bars in a bar chart, the thickness and pattern of the line that surrounds the bars, or the border and fill settings for any data series in any type of chart. To change the color or pattern of a data series:

1. **With the chart selected, click the box in the legend next to the data series you want to change.**

   A small circle appears in that box, indicating that any changes affect that data series.

2. **Use the color controls in the Accents window to select a new setting for that data series.**

   Set the pen to create and modify outlines. Use the color, pattern, wallpaper, or gradient to change the filled-in areas, just like changing a draw object.

Updating the chart with new numbers

Your chart is actually tied to the spreadsheet cells that created it. When you change the information in those cells, the chart is automatically updated. You can even add more cells to the chart range. Just use the General area of the Modify Chart dialog box to enter the new range. The tie-in ends, though, when you cut the chart. Copies of your chart also are not linked to the originating spreadsheet.

If you cut your chart and then paste it anywhere, it loses its link to the spreadsheet cells it was created from, so the chart isn't updated when changes are made in those cells. Instead, the chart becomes a group of draw objects that you can change manually if you want. If you need to update the chart, make a whole new chart.

Adding your own picture to a pictogram chart

One of the best-looking chart types is the pictogram chart, especially when you add your own picture. To create your own pictogram chart, follow these steps:

1. **Choose Edit⇨Copy, ⌘-C to copy a draw or paint graphic.**

2. **Bring up the Chart Options dialog box and then click Series to go to the Series area, shown in Figure 17-4.**

   For fastest access, double-click the box next to the series label in the legend to get to the Series area.

3. **If the series is not already displayed as a pictogram, choose Pictogram from the Display As pop-up menu.**

4. **Click the Pictogram Sample area.**

   A dark square surrounds a selected sample.

5. **Paste your graphic.**

   Click the Paste button, select Edit⇨Paste, or press ⌘-V.

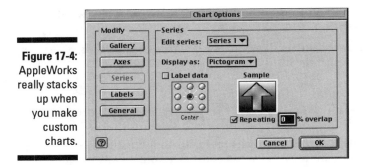

Figure 17-4:
AppleWorks
really stacks
up when
you make
custom
charts.

If you want the pictogram to be stacked in the bar, check Repeating. Otherwise, the graphic stretches or shrinks to fit the bar.

Resizing, Moving, and Deleting Charts

In a way, a chart is a big draw object. A chart floats above the spreadsheet in its own layer, like a draw object. You can move, resize, or delete it, just like any other rectangle you make with a draw tool:

- **To move your chart,** position the pointer anywhere inside its border, hold down the mouse button, and drag the chart to a new location.

- **To resize your chart**, drag any corner handle. The objects in the chart are scaled to fit within the new border.

- **To delete your chart**, click it to select it; then either press the Delete key or choose Edit➪Cut or Edit➪Clear.

Making Charts in Other Document Types

Charts can be made in any type of document that lets you make a spreadsheet frame, except a paint document. That leaves text, draw, database (in layout mode), presentation, and spreadsheet documents. Normally, when you make a chart from data in a spreadsheet frame, the chart appears in the document in its own layer, separate from the spreadsheet frame. Don't worry — the chart is still linked to the data in the spreadsheet frame.

To have the chart appear inside the frame with the spreadsheet, open the frame by choosing Window➪Open Frame before you make the chart.

After you cut the chart, its links to the spreadsheet cells that created it are severed. Copies are never connected. They are separate draw objects.

Chapter 18

Making It All Add Up with Formulas and Functions

*H*ere's a scary thought: Spreadsheet formulas come pretty close to actually programming your computer. You actually type in calculations you want the spreadsheet to perform.

Don't worry if this sounds a little daunting. We start by showing you a really important formula — and it's really easy.

First, a couple of definitions are in order. A *formula* is a series of instructions that you enter into cells to tell AppleWorks to make a calculation. A *function* is a predefined shortcut for doing complex calculations that you can include in your formula to make life easier. A formula can include functions that help it perform your calculation.

The AutoSum Shortcut — First and Finest

The majority of math in spreadsheets seems to be the adding of columns or rows full of numbers — sometimes incredibly long rows full of numbers. If this is as far as you want to go with spreadsheet formulas, you're just about finished with your lesson for today. Lesson one and only — the AutoSum button.

Σ AutoSum automatically adds up a row or column of numbers, dumping the result into an empty cell at the bottom of the column or at the end of the row. All you have to do is select the cells to add and click AutoSum on the button bar. Here's how:

1. **Select the cells you want to add (the *range*), along with an empty cell at the end to hold the result (see Figure 18-1).**

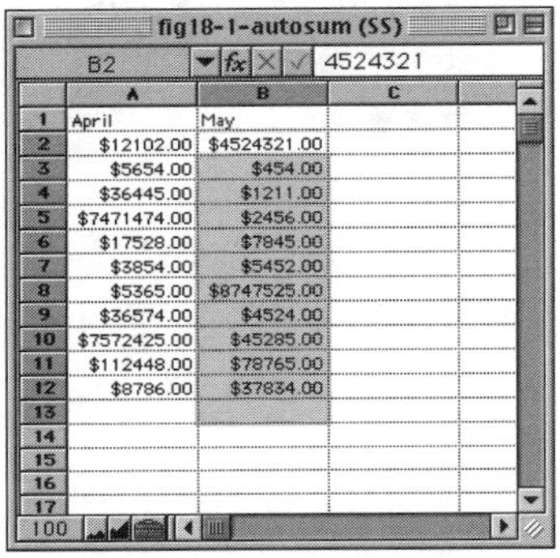

Figure 18-1:
Totals with a
tap — on
the
AutoSum
button.

2. **Click AutoSum.**

   The result appears in the empty cell.

   AutoSum actually creates a formula that adds the range of cells you selected and places the result in the empty cell. If you change a number in one of the cells, the total updates automatically as long as you have the Auto Calc option checked in the Calculate menu.

   You can use the AutoSum shortcut to fake your way through most of what you're likely to do with a spreadsheet. If you need to do more complex calculations with formulas, keep reading.

Warning: Thinking zone ahead

The rest of this chapter should be marked with the Technical Stuff icon. Using formulas in a spreadsheet is pretty heady stuff. If you're math-phobic and there's any way to get out of doing this math stuff, find it. But if you're into math or can get into trying, you'll get used to this stuff and, who knows, maybe even come to love it.

Here's some good news: If you took Algebra in high school and wondered, "What good is this going to do me in the real world?" — you finally have the answer.

Entering Formulas

Here's the number one rule of formulas: They always start with an equal sign (=).

This rule is set in stone. If it doesn't start with an equal sign, it's not a formula. The equal sign tells AppleWorks that a formula follows. Remember it this way: "The number you see in this cell equals the result of this formula." A typical formula looks like =A1+A2. This formula adds the contents of cell A1 to the contents of cell A2 and displays the result in the cell containing the formula.

Math operations

You can do basic math as well as more complex things in formulas. Table 18-1 offers a list of some math calculations you can do, the symbols they use, and the order in which each calculation happens in the formula. Remember from high school Algebra all those parentheses around parts of long, complicated equations? Remember how it really mattered where those parentheses went and what parts went where? This stuff is that stuff: Right here, right now. The order in which calculations happen affects the result of the calculation. For example, the result is different if you add first and then multiply versus if you multiply and then add.

Table 18-1	Math Operations in AppleWorks Formulas	
To Do This Operation	*Use This Symbol*	*Order in Which AppleWorks Performs This Kind of Operation*
Divide number by 100 percent	%	1
Raise a number to a power (exponent)	^	2
Multiply	*	3
Divide	/	3
Add	+	4
Subtract	–	4

Operations that have the same order number are evaluated from left to right. You can change the order of calculations by using parentheses. If parentheses are present in a formula, AppleWorks calculates the contents of the inner-most set of parentheses first and works its way out. Parentheses are really handy for simplifying what you're doing.

Entering cell references

The easiest way to tell AppleWorks which cell you want to use in your formula is to click it. Anytime the cursor is in the entry bar and you click a cell, the name of that cell is added into the entry bar. For example, to get =A1+A2 to appear in the entry bar, type an equal sign, click cell A1, type a plus sign, and then click cell A2. If you want a range of numbers, just drag across the range and select them, and the range appears in your formula.

Of course, you can always type in a cell name, but clicking the cell eliminates any typing errors that may sneak in.

Naming your cells

In standard spreadsheet language, instead of calculating something like "Total Income" minus "Total Expenditures," you normally end up with something like =D97–M84. The first way is a tad more friendly and easier to track, though, isn't it? Apple thought so, too, so it let us name our cells. Nice and friendly.

To name a cell, follow these steps:

1. **Select the cell (or range of cells) that you want to name.**

2. **Click the arrow in the entry bar and choose Define Name.**

   The Define Named Range dialog box shown in Figure 18-2 opens.

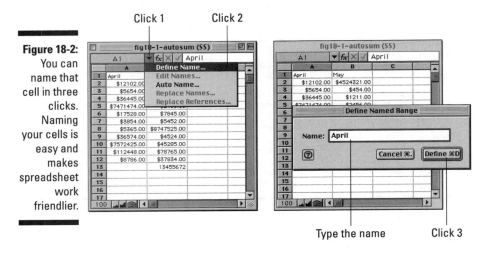

Figure 18-2:
You can name that cell in three clicks. Naming your cells is easy and makes spreadsheet work friendlier.

3. **Name your cell and then click Define.**

   This cell has the same name as the heading, but yours doesn't have to.

Notice in Figure 18-2 that the cell reference is A1. It's in the top corner — the leftmost element of the entry bar. After the cell is named, selecting that cell presents its name instead of its column and row address.

You can also select an entire range of cells and give them one collective name. Notice that the Edit Names dialog box in Figure 18-3 shows a range of cells called "Monthly total." We help you navigate the Edit Names dialog box in the following section.

Editing cell names

Whether you make a mistake naming your cell or just want to change its name for clarity, you can do so easily by following these steps:

1. **Click the arrow in the entry bar and select Edit Names.**

   The Edit Names dialog box, shown in Figure 18-3, comes up.

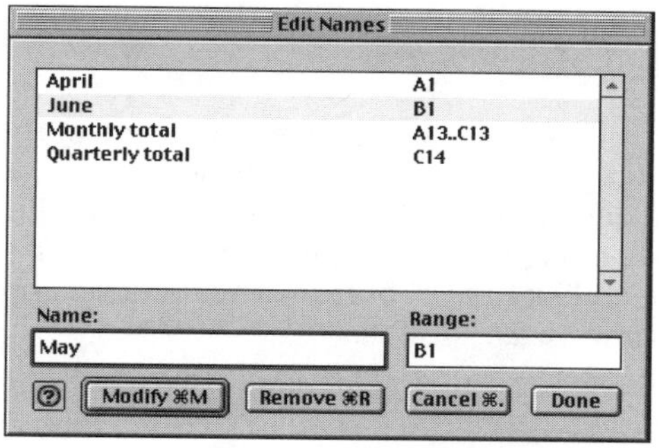

Figure 18-3:
The Edit
Names
dialog box.

Edit Names	
April	A1
June	B1
Monthly total	A13..C13
Quarterly total	C14

Name: May   Range: B1

[?] [Modify ⌘M] [Remove ⌘R] [Cancel ⌘.] [Done]

2. **Click once on the name to be changed.**

   That name appears in the Name field below the list of named cells.

3. **Enter your new name and click Modify.**

   If you want to change more names, repeat Steps 2 and 3. If not, click Done.

Creating formulas is much easier now. While you're in the entry bar creating your formula, you can pick a cell by name instead of scrolling all around looking for it. More about formulas is coming up.

From now on, when you want to go to a named cell, just select its name from the pop-up menu on the entry bar. You're there in a zip.

You can also reassign a name from one cell or cell range to another. For example, say you give the name "Holiday" to cells G3..G5 and then check a calendar and realize your mistake. You can switch the name "Holiday" to refer to G8..G10. Reassigning a name is similar to editing a name, except that you change the cell address in the Range field, ignoring the Name field. To assign a range of fields, enter the first cell address, type two periods, and then type the last cell address.

Using Functions

At the beginning of the chapter, we say that a function is a built-in shortcut for doing complex math calculations in spreadsheet formulas. One of the best examples of a function is the SUM function. If you want to add up the contents of ten cells, instead of typing **=A1+A2+A3** and so on, you can type **=SUM(A1..A10)**. This format automatically adds up the contents of the ten cells. AutoSum uses the SUM function in this way.

AppleWorks has more than 100 built-in functions that fall into eight general categories: Business and Financial, Date and Time, Information, Logical, Numeric, Statistical, Text, and Trigonometric.

The best way to add a function to your formula is to use one of the built-in AppleWorks functions. Enter your formula until you get to the place where you want a function. Then click the fx button in the entry bar. The Paste Function dialog box, shown in Figure 18-4, appears. Scroll through the list and select the function and then click the OK button. The function appears in your formula where the cursor was.

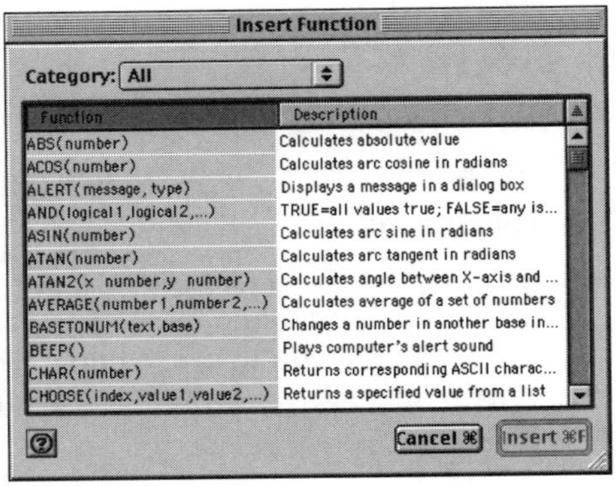

Figure 18-4:
Even the
funkiest
function is
just a click
away.

Insert Function	
Category:	All
Function	Description
ABS(number)	Calculates absolute value
ACOS(number)	Calculates arc cosine in radians
ALERT(message, type)	Displays a message in a dialog box
AND(logical1,logical2,...)	TRUE=all values true; FALSE=any is...
ASIN(number)	Calculates arc sine in radians
ATAN(number)	Calculates arc tangent in radians
ATAN2(x number,y number)	Calculates angle between X-axis and ...
AVERAGE(number1,number2,...)	Calculates average of a set of numbers
BASETONUM(text,base)	Changes a number in another base in...
BEEP()	Plays computer's alert sound
CHAR(number)	Returns corresponding ASCII charac...
CHOOSE(index,value1,value2,...)	Returns a specified value from a list

Cancel ⌘   Insert ⌘I

We'd love to tell you all about each of those functions, but that goes way beyond the scope of this book. The online help system is pretty good about explaining all the functions. AppleWorks includes an entire "Alphabetical list of functions" in the Help feature. Enter "Alphabetical list of functions" in the index, or click the Help icon in the Paste Function dialog box. Anytime you want to do a complex calculation, take a look to see whether AppleWorks provides a function that does it for you.

These three functions give you some ideas about what you can do with a spreadsheet. You can find more information about these and other functions in the online Help system.

- **AVERAGE:** This function works just like the SUM function, except that it calculates the average value of the contents of a range of cells. A typical AVERAGE function in a formula looks like this: =AVERAGE (A1..A10). AVERAGE is probably the second-most-used AppleWorks function and purists call it the "arithmetic mean."

- **IF:** This function tests to see whether a condition is true or false; it returns one value for true and another for false. This one function opens the door for a spreadsheet to make decisions based on the data in the spreadsheet. For example, you can have it check to see whether it's Wednesday and, IF it is, have it then recalculate all prices in a list to reflect a 10 percent discount. This is one powerful function.

- **MACRO:** This function lets a spreadsheet activate a macro you've recorded, press a button, or perform an AppleScript. It lets AppleWorks pull its own strings. The combination of the IF and MACRO functions is what enables people to make games in spreadsheets.

Functions can be extremely powerful tools for manipulating data in a spreadsheet. By using the right functions, you can have a spreadsheet make decisions based on the data you enter. The possibilities are limited only by your imagination. We've seen spreadsheets that do everything from play blackjack to analyze stock trends.

Relative versus Absolute References

To create your own formulas, you need to know how to specify which cells you want your formula to use for its calculations. For example, suppose that looking at the formula that AutoSum puts into cell B26, you see something like =SUM(B15..B25). This formula tells AppleWorks to add up the sum of the contents of cells B15 through B25 and put that number into the cell containing the formula.

However, if you copy and paste that formula into another cell, the range changes to reflect the move. That's because the formula uses a relative reference to decide which cells to add. What really happens is that the formula tells AppleWorks to add up the total of the eleven cells above the cell containing the formula. If you paste the formula into cell C26, it changes to =SUM(C15..C25); in D26 it would be =SUM(D15..D25); and so forth.

Relative references make a formula portable so that you can easily use it in another part of your spreadsheet. Relative references are the standard way of setting up formulas in AppleWorks because they give you so much flexibility to copy and paste the formula to other parts of a spreadsheet.

Absolute references refer to a specific cell, row, or column and don't change when moved. To make a cell reference absolute, all you have to do is put a dollar sign in front of each part of the cell name — for example, B26. If you put B26 into a formula, that formula always gets the contents from cell B26, no matter where the formula moves in the spreadsheet.

You can also mix the reference types to constrain just the column or row, like $B26, or B$26. The first example is constrained to column B, but the row reference changes as the formula moves up or down. The second example is constrained to row 26, but the column reference changes as the formula is moved right or left.

Part V
Working with Files: Smoothing Out the Rough Edges

The 5th Wave — By Rich Tennant

"Your database is beyond repair, but before I tell you our backup recommendation, let me ask you a question. How many index cards do you think will fit on the walls of your computer room?"

In this part . . .

Databases are magic. They make all the boxes full of business cards disappear, leaving in their place one slim, nonexistent (sort of) file. Amazing. They also do hours of redundant writing, copying, and pasting over and over again with a few clicks of a button. They make labels and sorting and all kinds of stuff just go away.

But the word — database — sounds kind of techy and scary, doesn't it? We thought so, too — once upon a time. But now we're cool and fearless, storing anything we can in these great things. But it's no fun to be cool and fearless alone. We want you there, too.

In this part, we show you what databases are and what they can do for you. You see how to enter, sort, and find information in a database; how to create a database; how to print records; and how to make your own form letters to send out to your friends during the holidays. Databases give you more scope for your genius!

Try 'em. We think you'll like 'em.

Chapter 19

Your Rolodex Revisited: Database Basics

*T*he database environment is one of the most overlooked and underused parts of AppleWorks, but this environment has a lot of power. The AppleWorks database environment was designed and developed by the publisher of FileMaker Pro, the most popular database on the Mac, and which is gaining a wide following in Windows. This chapter shows you how to get to first base with databases (and what not to do on a blind data).

Deciding When to Use a Database

Databases are used to collect and store information. A perfect example of a real-world database is the card catalog at the library. You remember card catalogs, don't you? They had all those funny little drawers filled with cards listing each book by title, author, or subject. Why don't you see those old catalogs anymore? Most libraries have put the card catalog on a computer using a database program. Computerized card catalogs are easier to update, easier to search and they save paper, too.

The card catalog is a collection of similar information: Each card has spaces for the author, title of the book, publisher, and so on, which makes it a perfect candidate for a database. You can use a database for any collection of information with similar items, such as:

- ✔ An address list (the most popular use for the database environment)
- ✔ A job/client file
- ✔ A recipe file
- ✔ A catalog of your videotape collection
- ✔ A catalog of your Beanie Babies collection
- ✔ A list of which Versace suits go with which Chanel handbags

The database environment has the power to produce sophisticated reports about the data it contains. In this chapter, we show you the basics so that you can enter information into an existing database, such as the name-and-address list provided with AppleWorks, and organize the information the way you want it.

The best way to learn about databases is to play with an existing one. If you don't happen to have one, you can create one easily by using the Address List Assistant. While you're it, instead of just playing around with it, why not use it for real? You can use it as is or customize it in any way.

You can only use the database environment in a database document. Database frames don't exist.

Database Records

A database *record* is a set of information. In a card catalog, one card is the equivalent of one database record. A record is like a form that you fill out and file into the database. After you enter your information, you can sort the records or search for records that contain specific items. This is one of the many places a database improves on the traditional card catalog — with the database you create one record and search for data in a specific field (see below) and with the card catalog you had to create a title card, an author card, etc.

You can think of the records in the database as cards in a stack. You can arrange them alphabetically, by number, by date, and so on. You can even separate a group of cards from the stack and just work with the smaller group. Figure 19-1 shows you a sample database record.

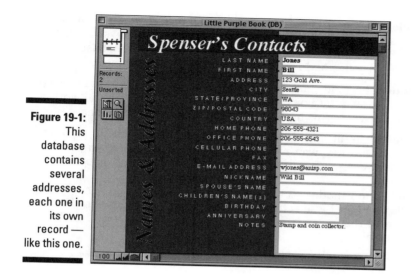

Figure 19-1:
This
database
contains
several
addresses,
each one in
its own
record —
like this one.

Database Fields

Each database record is made up of several pieces of information. Each of
these pieces is a *field.* Every record in the same database has the same fields.
A field can contain text, a number, a date, multimedia, a formula that makes a
calculation based on information in other fields, or a field that summarizes
other data.

Take another look at Figure 19-1. See the different spaces for each piece of
information? Those are the fields in that database. When you enter information in a database, you type it into fields. You find out more about fields in
Chapter 20, which is about designing a database.

Browse, Find, and Layout Modes

The AppleWorks database environment has four modes: browse, list, find,
and layout. Each mode enables you to work on a different aspect of the same
database document, and each has its own tools and commands. The following list describes these modes:

 ✔ **Browse mode:** This mode is where you or your user enters, views, and
sorts data.

✔ **List mode:** This mode enables you to view all the records in your database in a spreadsheet-like list made up of columns and rows. Use list mode for a quick overview of all the information in the database. You can also quickly find and select individual records in list mode.

 ✔ **Find mode:** This mode enables you to search for records containing specific information. After you find a set, you can save that set and work just within that set. This button is not on the default button bar.

 ✔ **Layout mode:** In this design mode, you create new layouts for viewing your records in a new way, modify existing layouts, or delete layouts you don't want anymore. This button is not on the default button bar.

You can switch to any mode by clicking its button in the button bar, by using a keyboard shortcut, or by selecting the mode from the Layout menu. Layout is an odd name for that menu because layout is also a mode of its own. Don't let that confuse you.

Entering Data

Whenever you enter data or work with data in any way, make sure that you're in browse or list mode. One way to be sure that you're in browse or list mode is to look at the left side of your AppleWorks window. At the top of the controls is a *Record book* — your control for moving through records. In browse or list mode, you can see a bookmark at the right of the Record book, as shown back in Figure 19-1. In the other modes, the bookmark doesn't show. We talk about the Record book and bookmark's functions very soon.

To enter browse mode, click the button, choose Layout⇨Browse, or use Shift-⌘-B.

You can also work with data in list mode, although traditionally all fields of information aren't in the layouts that are used for lists. To enter list mode, click the button, choose Layout⇨List, or use Shift-⌘-I.

Adding a new record

 The first thing you want to do is add a new, blank record to hold your information. The easiest way to accomplish this is to click New Record on the button bar. If you prefer, you may choose Edit⇨New Record or press ⌘-R.

When a new record is similar to the information in an existing record, choose Edit⇨Duplicate Record to copy that record. Doing so puts you in the new, duplicate record. Just change any information that's different. This command is very handy when entering corporate contacts because many people have the same corporate address. There is no button to duplicate a record. The keyboard shortcuts are ⌘-D.

Deleting records

 To remove a record forever, select it by clicking anywhere in its background, and then use the Delete button or choose Edit⇨Delete Record. When you delete a record, all the information contained in its fields is deleted. If your sample database comes with any fake data, try the Delete Record command on those records — after you've seen how the system works or replaced it with a few records of your own.

Filling in text fields

When a new record appears, the cursor is in the first field. Type the information for that field. The fastest way to move from field to field within a record is by pressing the Tab key. You can also click any field with the arrow pointer to position the cursor in it. To move back a field, use the mouse or press Shift-Tab.

Pressing the Return key in a field adds a line to that field — which is not what you want to do unless you're starting a new paragraph! On-screen, the extra line may cover up another field, but that's the least of it. An extra return messes up your labels, envelopes, merges, and more. As in word processing, pressing the Return key is a habit to be broken. If you press the Return key by mistake, use Delete to remove the extra line. Do it right away, before you have to waste hours later trying to figure out what's wrong.

Using multimedia fields

To place media (stills or movies) in this field, use the browse mode, as with all other data entry. For media, you should move your movies into the same folder as the database before you insert the movies. This saves you a lot of grief when you have to move your database or transfer it to another computer.

To insert still images, select the multimedia field, choose File⇨Insert, navigate to the desired image, and then click Insert. Your still image is now part of the database. That's it. You're done. If you're working with movies, read on for everything you need to know.

To insert QuickTime movies select the multimedia field, choose File⇨Insert, navigate to the desired movie, and then click Insert. Your movie is now part of the database. Your QuickTime movie now appears in the field, waiting to be played. However, you must have QuickTime installed on the computer for a QuickTime movie to play. If you don't have QuickTime installed, the image shows but doesn't play when clicked. To run a movie, double-click anywhere in the frame.

To easily locate and select a movie, select QuickTime from the Show pop-up list.

It's best to store media files in the same folder as the database because AppleWorks must find the file in order to play it. AppleWorks doesn't actually embed the media file into the database — that would swell your files beyond belief. Instead, AppleWorks uses *pointers* to files. Pointers to files are relative to the location of the database. If you move the database to another computer, the path to that file breaks, and AppleWorks asks you to locate that file and gives you an Open dialog box when you try to play it. If you keep the media in the same folder and move the folder, the path doesn't break. This ensures that, when moving the database to another computer, you move all necessary media files.

You can also insert other movie types.

✔ You can place QuickTime VR movies using the same steps as those for inserting a regular QuickTime movie. In the database, it plays and functions the same as anywhere else — double-click the image, and your cursor becomes a small circle. Move the circle to move around in the image.

✔ You can place sound clips in a manner similar to inserting a QuickTime movie.

Navigating through a database

As your database becomes larger, moving from record to record becomes more of a hassle. Your best navigation tool is the Record book. You can also use the scroll bar if you're in list mode or showing multiple records at once.

Click the top page of the Record book to move back a record. Click the bottom page of the Record book to move forward a record. Use the slider to move past many records quickly. To move the slider, click and drag it. In the lower-right corner of the Record book, you see the record numbers change, telling you where you are. You can also select the record number and type another number in its place and then press Enter to get to that record. The numeric Enter key is safer than the Return key when dealing with data, because the Return key creates a new, often unwanted, line when you're in a field.

Importing data from other databases

Another way to enter information into a database is to import it from a database created by another application, like FileMaker Pro. You can import data from any file that AppleWorks can read, including other AppleWorks files and the file types we list in Step 2 below.

Follow these steps to import a database document from another application:

1. **Open the AppleWorks database into which you want to import the data.**

   You can add to a database that has existing records or add data to a blank one.

2. **Choose File⇨Insert. Select the file type you want to show (depending on the type of database you're trying to open).**

   (If you're not sure what the file type is, try each.) Navigate to the location of the document you want to insert, select it, and then click Insert.

   If you don't see the file, open the file in the application that created it and export the document or records you want by saving them or exporting them in the format that AppleWorks can import, tab-delimited (ASCII). Then return to Step 2.

3. **Choose File⇨Insert. Navigate to the document you created in Step 1, select it, and then click Insert.**

   This action brings up the Import Field Order dialog box shown in Figure 19-2. The left side of the dialog box shows the data in the file you're importing. The right side of the dialog box shows the fields in your AppleWorks database document.

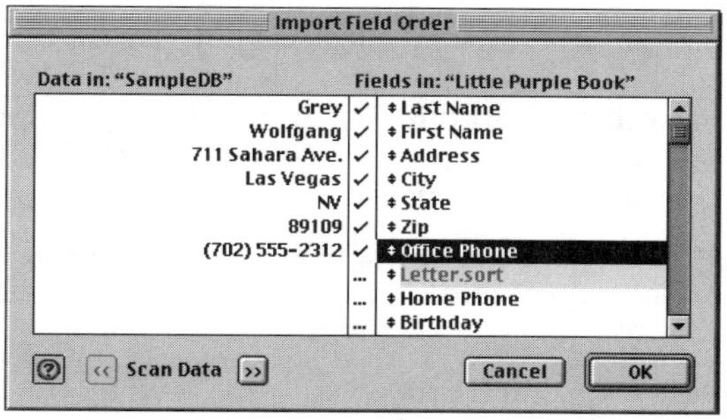

Figure 19-2:
Ever wanted to try your hand at the import business? Try the Import Field Order dialog box and see how you like it.

Import Field Order

Data in: "SampleDB"

Fields in: "Little Purple Book"

Grey	✓	‡ Last Name
Wolfgang	✓	‡ First Name
711 Sahara Ave.	✓	‡ Address
Las Vegas	✓	‡ City
NV	✓	‡ State
89109	✓	‡ Zip
(702) 555-2312	✓	‡ Office Phone
	...	‡ Letter.sort
	...	‡ Home Phone
	...	‡ Birthday

? ‹‹ Scan Data ››   Cancel   OK

4. **Drag the fields on the right side of the dialog box up or down so that they match up with the data on the left side.**

   Check marks identify fields that will be imported. Fields that won't be imported have three dots instead. You don't have to import the data from every field: Click in that column to add or remove a check mark.

   If your destination database doesn't have enough fields to import all the data, you can cancel the import process and add more fields to your database. See Chapter 20 for more information on adding fields.

5. **When you're happy with the match-up, use the Scan Data buttons to verify a few records.**

   Make sure that the data is going into the correct fields.

6. **Click OK to import the data.**

You can also export data from AppleWorks by saving a database document as an ASCII text file. Doing so enables you to use your database with another application, like FileMaker Pro or Excel. If you need a refresher on how to save a document in a different format, pop back to Chapter 2.

Sorting

Sorting is one of the things databases do best, which is why you use a computer instead of a card catalog. Want to alphabetize by a last name field? Just a few clicks and a few seconds later, you have your alphabetized list. How? You have a few choices. The really fast way is by using a button. For more control, you can use Organize➪Sort Records, which we show you soon.

Button sorts

When time is short and you need to sort, click one of these buttons:

 ✔ **Sort Ascending:** To quickly sort one field from A to Z, position your cursor in that field (within any record in the set) and click Sort Ascending in the default button bar.

 ✔ **Sort Descending:** To sort from Z to A, position the cursor in that field (within any record in the set) and click Sort Descending in the default button bar.

 ✔ **Sort Again:** To use the field and order that were used by the last sort, click this button. This is most useful after you set up a sort order that includes subsorts, by using the longer method of sorting, which we cover in a moment. This button is not on the default button bar.

The Sort Records dialog box has some benefits. Suppose you had to sort by last name in ascending order (A to Z). Then suppose some people had the same last name. With this dialog box, you can place the First name field second in the sort to sort records that have the same last name alphabetically by first name. With this in mind, take a look at the next sort option.

Saved sorts

To set up a sort you can save and reuse, take advantage of the Fast Report pop-up menu to create a named sort. Besides being reusable, named sorts also have the advantage of being able to subsort other fields, unlike the buttons' one-field sort ability. Follow these steps to create a named sort:

1. **Find the set of records to be sorted.**

2. **Choose New Sort from the Sort pop-up menu on the Tool panel, as shown in Figure 19-3.**

   This brings up the Sort Records dialog box, also shown in Figure 19-3.

Figure 19-3: Use the Sort pop-up menu to create a named sort.

3. **Name your sort in the Sort Name text box.**

4. **Set up a sort.**

   • From the scrolling Field List on the left, click the field you want to sort on, and then click Move (or double-click the field). The selected field moves to the Sort Order list on the right.

   • With the field name still selected in the Sort Order list, click the Ascending or Descending button to set the order of the sort.

   • For text, A–Z is ascending, and Z–A is descending. For numbers, ascending is 1-2-3 . . . and descending is 10-9-8. . . .

• Add fields that you want to subsort by repeating the last two steps as many times as necessary. To remove a field from the sort, select the field in the Sort Order list and click Move (or double-click the field).

5. **Click OK to save the sort.**

Your named sort now appears at the bottom of the Sort pop-up menu on the Tools panel, as in the pop-up menu on the right in Figure 19-3.

To use your named sort, choose it from the Sort pop-up menu on the Tools panel, shown in Figure 19-4. To change the sort later, choose Edit Sorts from the Sort pop-up menu, select the sort, and then make the changes.

For faster sorting action, try these field selection tips:

✔ To select several contiguous field names from the Field List at once, press Shift and click the first and last item, or drag over several items while holding down Shift.

✔ To select noncontiguous items, press ⌘ and click each item.

To print mailing labels, you can sort by state, zip code, last name, and first name to group your labels by state and zip with all the names in each zip code in alphabetical order. You can have as many items in the Sort Order list as there are fields in your database.

As you sort records, be aware that their numbers change relative to any found set and sort. Don't count on them to remember where a record is. They are not for record identification. For that, use a serial number field, as discussed in Chapter 20.

The Sort command ignores hidden records and those not part of the current found set. If you want to search just a subset of your database, hide the ones you don't want to include. You can choose Organize⇔Hide Unselected or click the Hide Unselected Records button (shown to the left of this paragraph) to exclude the records you don't want to include. Then do the search. The Hide Unselected button is not on the default button bar.

You can do a Find search to pick out a subgroup of records for your search. Check out "Finding," later in this chapter, to see how the find mode works.

Old sorts

The final sort option has the least benefit and is the oldest way to sort. You get to it by choosing Organize⇔Sort Records. This sort works the same as a named sort, but you don't get to name it, save it, and reuse it. We just want to point it out so that you don't go through the trouble to set it up only to find that you can't save it.

Finding

You can flip through your database manually when you need information, or you can use the find mode to search for specific information.

Find mode

To enter find mode, click the Find Mode button, or choose Layout⇨Find. The keyboard shortcuts are Shift-⌘-F. In find mode, you see what looks like a new, blank record. This is actually a Find Request form, like the one shown in Figure 19-4. Type the information you want to find into the appropriate field.

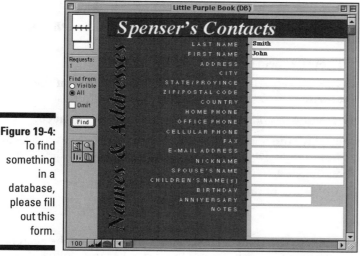

Figure 19-4: To find something in a database, please fill out this form.

Narrow your search

Take a look at the left of the Find Request form in Figure 19-4. It has a couple of options to help you with your search. At the bottom is the Omit check box. If you select this box, AppleWorks finds all the records that don't match the information you typed into the fields on the form.

You also have the choice of searching all records in the database or just the visible records. When records are found that match your search criteria, all other records in the database are hidden. You can use one find session after another to keep narrowing down the possibilities. For example, you can first find all records that contain the name John; then type in your state, check the Omit button, and do another search to find all the Johns outside your state. That way, you can easily find your friend John who moved out of state, even if you don't remember which state he moved to.

You can further narrow your search by filling in more fields. That way, you can search for records that contain John in the first name field, Utah in the state field, and Smith in the last name field. This search yields only records for the John Smiths who live in Utah that you have in your database. The more fields you fill in, the fewer records your search turns up.

Broaden your search with multiple requests

You can use multiple Find Request forms to broaden your search to find more records. One of the examples we cite in the previous section enables you to narrow your search to records with a first name of John and the state of Utah. What if you want to find all your friends named John and all your friends who live in Utah at the same time? You can use multiple Find Request forms to create a search that finds John in the first name field or Utah in the State field. Here are the steps to follow:

1. **Enter find mode (use the button, menus, or keyboard).**

2. **Type your first search criterion in the appropriate field on the Find Request form.**

3. **Choose Edit⇨New Request or press ⌘-R.**

4. **Enter the second search criterion in the appropriate field on the new Find Request form.**

5. **Repeat Steps 3 and 4 to add as many request forms as you need.**

   AppleWorks displays the number of request forms in this search next to the word *Requests* on the left side of the window. Remember, the more forms you add, the broader your search.

6. **Click the All or Visible button to search the database.**

Save your search

You can set up a search to save and use later without re-creating the search forms. This is called a *named search*. To create a named search, follow these steps:

1. **Choose New Search from the Search pop-up menu on the Tools panel, shown in Figure 19-5.**

Figure 19-5:
The Search
pop-up
menu.

2. **In the dialog box that appears, type a name for your new search.**

3. **Use the techniques described on the last couple of pages to create a search.**

4. **Click the Store button that appears in the Tools panel or press Enter to save the search.**

    Your new search now appears at the bottom of the Search pop-up menu on the Tools panel.

To use your named search, just choose it from the Search pop-up menu.

Match records

This section is only for people needing massive database-searching power. Pregnant women and people with heart conditions should skip this section.

The Match Records command, Organize⇨Match Records (⌘-M), is like the find mode on steroids. You can actually use the Match Records command to find all records that meet the following criteria:

- Contains *barb* somewhere in the First Name box
- Has a last name that starts with *L*
- Was entered before last Tuesday
- Has an address that's the square root of the zip code

If you need the really big guns for your search, you've come to the right place. Just take a look at the Enter Match Records Condition dialog box in Figure 19-6. Sheesh, even the name of the thing is scary.

Unlike a Find search, the Match Records command doesn't hide records that don't match the search criteria; the Match Records command selects all matching records instead. Match Records searches only visible records, so if you want to search your whole database, choose Organize⇨Show All Records or press Shift-⌘-A before you search.

In the previous bulleted list, we mention finding records where the address is the square root of the zip code. The formula in Figure 19-6 does just that. That's right — a formula. This formula stuff goes way beyond the scope of this book. We just thought we'd show you what you're missing.

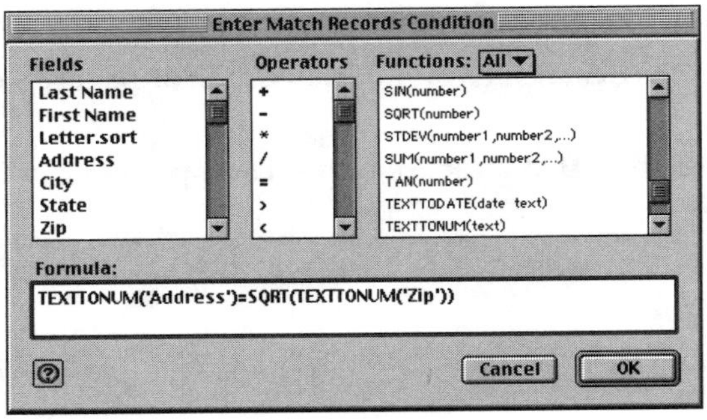

Figure 19-6:
Fear the
mighty Enter
Match
Records
Condition
dialog box!

> **Enter Match Records Condition**
>
> | Fields | Operators | Functions: All ▼ |
> |---|---|---|
> | Last Name | + | SIN(number) |
> | First Name | - | SQRT(number) |
> | Letter.sort | * | STDEV(number1 ,number2,...) |
> | Address | / | SUM(number1 ,number2,...) |
> | City | = | TAN(number) |
> | State | > | TEXTTODATE(date text) |
> | Zip | < | TEXTTONUM(text) |
>
> **Formula:**
> TEXTTONUM('Address')=SQRT(TEXTTONUM('Zip'))
>
> [Cancel] [OK]

If you type your own formulas, remember to enclose the text in double quotes. Field names need to be enclosed in single quotes. Don't forget to close the parentheses.

Searching Shortcuts

Four buttons are available to enable you to do one-click searches in your database. All four require that you use an existing record as an example to let AppleWorks know what you want to search on. All you do is click a field that contains the information you want to use, and then click one of these buttons (assuming that you added them to the button bar, because they aren't there by default):

=	✔ **Match Equal:** Finds all records that have matching information in the selected field. For example, equals (=) and no typing finds blank fields.
≠	✔ **Match Not Equal:** Finds all records that don't match the information in the selected field. For example, equals (=) and 3 finds all records in which this field doesn't have a 3.
<	✔ **Match Less Than:** Finds all records that have information that is less than the information in the selected field.
>	✔ **Match Greater Than:** Finds all records that have information that is greater than the information in the selected field.

For greater than and less than, letters at the beginning of the alphabet are considered less than letters at the end. If you select a field containing text that starts with C and then click Match Less Than, only records containing text that starts with A or B in the selected field will be found.

Like the Match Records command, these buttons search only visible records. To search your whole database, show all records before you click the button.

Chapter 20

Designing a Database

· ·

· ·

Do you keep all your really important information on little slips of paper that always get lost? Well, if you do, maybe you should think about creating a custom database to organize and sort all your little slips. Having important client information, that superb casserole recipe, or all your research notes at your fingertips is much nicer than having to go through all the pockets of your dirty clothes looking for that one scrap of paper with the vital information on it.

Creating an AppleWorks database can be easy at the simplest level, but you can get into some fairly heavy stuff. For ease, your best bet is to use an Assistant or template — at least to get started. Plenty of other templates abound. Of course, the first place to check is the Templates button on the Web page of Starting Points. The AppleWorks User Group (http://www .awug.org), local Mac User Groups (http://www.apple.com/usergroups), and other computer user groups are also sources for database templates. The Apple Web site (http://www.apple.com/appleworks) leads to related products and resources as well.

That said, creating a database is really cool. Why not take a stab at it?

Planning the Database

The first step in creating a database is planning. Sure, you can always go back and add things later, but if you plan beforehand, you won't have to go back and move data around to fix things. Ask yourself these kinds of questions as you design your database:

- ✔ **What will you use the database for?** Will you use it mostly on-screen, or do you want to organize information for printed reports or labels? Make the form fit the function.

- ✔ **How many fields do you need to put information in?** Make a list of all the information items you want to include. Split items into their smallest parts, like using a first name and a last name field rather than just a name field. Joining information together later is much easier than picking out different items in one field.

- ✔ **What kind of information are you going to store?** A database for storing research notes for a term paper is quite different from a contacts database.

- ✔ **How do you want to access the information?** You can add more fields for keywords or categories that can help you sort or find information in the database. For example, do you want to look up a recipe by a type of ingredient or by the number of people it serves?

- ✔ **Do you want to include special fields that automatically enter the date, time, or serial number for a record?** How about using a pop-up menu to limit entries in a field to a preset list? (Find more about these special field options later in the chapter in the section "Mastering Special Field Types.")

- ✔ **How many different layouts do you need?** Do you want one layout for entering data and another for printing the contents of your database? How about a layout for printing labels? Actually, this isn't so important because you can always add layouts later. See the section "Laying Out the Database," later in this chapter, for more information on layouts.

If you don't understand what some of these questions mean, keep reading; the technical ones are explained in this chapter. After you get an idea of what you can do with a database, jot down your answers to these questions and sketch out how you want the layout to look. Visualizing what you want before you sit down at the computer makes the design process much easier.

Defining Fields

Where paper forms have blanks, database records have fields. Before you can enter information into a database, you have to create the blanks to hold the information. Each record is made up of several fields into which you enter the information in the database. The first step in making a new database is telling AppleWorks how many and what kinds of fields you want.

The first thing you see when you open a new database document that isn't based on a template or an Assistant is a Define Database Fields dialog box like the one in Figure 20-1. After all, you don't have a database until you have a place to put your data.

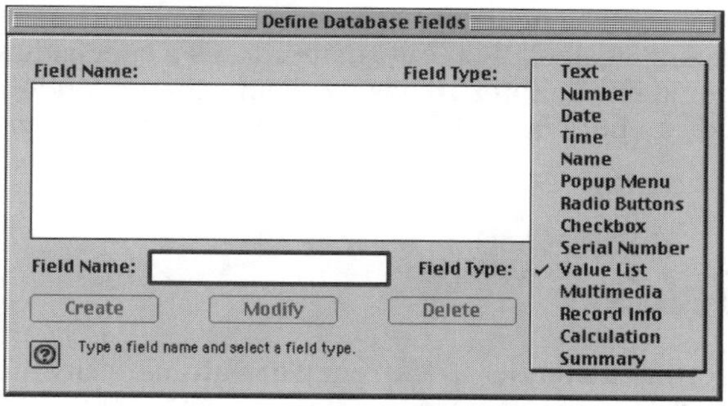

Figure 20-1:
The Define Database Fields dialog box and all the field types.

Define Database Fields
Field Name: **Field Type:**

Text
Number
Date
Time
Name
Popup Menu
Radio Buttons
Checkbox
Serial Number
✓ Value List
Multimedia
Record Info
Calculation
Summary

Field Name: [   ]   **Field Type:**

[Create]   [Modify]   [Delete]

Type a field name and select a field type.

Here's how to create your database fields — after you read about each field type:

1. **Name your Field in the Field Name text box.**

2. **Select the type of field you want from the Field Type pop-up menu.**

   We go over these in a moment.

3. **Click Create to define the field.**

   Depending on the type of field you picked, you may see an Options dialog box at this point. You can choose options for your field now or come back to it later. Click OK in the Options dialog box to create the field.

   The field now appears in the list at the top.

4. **Repeat Steps 1 through 3 to define all the fields in the database.**

5. **Click Done when you finish adding fields.**

As you repeat Step 4, make sure that you don't click Modify rather than Create, or you'll rename one field over and over again instead of adding new fields.

Mastering Basic Field Types

You may wonder, "What are all those different types of fields for?" So we've got the lowdown on each one right here. After we explain each field, we go over the options for the field and how to use them.

Text fields

Text is the general format for most information. You can put almost anything in a text field, including numbers. However, if you enter numbers into a text field, AppleWorks sees them as text, so they sort as text (1, 11, 12, . . . 2, 21, . . .) rather than numerically (1, 2, 3, . . .), and you can't do calculations with those numbers, such as figuring elapsed time. (You can convert this text into numbers to use in a calculation, but that requires a special function to convert them to numbers. Chapter 18 has more information on functions.) By the way, a text field can hold up to 1,008 characters, depending on the text formatting within it.

Number fields

To automatically format a number as currency or automatically include commas, use number format. Also use this field type if you want to use the contents of the field for a calculation in another field. You can't put text in a number field, so if you're using the field for zip codes, the field won't work when you enter a Canadian address. Don't even try a phone number here. The dash is not permitted in a number field.

Date fields

The advantage of a date field is the ability to use it in calculations. Whether you have the user enter a date or you take advantage of the auto-enter ability, this field can help you know when invoices are overdue, when something has expired, and so on. The user can type the date numerically, or enter something like Aug 12 and have AppleWorks convert it to 8/12 automatically. As a convenience, you don't have to enter the year when hand entering a date. AppleWorks assumes the current year and adds it for you. If your date is not for the current year, be sure to enter the year. For example, enter **8/12/93**.

You can set the date field to have the date appear in any of the standard date formats when it prints. We cover that in the section "Laying Out the Database," later in this chapter. Several validation options are also available. See "Setting Options for Fields," later in this chapter.

Time fields

This field type acts just like the date field except that you use it to store and calculate time rather than dates. The field also has validation options, discussed in the upcoming section, "Setting Options for Fields."

Name fields

This is for entering a first and a last name in the same field. No database developer worth anything would let you do that, though. What happens when you want to create a mail merge that says, "Dear Mr. Smith?" You can't. And "Dear Mr. Bob Smith" doesn't cut it. One thing you may want to use this field for is to have it automatically enter the user's name, which is the name AppleWorks sees from your computer setup. If people share the computer that the user's name is stored on, the user name isn't always accurate, but you can still use it to have an idea of who is entering what in your system.

Don't use the name field to place names, except to auto-enter the user's name or some other use where you always want only the full name, never the given name or the surname. For all other names, create these regular text fields: a first name field, a last name field, and, optionally, fields to hold prefixes and suffixes, such as Dr. and III.

Serial number fields

This field enables you to automatically number your database records. This ability is a database creator's *must*. Never create any database without giving each record its own permanent, unique ID (some people call it a *key*) number. A unique ID number enables you to find the order in which you originally entered your data even after you've sorted and re-sorted your data. All you have to do is sort on the serial number field. You can also use this list to quickly determine whether a record has been deleted because that serial number is no longer present. Someday you'll thank us for this advice.

You may also use this field type to assign customer or invoice numbers. If you've been using a paper-based system and are switching to a database, you can even start your numbers where the paper system left off.

You can enter only numbers in a serial number field. Upon creation, AppleWorks automatically enters the number 1 in the first field you create, continuing to increment record numbers by one. (The second field is 2, then 3, and so on.) You can click the Options button and change this numbering system in the Options dialog box. In the Next Value text box, enter the number to give the next record you create. In the Increment text box, enter how much higher the subsequent numbers should be.

Multimedia fields

The coolest! This field can hold most graphic formats, QuickTime movies, and QuickTime VR. That means that it can display a picture — or movie — that can play inside your database! You don't have to do anything special or fancy to create this type of field. Its power is in the types of files it can contain. The field has no options or special settings. Just create the field, size it to your liking in the layout, and enter browse mode later to place your media or image files. We discuss file placement options and considerations in Chapter 19.

You can use this field type to do all kinds of cool things. For example, you can make photo ID employee badges right from your employee database. Or, if you have a company catalog, you can store videos of the items you carry, distribute the database for customers to view, or create a print catalog. In the print catalog, one frame of the video shows so that customers can still see an image of the item.

Record info fields

You can set up record info fields to automatically insert the time and/or date the record was created or modified; or, you could also keep track of the person who modified your database. You *always* want to record the date created and date modified so that you can find out how current your information is. You can also enter a record info field that enables you to find out who made changes to your data so that you can discuss the accuracy of the changes with that person. Used in this way, record info fields are troubleshooting aids. You can also use record info fields in a message-taking or note-taking database because this data type can add time or date stamps to your messages or notes for you.

Setting Options for Fields

As you define your fields in the Define Database Fields dialog box, you can set up options for making them enter information automatically or verify that user input meets your criteria. These are some of the bells and whistles of databases.

Each type of field has its own set of options that enhance its functionality. Create one of each and explore to get the idea. Figure 20-2 shows an Options dialog box (this one is for the text field called "First name").

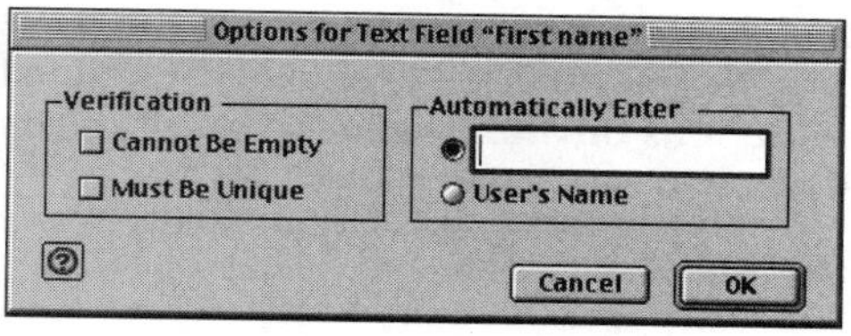

Figure 20-2:
Your first
Options
dialog box.

The options are as follows:

- **Automatically Enter:** When any new record is created, whatever you enter in this option box is auto-entered for you. For example, in a regular text field, you may expect that someone lives in New York, so this option can auto-enter **NY** in a state field. If he doesn't live in New York, just change it. If he does, you save a lot of typing. In a date field, this option can enter the date for you. In a serial number field, it can enter the next serial number for you. And so on. Alternatively, you can click the radio button by User's Name and AppleWorks will fill in the name stored as the user — that's the Owner name for OS releases before MacOS 9, and even for MacOS 9 if you haven't enabled Multiple Users. If Multiple Users is in effect, it is the login name of that user.

  Automatic data entry of some sort or the other is available for the following field types: text, number, date, time, name, serial number, and record info.

- **Cannot Be Empty:** This option forces the user to enter something in the field (or the user can't do anything else). Put a check mark by this one to put it into action. If it makes you crazy, come back later and turn it off. This option is available for the following field types: text, number, date, time, name, and serial number.

- **Current Date:** This option automatically enters the date and is only available for the date field type.

- **Current Time:** Current Time automatically enters the time. This option is available only for time fields.

- **Must Be Unique:** This makes sure you don't have two records with the same exact information (or AppleWorks won't let you go on). Put a check mark by this option to turn it on. This option is available for the following field types: text, number, date, time, name, and serial number. You don't really want two or more records for the same customer, do you?

- **Range:** Use this option to specify that a number be within a range that you specify. This is good for inventory control, invoices, or even ages. This option is available for number, date, and time fields.

Auto-enter data and data validation only work in a field if the option is on when the field is created or if the information is entered at a time that the option is on. Turning these options on after the fact doesn't retroactively look at, change, or enter data.

Mastering Special Field Types

The following fields are created in the same dialog box as the others, but each has a specific look to it and all are for entering predefined data. You enter this data as you create your database, so the user is limited to the choices you provide. Database people call predefined data *value lists*. You predefine values for your users to choose from via the Options dialog box.

Pop-up menu and radio button fields

Pop-up menus and radio buttons have the same effect: They force your users to select one choice from your value list. The main difference between pop-up menus and radio buttons is the amount of room each takes up on-screen. Radio buttons enable the user to see all choices at a glance, while pop-up menus show only one until it's clicked to reveal the rest of the values. These fields are life-savers. Just imagine a database where you or your staff enter plain text. One day someone writes LA in the City field. The next person writes L.A., while someone else writes Los Angeles. If you search for "LA," you miss those other entries. A value list limits the deviations by standardizing entries.

To set up a pop-up menu or radio button field, follow these steps:

1. **Select the field in the Define Fields dialog box and click Options to bring up a dialog box like the one in Figure 20-3.**

   This step is important: AppleWorks starts you off with one or two placeholders (depending on your field type). Change the pre-entered values, or you'll look like a goofy monkey when users see Item 1 in their list of choices.

2. **Click Item 1 in the Items for Control box to select it, and then type your first value.**

   The first value shows up in the Item Label field.

3. **Click Modify.**

   This action changes Item 1 to your value. Do the same for Item 2 if one was supplied.

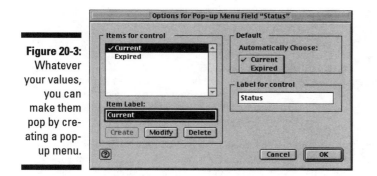

Figure 20-3: Whatever your values, you can make them pop by creating a pop-up menu.

4. **Continue entering as many values as you like by simply entering the value in the Items for Control box and clicking Create after entering each one.**

   When they're all created, click the pop-up menu in the Default section of the dialog box and select the one you want to have appear automatically. You may want to make a value that says, "Pick one, please," so that people know to select one, and you know whether they did. The last section of the dialog box shows you the name of the field you're working in, which you can change if you wish a different label put on your layouts for this field.

Value list fields

This list would be more aptly called a scrolling list, but alas, it's not. It works almost like the other value-list types, having users select from a scrolling list, except that it gives you the opportunity to allow the user to type anything else in the field as well — with control. By checking Alert For Unlisted Values, a warning appears: The value entered is not in the accepted list, asking whether to Continue, Accept (the value and move on), or accept it and Add to List. Continue enables the user to try another entry. If the old value is left, the box keeps reappearing. Additionally, you can demand that the value not be left empty and/or be unique. The warnings appear when the user exits the record, not the field.

Checkbox fields

This option creates a field in which the user either checks or unchecks the value. It is limited to one value, not a list. You determine whether the value is initially checked or not. The word the user sees by the checkbox is whatever you enter in the Label for Checkbox area of the Options dialog box, not the name of the field. Checkbox fields are used for yes/no, true/false, on/off, and other binary choice (one of two) fields. Some examples are: Married, U.S. Citizen, and so on.

Fields that (kind of) think for you

You can set up two kinds of fields to perform some function or manipulation to your database information and display the result. These are calculation fields and summary fields.

✔ **Calculation fields:** The content of a calculation field is the result of a formula you create for the field — such as searches for matching records and spreadsheets. When you create a calculation field, the Formula dialog box appears. If you haven't thought of a formula yet, just put two quotation marks there to keep the field defined. You can write yourself a message between the quotation marks if you like. Not all calculations are numeric. The figure below shows a *concatenation* of text — it joins together the contents of two text fields. This power is very handy. The concatenation shown below also happens to be one of the handiest and most-often-used database calculations around.

✔ **Summary fields:** A summary field is a special calculation field that accesses data from several records at once. Use a summary field to compute totals and averages for all the records in the set you are working in. Summary fields are handy to include on printed reports. Summary fields are odd birds — their results show only on-screen in Page View or when you print. For more information on narrowing your search, see Chapter 19.

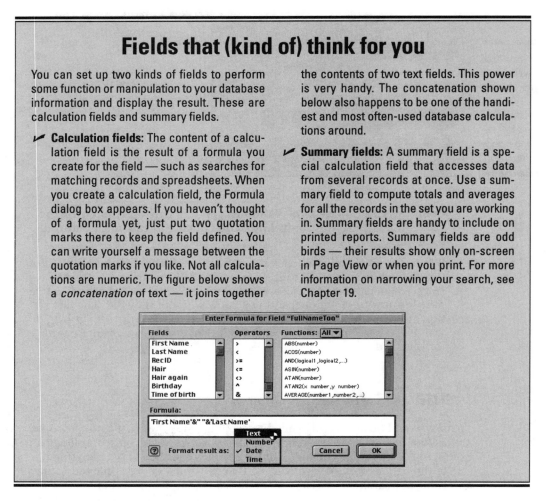

Don't believe the Help file when it tells you that the field can contain multiple checkboxes, enabling you to select multiple items in a set of field values. To accomplish this, you need to create multiple checkbox fields and group them on your layout.

Laying Out the Database

After you define your fields, they show up on a generic record, stacked one on top of another. This arrangement may suit your purposes just fine, or you may want to rearrange things according to your own taste.

If you want to change the way a record looks, you need to use layout mode. You can turn on layout mode by clicking the button shown in the left margin (which you'll have to add to your button bar; see Appendix A if you don't know how to add a button) or by choosing Layout➪Layout. You may also use the keyboard shortcut: Shift-⌘-L.

Layout mode works just like the draw environment and gives you access to all the draw and frame tools by replacing the status area at the left of the database window with the standard Tools panel. Everything in layout mode is treated as a draw object, including the fields and their labels, as shown in Figure 20-4. Anything you do to one record appears on all records.

In layout mode, the name of the field is displayed in the box representing the field. The field label appears in a separate text frame. The names in the field disappear when you switch back to browse mode.

 Labels are not attached to any particular field and do not affect the field's contents. As you move fields around, make sure that you move the label as well. You can change the label for a field to anything you like — the label is just a text frame. Most people use labels to tell users what data belongs in each field. Notice how we connected three labels together when we placed the city, state, and zip fields next to each other.

If you want to change the way a number, date, or time appears in a field, double-click the field to bring up the Format dialog box. Remember, you can't change the text formatting in all types of fields by double-clicking, but you can always use the commands in the Format menu.

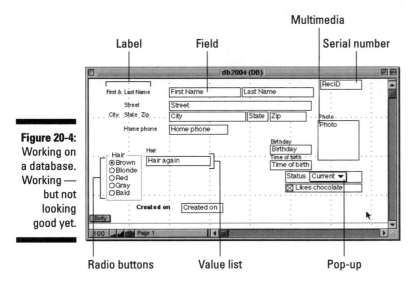

Figure 20-4: Working on a database. Working — but not looking good yet.

You can draw graphics or add clip art to the background to make it more lively. You may want to put colored rectangles behind different groups of fields to make them stand out more. Be as creative as you like — you can do anything in a database layout that you can do in a draw document.

You can make a colored background for the layout by drawing a colored rectangle that covers the whole record area. Choose Arrange⇨Move to Back to put the rectangle behind the fields, labels, and other graphics. You can also use the Arrange buttons. In Chapters 12 and 13, we discuss these buttons and other techniques that you can use to design your layout.

When you color the background, the fields appear as white. If you want them to blend in with the background, select the fields and use the fill tool to make them transparent.

If you want a larger area for your record, drag down the line labeled Body to make more room. A record can be as large as you like, but for entering information, make sure it all fits on the screen. It's better to switch layouts than to scroll. Database designers create one layout for each group of data and place it logically. Here are some ways to get fields into and out of your layout:

- ✔ To remove a field from a layout, select the field and press the Delete key.

- ✔ Choose Layout⇨Define Fields to create new fields, or to change existing fields to other types or alter values or formulas.

- ✔ Choose Layout⇨Insert Field to add an existing field to a layout.

Figure 20-5 shows you what the sample database looks like after a background and some graphic accents have been added.

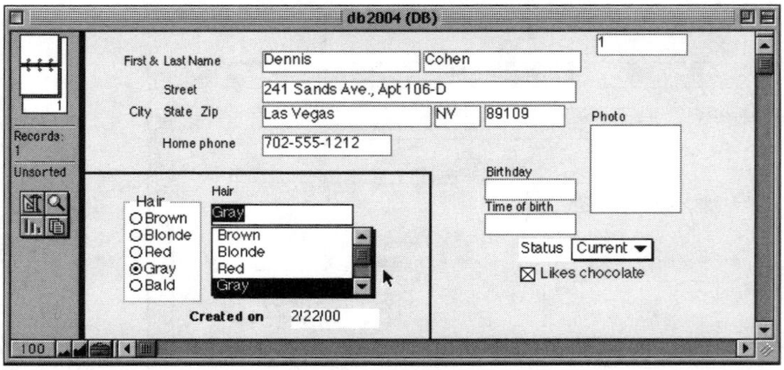

Figure 20-5:
The same database — what a difference some color and lines make.

[Figure 20-5: Screenshot of db2004 (DB) database window showing a record layout]

First & Last Name	Dennis	Cohen
Street	241 Sands Ave., Apt 106-D	
City State Zip	Las Vegas	NV	89109
Home phone	702-555-1212	

Photo

Hair: ○ Brown ○ Blonde ○ Red ⊙ Gray ○ Bald

Hair: Gray / Brown / Blonde / Red / Gray

Birthday

Time of birth

Status: Current ▾

☒ Likes chocolate

Created on 2/22/00

Adding Summary Reports for Printing

Databases can have more than one layout. All the layouts in a database share the same information, and you can enter information into the database in any layout. Layouts are just different ways of viewing the same information. For example, your address database can have one layout to make it easy to enter data on the screen, another layout that you use to print a phone list, and yet another layout for printing address labels. The data entry layout would include all the fields in the database, arranged to make entering data easy. The layout used to print the phone list just has the name and phone number fields on a short body; it should be easy to read when printed. The address label layout needs to fit on standard laser labels and needs to include only fields with address information.

Most databases have at least one layout used only for printing a report of the records. A handy thing to include in a layout for printing reports is a section that sums up the information in the records. Summary parts enable you to include things like totals or averages either for all the records in a database or for certain subsets of records.

Summary parts don't show up in browse mode unless you have page view turned on. They're designed to be printed out with the report of the database, not to be viewed on-screen. You can use page view to preview what your report will look like when printed.

Adding a grand summary part

Actually, there are two kinds of grand summary parts: the *Leading* grand summary part, which appears once at the very beginning of a report, and the *Trailing* grand summary part, which appears once at the end of the report.

You generally use grand summary parts to create totals, averages, or summaries of information for the entire database. An example is a Trailing grand summary part that contains a summary field totaling the sales figures from every record in a database. Using that summary field, you can print a monthly sales report that has the total sales for the month printed at the end of the report — the Trailing grand summary. Or, if you want the good news right up front, you can use a Leading grand summary part.

To add a grand summary part:

1. **Click the (optional) button to switch to layout mode, choose Layout⇨Layout, or press Shift-⌘-L.**

2. **Choose Layout⇨Insert Part.**

   This command brings up the Insert Part dialog box shown in Figure 20-6.

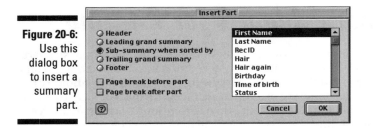

Figure 20-6:
Use this
dialog box
to insert a
summary
part.

3. **Choose Leading grand summary or Trailing grand summary.**

4. **Click OK to insert the part.**

In addition to adding a summary part, you have to add a summary field to your database that includes a formula to get a total or an average. Then use the Insert Field command to put the summary field onto your layout. Although you can place the summary field anywhere in the layout, putting it in the summary part makes the most sense.

To get a total or an average for a certain field across all records in a database, create a summary field using the SUM or AVERAGE function that uses a field name for its input, like this: SUM(<field name>). Typical formulas look like this: SUM('Amount') or AVERAGE('Count'). Of course, you can create formulas to show anything you like in a summary field.

Adding a sub-summary part

A sub-summary part enables you to get subtotals or other information for a subgroup of sorted records. The sub-summary part works like the grand summary part, except that it appears before or after every subgroup of records instead of at the beginning or end of the whole database. Also, the sub-summary part shows up only when your database has been sorted.

Adding a sub-summary part is a bit different from adding a grand summary part. We step you through it:

1. **Click the button to switch to layout mode, choose Layout⇨Layout, or press Shift-⌘-L.**

2. **Choose Layout⇨Insert Part.**

   This command brings up the Insert Part dialog box (refer to Figure 20-6).

3. **Choose Sub-summary When Sorted By.**

   Pick a field from the scrolling list on the right. The sub-summary appears in the report only when the database has been sorted by the field you pick here.

4. **Click OK.**

5. **A dialog box appears, asking you whether you want the sub-summary above or below the subgroup of reports. Select one to place the part into your layout.**

To get something to print out in the sub-summary part, you need to insert a summary field and create a formula for that field. Skip back to the end of the previous section, "Adding a grand summary part," for a tip on a couple of commonly used formulas.

A sub-summary appears only if the database is sorted by the field you specified when you inserted the sub-summary part.

Understanding header and footer parts

A difference exists between header and footer parts in a database layout and regular headers and footers. A database can have both layout and regular headers and footers, and each does something different. Here are four fundamental differences between layout header and footer parts and regular headers and footers:

- ✔ Layout header and footer parts can contain summary fields with formulas for summarizing field information. Regular headers and footers can't.

- ✔ Layout header and footer parts appear only on pages printed using the layout that contains them. Regular headers and footers appear on every page printed with any layout in the database.

- ✔ Layout header and footer parts use the draw environment. Regular headers and footers use the text environment.

- ✔ You can only add layout header and footer parts in layout mode. You can only add regular headers and footers in browse mode.

Also, a regular header appears above a layout header part, and a regular footer appears below a layout footer part.

Here's a special treat! Figure 20-7 shows you a sample layout that contains all the parts covered in this chapter.

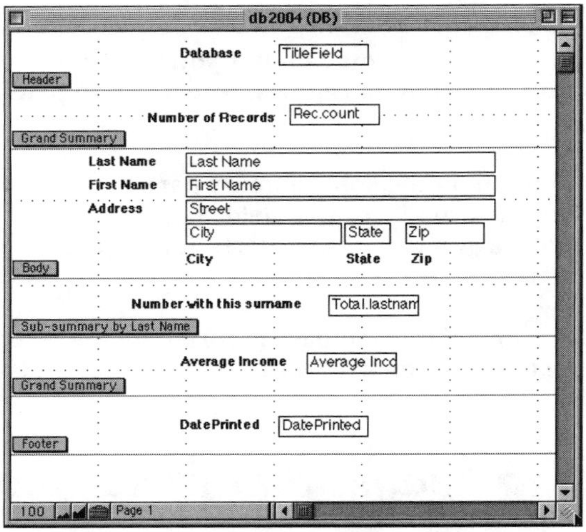

Figure 20-7:
Covering all
the bases:
This layout
has every
possible
part.

Chapter 21

Printing a Database

In This Chapter

▶ Adding layouts to your database just for printing

▶ Printing labels

▶ Using standard labels

▶ Working with custom label layouts

▶ Closing up space when you print a layout

▶ Using AppleWorks reports

*W*hat do you do with the data in a database? Well, you can look at it on-screen, or you can print it. This chapter deals with the second option. Usually, you want things to print out a little differently than they appear on the computer screen. Sometimes, a lot differently. Take labels, for example: You've got to take the address information that fills up practically your whole screen and cram it onto a 1-inch label. That job calls for a new layout.

Adding Layouts for Printing

The first thing to do if you want to use a different layout for printing is add a new layout to the database. After you add a new layout, you can set up the way you want the report to print. To add a new layout for printing, just follow these steps:

1. **Access the Layout pop-up menu from the Tools panel, as shown in Figure 21-1, and choose New Layout, or choose Layout⊏>New Layout.**

   The New Layout dialog box appears, as shown in Figure 21-2.

   You can get to the New Layout dialog box by Control-clicking the layout (you must be in browse or list mode for the contextual menu to be available) and selecting New Layout from the contextual menu.

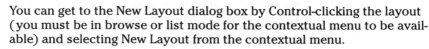

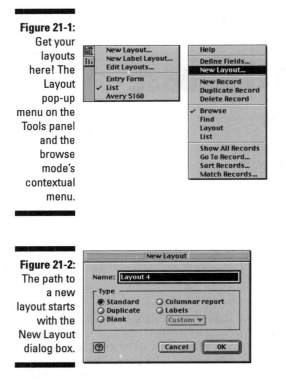

Figure 21-1:
Get your layouts here! The Layout pop-up menu on the Tools panel and the browse mode's contextual menu.

Figure 21-2:
The path to a new layout starts with the New Layout dialog box.

2. **Enter a name for your layout in the Name field within the New Layout dialog box.**

3. **Select a layout type from the available layout options.**

   You can choose from several layout options:

   - *Standard:* This layout option is the standard layout; it stacks the fields one on top of another and places all fields on the layout.

   - *Duplicate:* This layout option copies all the formatting of the current layout into the new layout.

   - *Blank:* This layout option is — you guessed it — empty, zilch, nada, the big nothing.

   - *Columnar Report:* This layout option tries to arrange all the fields you specify onto a single horizontal line. The columnar report includes a header containing the field labels so that column titles print across the top of each page. Each record is represented by a single horizontal row of data, which is good for printing large databases.

   - *Labels:* This layout option has a pop-up list of many label options. Most of this chapter explains how to work with this type of layout.

4. Click OK to add the new layout to your database.

If you choose Columnar Report or Labels, when you click OK, the Set Field Order dialog box appears. Choose which fields you want to use in the layout and in what order you want them to appear. Figure 21-3 shows the Set Field Order dialog box.

Figure 21-3:
Get your
fields in
order with
the Set Field
Order dialog
box.

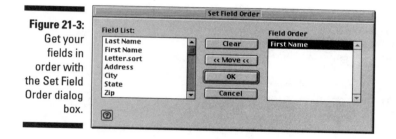

To set up the fields for the new layout, click a field in the Field List box, and then click Move — or just double-click the field in the first place. This action adds the field to the Field Order list on the right. Remove items from the Field Order list by selecting them and clicking Move to put the fields back into the Field List box. (The Move button is smart. It changes direction.) You can also hold down Shift and then click to select several consecutive items in either list and move them all at once, or you can hold down the ⌘ key and select several not necessarily contiguous items in either list and then move those. When the Field Order list looks the way you want, click OK to add the layout to your database document.

Most new layouts need some tinkering. Check out Chapter 20 for more information.

Printing Labels

AppleWorks comes with prepared layouts for more than 100 popular sizes and shapes of Avery labels — okay, it's only one more at 101. You can also make your own custom sizes. Look for the 8½ x 11-inch sheets of self-sticking labels that say they are laser printer or inkjet compatible.

The easiest way to add a new label layout is to use the Create Labels Assistant, which steps you through the process of setting up a label layout. You can find the Create Labels Assistant as New Label Layout in the Layout pop-up menu and as Layout⇨Create New Label Layout. (You have to be in a database for this Assistant to be available and in browse or list mode for the

Layout pop-up menu to be there.) The Assistant is so easy to use that you could skip the rest of this chapter — but don't! Figure 21-4 shows you some of the screens the Assistant uses to walk you through the label-creation process.

When you create labels with the Assistant, calculation fields are added to your database for each line of the label. The name is very descriptive — for example, `Line 3:City+State+Zip`.

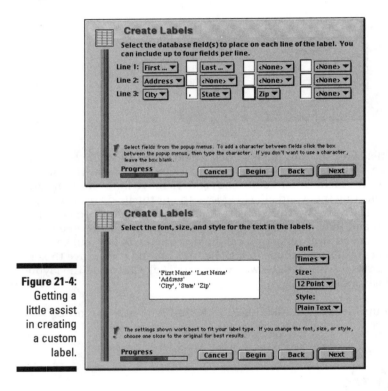

Figure 21-4: Getting a little assist in creating a custom label.

Using standard Avery label layouts

The quickest and easiest way to set up a label layout is to use one of the pre-pared layouts for Avery labels. Product codes on these labels correspond to the label choices in AppleWorks. Follow these steps to create your new layout specifying one of these label standards:

1. **Bring up the New Layout dialog box using the pop-up menu in the Tools panel, or choose Layout⇨New Layout or, if in browse or list mode, choose New Layout from the contextual menu.**

2. **Choose Labels as your Type, and then select the product number for your labels from the pop-up list under the Label option.**

3. **Click OK.**

4. **In the Set Field Order dialog box that appears, choose which fields you want on your labels, and then click OK.**

You may have to move and resize the fields to fit them on the label. See "Closing up space when you print," later in this chapter, for information on how to make text slide over and eliminate empty space between fields.

If the information at the edges of your labels gets cut off, use the Document dialog box to set the margins for the layout as close to the label edges as your printer allows. Choosing Format⇨Document opens the Document dialog box. If things still get cut off, adjust the layout to leave more room around the edges.

Customizing label layouts

If you can't find the product number that matches your labels, or if your labels don't have a matching number, create a custom label layout by following these steps:

1. **Open the New Layout dialog box (refer to Figure 21-2).**

   Use the pop-up menu in the Tools panel, the contextual menu, or choose Layout⇨New Layout.

2. **Name your new layout.**

3. **Choose Labels as the Type, choose Custom from the pop-up list, and then click OK.**

   This step brings up the Label Layout dialog box shown in Figure 21-5.

4. **Enter three pieces of information about your labels: the number of labels across the page, the label width, and the label height; then click OK.**

5. **In the Set Field Order dialog box that appears, choose which fields to include, and then click OK.**

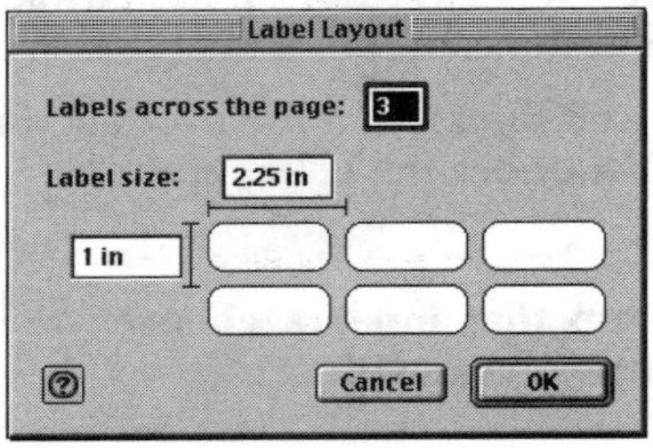

Figure 21-5:
Use any size
labels you
want by
making a
custom
layout with
the Label
Layout
dialog box.

Label Layout

Labels across the page: `3`

Label size: `2.25 in`

`1 in`

Cancel   OK

When you measure the label width and height, measure from the edge of the label to the beginning of the next label, including any blank space in between. You can make up for the extra space between the labels by leaving room around the edges of the fields in your layout.

If you want to use your custom label layout again in other databases, save a blank copy of the database document containing the layout as a template. See Chapter 2 for more information on working with templates. After you create a layout, it appears in the Layout menu and in the Layout pop-up menu on the Tools panel. The Edit Layouts command also appears in both places. You can use Edit Layouts to change the layout name at any time.

Closing up space when you print

You can set up a layout to slide text up or over to close up blank space in a field when you print. How you actually get this feature to work can be a bit confusing, so we can clear that up right here.

1. **Choose Layout⇨Edit Layouts.**

   The Edit Layouts dialog box (shown behind the Layout Info dialog box in Figure 21-6) appears.

2. **Select the layout to edit and click Modify.**

   The Layout Info dialog box, shown in the foreground of Figure 21-6, appears.

3. **Check the box next to one or both of the slide options.**

   Here's the tricky part. The fields must meet the following conditions for sliding to work:

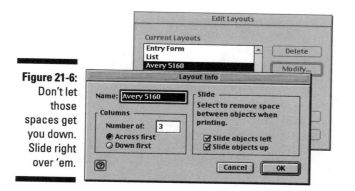

- Fields only slide left toward other fields the same size or larger. A field can't slide toward one even slightly shorter than itself. A field can also slide up — but not toward another field that's even slightly narrower than itself.

- The fields need to be precisely aligned at their top edges to slide left and at their left edges to slide up.

- The fields can't touch, or they won't slide.

These idiosyncrasies can work to your advantage to prevent some fields from sliding. For example, if you don't want a field to slide left, make it slightly larger than the field to its left.

Using Reports

The Report feature enables you to select a named sort, a named search, and a specific layout to use together to create a custom set of information from your database. See Chapter 19 for more information on named sorts and searches.

To create a new report, choose New Report from the Report pop-up menu on the Tools panel. The New Report dialog box opens.

Give your report a name, and then choose the layout, sort, and search options for your report. Check the box next to Print the Report for your report to automatically print when selected. Then click OK. Your report now awaits you at the bottom of the Reports pop-up menu.

Chapter 22

Using Mail Merge: It's One Cool Trick

· ·

· ·

Have you noticed that since computers became popular, everyone is sending you personalized sweepstakes letters? That's mail merge at work. But a sweepstakes letter is a really tacky example of what you can do with mail merge. Mail merge is actually a powerful tool for creating *good-looking* personalized business letters, invoices, and more.

What Is a Mail Merge and What Can It Do for Me?

If the phrase *mail merge* only conjures up images of dozens of postal trucks weaving together on a crowded freeway, you probably need an explanation of what mail merge is all about. A mail merge is what happens when you take a form letter or a similar document and insert information from a database to print large numbers of "personalized" documents.

You may be wondering whether this can really help you.

Have you ever had to send out newsletters by printing separate labels and sticking one on every single newsletter? Or, have you had some other mailing for which you had to print the labels, sort through piles of letters, and match the labels with the correct letters — sticking a label on every single letter? With mail merge, you can print the address right on the newsletter or letter!

Have you ever created a price list from an inventory database, looking at the inventory information and retyping it into your price sheet? Or copying and pasting it in? By merging, you can avoid re-entry of information.

And, of course, don't forget the good old holiday cards or letters. In this busy world of information overload, you may just want to save hours every year by merging the same *special* holiday greeting to every member of your family. Of course, you want to personalize it with a few custom fields inserted.

So . . . do you think it sounds good? When you see how this works, you'll probably think of a few things you can use it for. Or maybe not. Either way, this chapter tells you how to set up and print a mail merge.

Creating a Merge Document

You can merge data into any word-processing document, a text frame in a drawing document (like the one shown in Figure 22-1), or a spreadsheet document or frame.

Create your document as you normally would, setting it up exactly as you want it to look. Enter anything that the merged data won't enter for you — anything you want to appear in every document. You don't have to leave gaps for the text to merge into. Later, when you tell the Mail Merge floating window that you want to insert a field, AppleWorks inserts a placeholder that grows or shrinks to fit the information being added. You don't have to enter any special codes, either. AppleWorks does that for you. (See "Merging the Data," later in this chapter, to find out how to use the Mail Merge window to insert placeholders.)

Selecting Records to Print

AppleWorks uses whatever records are visible in the database at the time you give the Print Merge command. It also uses them in the order they happen to be sorted.

In the database, use the Find or Match Records command to select a group of records that you want to use for the merge. Setting up a named search and/or sort is a good idea. If you use the Match Records command, make sure that you also hide unselected records (choose Organize➪Hide Unselected) so that only the selected records are visible. To use every record in the database, click the Find All button or choose Organize➪Show All Records. See Chapter 19 for more about the Find and Match Records commands.

Finally, sort the records you selected into the order in which you want them to print.

Preparing the Merge

After you have the merge document ready, choose the database from which you want AppleWorks to pull information.

To select the database, make the merge document the active window. Then choose File⇨Mail Merge. This brings up a very basic Open dialog.

Navigate through your hard drive until you see the database. Select it and click OK. If you don't see your database, perhaps it hasn't been saved yet. Click Cancel. Locate and open the proper database, make sure that it's saved, and try selecting the database again.

After you select a database, the Mail Merge window shown in Figure 22-1 appears. Use this tool to Insert placeholders into your document, choose a different database for the merge, or print the merged documents.

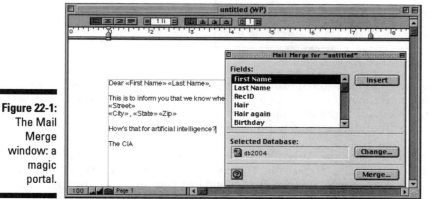

Figure 22-1:
The Mail Merge window: a magic portal.

You can move between your letter and the window. Position the cursor in the document where you want a placeholder inserted, and then move back to the palette. Scroll through the list of field names on the left, click to select the field you want to insert, and then click Insert. AppleWorks inserts the placeholder at the point where your cursor is placed in the document. The placeholder appears as the field name you chose surrounded by double angle brackets (refer to Figure 22-1). Go back to the document, type any spaces or punctuation you may need, and then — leaving the cursor where you want the next field's data to appear — return to the window to select the next field. You can also simply double-click the field name instead of clicking Insert.

If you don't like moving the mouse back and forth all that much, you can leave it specifically for the Mail Merge window and instead use the arrow keys to move around in your merge document or frame.

Merging the Data

Looking at placeholders can be less than ideal. When you click the Merge button, you are presented with the dialog box shown in Figure 22-2. You have three choices in how you want to merge the data.

Figure 22-2:
Destination,
please —
paper,
screen, or
disk.

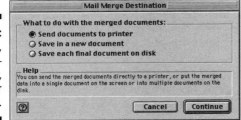

Choosing the first radio button prepares printed copies of the merge document for all the records in your found set. This action brings up your standard Print dialog box. Refer to Chapter 2 for general document-printing information. The second and third radio buttons are more interesting.

Before you print a mail merge with tons of records, test it by printing a small group of hand-selected records. That way, you can make sure that all insertions work as they should and that all the text is formatted correctly. Print one page as a test before you commit to a huge print job, such as your entire holiday mailing.

Selecting the middle button creates a new, untitled document consisting of the merge document with the placeholders replaced by live data *for every record in the found set.* These merged documents are separated by section breaks (refer to Chapter 5 for more about sections). Obviously, if you have a large merge document (say, a newsletter or something with lots of graphic elements) and/or a large found set, this could turn into a very large document, so make sure that you have enough memory allocated to AppleWorks if you're going to do this. This option is only available if the merge document is a word-processing document.

Finally, the last button creates an AppleWorks document on disk for each record in the found set and places them in a new folder. A Save dialog box lets you set the location and name for both this new folder and its contents. The document names are the same as that of the folder with sequential numbers appended. For example, if the folder were named Welcome Letter, the documents would be Welcome Letter 1, Welcome Letter 2, and so forth.

And now, some memorable merge facts:

- ✔ You can insert any type of field in your database, except for summary fields. See Chapter 20 for details about field types.

- ✔ Fields don't have to be visible on the layout to be inserted.

- ✔ You can use the same field multiple times in your document.

- ✔ You can insert up to 246 fields.

- ✔ Each field can have up to 1,000 characters (or slightly fewer characters if the field contains formatting).

Any font or formatting you apply to the placeholder affects the way the text from the database prints out. Apply the formatting you want to the whole placeholder, including the brackets at both ends.

Save the changes to your merge document after you insert all the placeholders. The document containing the mail merge will remember the database and can be used over and over.

Part VI

Mastering AppleWorks Internet and Automation Features

The 5th Wave   By Rich Tennant

"The new technology has really helped me get organized. I keep my project reports under the PC, budgets under my laptop, and memos under my pager."

In this part . . .

*W*hether you're a Net junkie or a Net novice, working with the Internet couldn't be easier than with AppleWorks. AppleWorks integrates Web capabilities right into your AppleWorks documents, launching your Web browser for you with the simple click of an AppleWorks button.

Want to establish your presence on the Web? AppleWorks enables you to save your AppleWorks word-processing documents as HTML files — ready for Web publication.

Want to automate those repetitive processes or create shortcuts to make some operations match the way *you* want to work? AppleScript and AppleWorks macros give you just those (super) powers.

Chapter 23

Connecting to the World the AppleWorks Way

*T*hat old saying about needing to be well connected to get ahead in this world has taken on new meaning since the Internet went public. And they thought no man was an island before modems and the Net! These days, no computer's an island, either. Whether you use AppleWorks as an office-based business tool, as a lone computer-based business tool, or for personal use, AppleWorks makes Internet connectivity a lot easier. In this chapter, we take you on an exploration of all the AppleWorks connectivity options.

First Things First — Getting Internet Access

This chapter is all about how AppleWorks takes you to the Web quickly and efficiently — with the click of a single button. However, before you go any-where on the Web or do anything like send e-mail or put up a Web page, you need a physical connection to the Internet.

If your computer is on an office network and your company provides Internet access, you can connect through the network. You don't need an ISP; skip the rest of this section. Ask your network manager to help set up your computer for Internet access.

If you have a home account, you probably don't have a dedicated connection like people using a network at the office; you usually have a *dial-up connection* (although cable modem, *Digital Subscriber Line* (DSL), and *Integrated Services Digital Network* (ISDN) connections are becoming more common), which is a modem connection over your phone line. Your Web browser can't display the Web site you want to see until you establish a modem connection to your ISP (Internet service provider). We bring this up because your interaction from AppleWorks to the Web requires you to have that Internet connection established and for certain settings to be in place. If you use a dial-up account, you need to remember that AppleWorks automatically connects your modem to your ISP's modem whenever you click a Web-related button or link. Don't forget to disconnect when you're done!

Changing Your Default Browser

 AppleWorks is preconfigured to call upon the browser set as your system-wide default browser; here's how to switch to another browser you've installed.

On a Mac running OS 8.5 or later, follow these steps:

1. **Add the Configure Internet button to your button bar.**

2. **Click the Configure Internet button.**

    In OS 8.5 and later, this launches the Internet Control Panel. You could have also replaced the first two steps with choosing ⌥⇨Control Panels⇨ Internet, but we wanted you to see that AppleWorks also gives you access.

3. **If the Edit Set area is collapsed, click the blue arrow next to the words "Edit Set" and then click the Web tab.**

4. **In the Default Web Browser pop-up menu, select the desired browser. All installed browsers should appear in this list.**

    If the browser you want is not there, choose Select and then navigate to, and choose, your browser.

5. **Close the window and save your changes.**

On a Mac running OS 8.1, follow these steps:

1. **Add the Configure Internet button to your button bar.**

2. **Click the Configure Internet button.**

    This action launches Internet Config, a separate little public domain program that enables your Internet settings and preferences to be accessible by almost every Internet application. Internet Config should open to the Internet Preferences dialog box, shown in the figure at the end of this sidebar, which is just a bunch of buttons.

3. **Click Helpers to open the Helpers dialog box.**

   Helpers are pointers to the applications you want your Internet applications to call upon. There's a Helper for each Internet access function.

4. **Scroll to http, select this line, and then click Change to open the Add Helper dialog box.**

   The http Helper is the application that's called when you request an address that begins with http — your Web browser.

5. **Click the Choose Helper button. The Open dialog box appears.**

6. **Navigate to the desired browser and then click Open.**

7. **In the Add Helper dialog box, click OK to close it and then close the Helper's window using the lose box in the top-left corner.**

8. **Making sure Internet Preferences is the active window, choose File⇨Save and then File⇨Quit.**

Several applications may install Internet Config. Each copy references the same preferences, which are called Internet Preferences and live in your Preferences folder within your System folder. It's okay to trash extra copies, but for the sake of AppleWorks, keep one copy or an alias to it in the AppleWorks folder. Figure 23-1 shows your Internet References.

Figure 23-1:
Coffee, tea,
or e-mail?

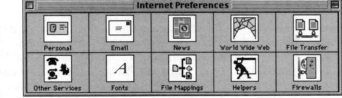

Using the AppleWorks One-Click Web Feature

Throughout this book, we show you how to use buttons to perform common AppleWorks tasks. Now it's time for us to introduce the Internet buttons and links — your one-click paths to Cyberspace.

You need to have a Web browser and a connection to your ISP to use the AppleWorks Web connection abilities. If you don't have a browser to launch, clicking the button doesn't do anything. If you aren't connected to the Internet, clicking all the Web connection objects in the world doesn't do anything more than launch your browser to an empty page or an error message.

You can reach your Web destination several different ways, and we explain those methods in this section.

Clicking the Launch Browser button

 One way to get to the Web is by clicking the optional Open Browser button, which launches your browser. Of course, you really want to go to the Web. And the Launch Browser button delivers — as long as you're connected to your ISP at the time. If you're not connected to your ISP and don't have your computer set up to connect you automatically, the Open Browser button simply launches your browser to a blank page, which may be a little anticlimactic. To find out how to set up your computer to connect automatically, check out the sidebar "For your Internet connection convenience."

So where in the World Wide Web does clicking the Open Browser button take you? That's a good question. It takes you to whatever page your browser calls home. Each browser has a *default home page* (possibly blank), or starting Web page, which you can change in the browser's preferences. You can hang out at this home page as long as you like. Or you can head to any place you want from within your browser.

Clicking the Open URL button

 If you come across a Web address in a text frame, document, or database, you can highlight that *URL* (Web address) and click the optional Open URL button. Your browser is called into action, taking you directly to the site you selected. The Open URL button is not available in paint or draw environments (except in text frames) because you can't select text in them, but the button is available in a database because you can insert URLs into the fields. The Open URL button is also available from any text frame or document, including a text frame within a drawing document.

Clicking a link

The advent of the Internet popularized a new way of non-linear reading. Hyperlinks — *links* for short — are underlined bits of text that instantly transport readers to another location, whether it's on the same page, on another page, or in another document entirely. Links are so handy that instead of remaining only in the realm of the Internet, they're now also used in regular documents. Links in AppleWorks documents can even connect readers to documents on the Web.

For your Internet connection convenience

You can set your dial-up connection to connect automatically when you call upon your browser. With this setup, clicking any Web button in AppleWorks is guaranteed to take you to your destination.

Your PPP software (Point-to-Point Protocol) found in your Remote Access control panel on OS 8.5 or later, which controls your dial-up, takes you to your destination. Choose ❖⇨Control Panels and then select either PPP (OS 8.1) or

Remote Access. Select the Options button, wherever that is, and then check the option to connect automatically. This option can be great — or it can drive you crazy. With this option checked, every single time you launch any Web-accessing program, your computer starts to connect. That's handy, but sometimes you just don't want to connect automatically. If connecting automatically makes you crazy, go back and turn off the option.

Click a link — a hypertext link, to be exact — and your browser pops up and delivers you directly to the linked page. Surfing the Web couldn't be easier, could it? Links in AppleWorks aren't limited to text. They can also be graphics. To find out how to create your own links, see Chapter 24.

Visiting a favorite site

You can create a button that takes you straight to a favorite site with a simple click (see the next section, "Customizing Your Button Bar for the Web," to find out how to create customized buttons). If you visit any sites on a regular basis, you'll love this capability. You can even give the button its own icon. Is the wisdom you glean from the site destined to become a part of a document? Great! Launch the site while you're in that very document. That way, your document is waiting for you, ready for you to gather facts as you write your report. You can even copy text from a Web page and paste it into your own document — provided that the information is just for your own notes and you aren't violating any copyrights. If you're running an office, small business, or classroom, you can create all types of custom buttons to take your users to the Web. The downside of this is that you end up having to scroll the button bar a lot. Each AppleWorks document can have its own custom buttons and, when you share that document with another user, they can use the document's custom buttons.

When you share custom buttons, any macros that they execute must also be stored in the document, and any documents, applications, or applications that they invoke have to also be available to the people sharing the custom button document.

An alternate approach is to create a document that contains all your favored sites as URL links. If you have Active Links turned on, all you have to do is click one with the Internet Link cursor. Or you can just keep a long list of URLs in an open document so that all you have to do is select one of them and then click the Open URL button.

Customizing Your Button Bar for the Web

If you use AppleWorks in a business or classroom environment, you'll have a field day customizing buttons for the Web. In addition to being more efficient, custom Web buttons also reduce the chances of users ending up at the wrong Web site — or wandering along the way.

For example, suppose you have an assistant at work who needs to go to a specific Web site every day. You can create a button to take your assistant directly to that site.

Follow these steps to create a custom button to take you to a specific Web site:

1. **Select Customize Button Bar from the button bar's contextual menu or select Edit⇨Preferences⇨Button bar.**

2. **Click the New button**

   The New Button dialog box, shown in Figure 23-2, opens.

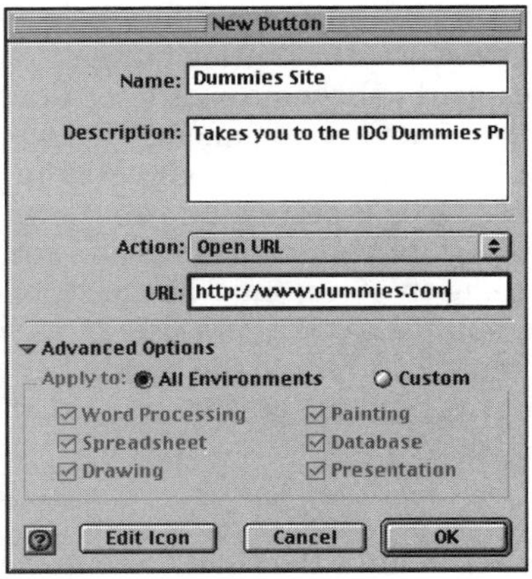

Figure 23-2:
Creating a custom button to get to the *For Dummies* Web page.

New Button

Name: Dummies Site

Description: Takes you to the IDG Dummies Pr

Action: Open URL

URL: http://www.dummies.com

▽ Advanced Options

Apply to: ● All Environments   ○ Custom

☑ Word Processing   ☑ Painting
☑ Spreadsheet   ☑ Database
☑ Drawing   ☑ Presentation

Edit Icon   Cancel   OK

3. **Enter a name for your new button in the Button Name text box.**

   In our example, our button takes us to the Dummies Web site, so we name our button **Dummies Site**. This is the name that shows in the balloon text when you rest your mouse on that button without clicking with ToolTips turned on.

4. **Enter a description for your button in the Button Description text box.**

   A good description helps you remember the button's function later. The description also shows in the button bar's info bar when you place your mouse pointer over that button.

5. **Choose Open URL from the When Button Pressed pop-up menu.**

   Choosing this option tells AppleWorks that you are creating a button that takes you directly to a Web site. (The URL is the address of that Web site.) Notice that you now have a field in which to enter the URL.

6. **In the URL field, enter the full address that you want to go to when this button is pressed.**

   In our example, we enter the full address of the *For Dummies* Web site (`http://www.dummies.com`).

7. **In the Apply To panel, select the environments in which you want this new button to show.**

   If you want your Web site buttons to show at all times, check All Environments as we do in Figure 23-2. (This setting is the default for URL buttons.) You will have to click the Advanced Options disclosure triangle to see this section of the dialog.

8. **Click the Edit Icon button to design your button.**

   The Edit Button Icon dialog box — a mini painting window — opens, as shown in Figure 23-3. You can design your button in the painting window or copy an image from somewhere and paste it in. Without closing this dialog box, we visited the *For Dummies* site and used our computer's Screen Capture command (Shift-⌘-4) to select and capture a part of the Dummies logo that we thought made a nice button to remind us of the button's function. Then we came back to the editor window and used the computer's Paste command to paste it in. Remember to get permission to use other people's art and to respect the copyright.

9. **Click OK to close the Edit Button Icon dialog box.**

   You now have a custom button to take you to the Web site.

See Appendix A for more information about creating other types of custom buttons and adding buttons to your button bar.

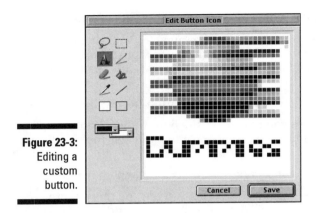

Figure 23-3:
Editing a custom button.

Launching Your E-mail Application

 Regular mail is great for lots of stuff, but e-mail is immediate and lets you send information that can be copied and pasted. With the Launch Email button, you get to your e-mail program any time, from any environment, no matter what you're doing in AppleWorks, with just the click of a button.

Launching your e-mail application

Clicking the optional Launch Email button opens your e-mail program. If you run OS 8.1 or later (and AppleWorks 6 requires 8.1 or later, so we know who you are), your default e-mail program is Outlook Express unless you've already changed it. If you don't have an e-mail program, clicking the Launch Email button has no effect.

If you want to add or change an e-mail program, follow the directions in the "Changing your default browser" sidebar, earlier in this chapter, and then do one of the following:

- ✔ If you're using the OS 8.5 or later Internet Control Panel, click the E-mail tab and then choose your e-mail program from the Default E-mail Application pop-up menu.
- ✔ If you're using Internet Config, select MailTo in the Helper list and make your change.

While you're in the Internet Control Panel or Internet Config, set up your e-mail address, if you haven't already. If you're using Internet Config from the main window, click Email and then enter the information you agreed upon with your ISP. Then close the window. In the main window, click Save and then click Quit.

Sharing Your Documents on the Web

You've seen those two buttons on the Web tab of your Starting Points window. One of them hooks into the Apple Web site and loads the AppleWorks newsletter, and the other brings up another AppleWorks document that points you toward more AppleWorks templates. Wouldn't you like to have similar buttons available as Starting Points from your Web site? Well, here's how you accomplish this feat:

1. **Create the document you want to share this way, using all the tools discussed in the rest of this book and save it with a name ending in .cwk (that's a period followed by the letters *cwk*).**

2. **Upload it to your Web site. If you're using MacOS 9, the Sites folder of your iDisk (you have signed up for iTools, haven't you?) is a good place.**

   AppleWorks provides an AppleScript to mount your iDisk for you.

3. **Create a Web location document — that's just a clipping file containing a URL. Give it a descriptive name.**

   To do this, type the document's URL in a text document, select the URL, and drag it to the Finder desktop.

4. **Stick this Web location document in your Starting Points folder.**

You can also share this Web location document with your friends and co-workers so that they have access to your templates and newsletters through the Web tab of their Starting Points windows.

You will sometimes get a blank thumbnail on the Starting Points Web tab or when clicking Search in Clippings doesn't seem to do anything. When this happens, make sure that you have an active connection to the Internet (this might mean that you have to do something with your Web browser to "validate" your TCP/IP network setting), control-click in the offending window, and select the item that starts with Reload. You might have to do this more than once.

Chapter 24

Publishing for the World Wide Web

In This Chapter

▶ Going behind the scenes of a Web page

▶ Creating your Web page with AppleWorks

*Y*ou've browsed the Web, gotten to know what's out there, seen what you like — and more important, what you don't like. Now it's time to establish your own presence on the Web. Ready? Here you go. . . .

Exposing the Secret Life of a Web Page

Things aren't always as they appear. That's the secret of magic — and of any Web page's magic. Actually, it's the secret of any word-processing document, too. Just as invisible characters hide in your word-processing document (see Chapter 5), still more hidden codes hide in a Web page. Imagine if you had to learn all those codes before you could even type a letter to your mom.

Luckily, when it comes to both word-processing documents and Web pages, AppleWorks does the work for you, embedding the codes each time you select a font attribute, set the alignment with the ruler, or do anything else to your pages. You can study these codes if you want, but because AppleWorks takes care of them for you, you aren't bothered with them here — at all. You're busy. You want a Web site, not a programming education.

"Those codes" are called *HTML tags,* and the language that brings those codes to life is called *HyperText Markup Language,* or HTML. The text you view is actually hanging out between a bunch more text that you don't see. This hidden text is the HTML tags, which hide between these pointy brackets: < >. These tags are all over the place, telling your browser the size at which it should show text on your page, where to align, when to start a new paragraph, and so on. If you wish to see (or change) what AppleWorks uses when translating your word-processing document to HTML, check out Edit⇨Preferences⇨HTML Import/Export. Unfortunately, you can only change the attributes that AppleWorks has and can't add any new ones (like OpenTable and CloseTable to the Import preferences).

Before you begin to build any Web site, ask your Internet service provider (ISP) what file-naming conventions to observe. Generally, keep your Web site's name short, and don't use spaces or other special characters. You definitely need to add ".htm" or ".html" as the extension so the browsers know that it's an HTML file and can find it. Your ISP can tell you which extension to use.

Creating Web Pages with AppleWorks

AppleWorks is great for creating Web pages because you can publish any existing documents to the Web. Here's the deal: Almost anything you can toss into your word-processing document can be part of your Web page. A few things are simply ignored. Nothing is unsafe or bad. Create your word-processing page, and you have your Web page. That's it. All you do is choose File⇨Save As; select HTML as the document type in the pop-up menu; give the page a precise title, adding ".htm" or ".html" to the end (ask your ISP which extension you should use); and then click Save. You're ready to transfer your page to your Web site. (Your ISP can give you the scoop on how to do this.)

If you think that you might modify or update this page later in AppleWorks rather than learning HTML and modifying the HTML files in a text editor or some other Web page-editing tool, be sure to also save a copy in AppleWorks format. Many of the HTML directives AppleWorks exports do not import, as a quick comparison of the Import and Export lists verifies.

Before you begin any Web page or Web site, get organized by creating a folder to house all of its elements. Create one folder for each Web site. In each site's folder, also create a subfolder called Art in which you can place your artwork. By saving the pieces of art, you can change the art later. Using folders and saving elements makes life much easier when it's time to edit or update your pages.

Adding elements

A Web page can be straight text, or it can be packed with charts, tables, multimedia, and graphics. The page can contain simple text links, or it can feature objects that behave like links (these are called *buttons*). After you create your Web page and input your text, you can jazz it up. After all, who wants a humdrum Web page? The following sections give you pointers on how to bring your Web page to life.

Adding font attributes

The ability to assign a font to a Web document is rather new and is of questionable value. After all, you have no way of knowing what fonts are on your viewers' computers. HTML is constantly evolving to deal with this type of issue, but for now, the AppleWorks solution is to translate any fonts you place in your document into the default font for your word-processing document when it saves your page as HTML. Here's some advice to save you time:

✔ If you're designing your document to be viewed solely within AppleWorks, design to your heart's content (but with taste) when it comes to using fonts. However, if you're designing your document solely to save it as a Web page, don't waste your time worrying about fonts.

✔ For the sake of good design, whether you're designing your document for AppleWorks or for the Web, skip underlines and stick to using bold and italic to emphasize words. Bold and italic look classy and translate well into HTML.

Only a few of the other attributes listed in the Style menu will make it through the translation — see the Advanced HTML Export preferences.

✔ Text alignment translates well — except justification, which becomes flush left (normal).

Using tables

AppleWorks tables make it through the HTML translation well. You definitely want to use them — not only for the typical reasons mentioned in Chapter 7 and in the spreadsheet chapters, but also for reasons you may have never thought of before.

Tables are a main source of placement control on the Web. In Chapter 5, we explain how to use tabs in word processing. On the Web, you get to forget about all that stuff and use tables instead. Suppose that you want a stair-step effect — the first line of text at the left, the next line farther right, the third even farther right.

Normally, tabs would do the job. However, on the Web, each tab just translates into a single space. Thus, to achieve the same result, create a table and place your text in the boxes to match the positioning you want. Then, turn off all the borders so the text looks more natural. AppleWorks spreadsheets can't contain graphics, though, so this layout method won't work with graphic elements unless you use the new Table frame type. See Chapter 7 for more about tables.

If you already created your text table with tabs, just select Table➪Convert to Table to create an instant table.

Adding bulleted or numbered lists

One of the most effective ways to present information is to use a bulleted or numbered list. All list styles translate perfectly and look great on the Web.

To create a list, enter at least some of the list's contents, pressing the Return key after each line. Select the lines of text and then select one of the list styles from the Style pop-up menu below the button bar. You can also use the Show Styles floating window to define your own list style.

After you apply the style, you can continue to add to your list by placing your cursor at the end of the last character in the list and pressing Return to carry the style down to the next line (as in any word-processing document). See Chapter 8 for more on lists.

Inserting images

AppleWorks supports most image formats. In other words, you can place a picture saved as PICT, TIFF, or EPS, and AppleWorks calls its file translators into action to make the picture work in the document.

The Web requires that images be one of three specific formats: GIF, PNG, or JPEG. Although almost nobody uses PNG yet, AppleWorks can create PNG files and put you ahead of the trendsetters. It also creates JPEG files. But for some reason, this version of AppleWorks doesn't create GIF files, even though you can create them in AppleWorks 5. Go figure.

Although no one has answered us directly, it is likely that the dropping of support for creating GIF files is a result of Unisys's licensing fee requirements for using its patented LZW compression technology — an integral part of the GIF format. It doesn't charge for decompression uses.

As you create your page, graphics remain in their original formats or the formats to which AppleWorks translated them. When you save your page as HTML, AppleWorks translates the images into the required PNG or JPEG format. For more on inserting graphics, see Chapters 7 and 13.

Images placed as objects (floating frames) aren't translated to HTML. Place your graphics inline with the text to be included in translation to the Web page.

AppleWorks translates all the images you place on your page (whether inserted, pasted, or created), into separate graphic files when you save your page as HTML. AppleWorks names these graphics sequentially: html1.png, html2.png, and so on. This is where having a separate folder for each Web page comes into play. You definitely want all these files to be kept together with your page, or Web users won't be able to find the images.

Showing QuickTime movies

You can insert a QuickTime Movie just as you insert any other graphic. At first, the movie looks just like a graphic, displaying the first frame of the video, but a small filmstrip icon appears in its lower-left corner. Clicking that icon brings up the movie's control strip. You should recognize the standard-style video controls from VCRs and tape recorders. The controls work the same way, too. Click outside the video area, and the controls disappear.

Adding other page elements

Table 24-1 shows you how common word-processing page elements translate to HTML and end up looking on the Web.

Table 24-1	Effects of HTML Translation
Before Translation	*After Translation (in HTML)*
Inline frames	Remain in the correct place. Tables and Spreadsheet frames become HTML tables.
Text frames as objects (floating)	Totally ignored.
Drawings/paint frames (floating)	Move to the closest side margin.
Soft return or column break	Line break , which begins a new line without adding space before the following line.
Soft hyphen	Totally ignored.
Header or footer	Headers show at the start, footers at the very end — both with a horizontal rule to separate them from the rest of the page. Only the first section's header and footer are recognized. The others are ignored.
Footnotes/end notes	Become numbered end notes.
Page and section breaks	Become horizontal lines.
Auto-enter date/time	The time that the document was saved.
Footnote indicator	Becomes a link to the end note and is turned into a superscript number in parentheses.
Auto-enter page number	Doesn't work — numbers just become generic number signs (#).

Don't use special characters such as <, >, &, ;, and / on your page. These characters are part of HTML code unless you encode them by their HTML names. For example, if you want a "&", then use "&".

Adding a background

Backgrounds can add interest and personality to your Web page. You can select a color for your background or use a graphic.

Using a color for your background

Follow these steps to use a color for your background:

1. **Choose Edit⇨Preferences⇨HTML Import/Export or, if you've customized the button bar, click the Configure HTML button on the button bar to open the Configure HTML dialog box.**

2. **Choose Export Preferences (Basic) from the Topic pop-up menu.**

3. **Select a color from the Color pop-up menu.**

The Color pop-up menu gives you only eight color choices. To use a color other than those on the list, you have to modify the HTML that is produced (which means finding the six hex-digit code for the color you desire, as well). Make a table and fill a cell with the color you want from the Accents window. Save your test document as HTML, and then look at the "bgcolor" generated for that cell in its <TD> directive. That is the number you're going to have to move into the BODY directive of your HTML page.

Using a graphic for your background

Follow these steps to use a graphic for your background:

1. **Choose Edit⇨Preferences⇨HTML Import/Export or click the Configure HTML button, if present.**

2. **Select Export Preferences (Basic) from the pop-up menu.**

3. **Click Set Background Image.**

   This action brings up an Open window and you can navigate to the folder containing the image you wish to use.

Backgrounds don't show up in the document; they appear only in your browser. To get an idea of how your page looks on the Web, click the Open File in Browser button. This action launches your default browser, opening a copy of the current file.

To remove a background, repeat Steps 1 and 2 to return to the Configure HTML dialog box and then click the Remove Background Image button. To remove a color, select None from the pop-up menu.

Creating links

Links can take your readers to another page within your site or to another location on the Web. Links aren't restricted to the Web, though: When inserted into a word-processing document, a link can take readers to another document or simply to another place within the open document. Whether you create a Web link or a document link, you can assign text or an object as the link. Objects that are links are called *buttons*. Whether you link from text or objects, the method is the same. The following sections tell you how to create both Web links and word-processing links.

Using buttons to create links to Internet locations

The easiest way to create Internet links is with buttons. If you don't want to use buttons, go to the section "Using the Links window to create links," later in this chapter.

Follow these steps to create a link that uses a button:

1. **In your AppleWorks document, select the object or text for your link, as shown in Figure 24-1.**

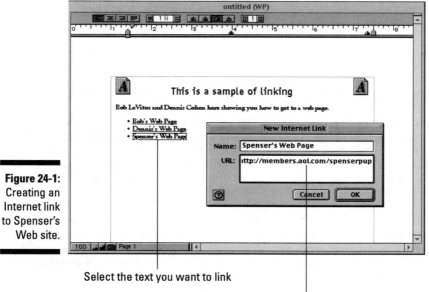

Figure 24-1:
Creating an Internet link to Spenser's Web site.

Select the text you want to link

Enter the Web address here (URL)

2. **Click the URL Link button on the button bar.**

The New Internet Link window opens. If your link is text, your selected text is automatically entered as the link's name in the Name text box. Change the name if you want. If your link is a graphic, enter a name for the link.

3. **Enter the destination Web address.**

Click in the URL field and type your destination. To link to a location on the Web, enter the address, or *URL,* for that location. (URL stands for *Uniform Resource Locator.*) Your selected text is underlined to tell readers that it's a link. Open the Links floating window (Format➪Show Links Window, Shift-⌘-M), shown in Figure 24-2, to show the links you've created for that document. That's it. You have a link.

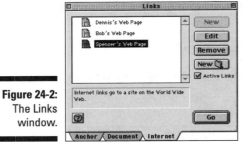

Figure 24-2:
The Links
window.

From a hard drive, AppleWorks always attempts to connect to a link if it's active. For the purposes of AppleWorks, an active link is a Web address that you want treated as a link rather than as editable text. If the link is active, AppleWorks calls up your browser — launching it if it isn't already running — and takes you directly to that location (see Chapter 23 for more information about launching Web browsers). For a link to behave as a link rather than as text, though, the active links feature must be turned on for that link. If this feature is not on, choose Format➪Turn Active Links On, click the Active Links button in the Links window, or click the Links On/Off button to turn it on. You know that a link is active when your cursor turns to a hand and globe when moved over the link.

To edit the words in the link, click the Links On/Off button to turn off Internet linking. Otherwise, clicking those words brings up the Web site — or at least tells your Web browser to try to bring up the site. *Note: Editing the words in the link is different from editing the link itself, which is the destination to which your browser jumps.*

You can actually create URLs that launch other Internet helper applications, such as Telnet, your e-mail application, the application you use for FTP, and so forth, if you prepend the URL type. For example, if you use Outlook Express for your e-mail, `mailto:steve@mac.com` launches Outlook Express and addresses a new mail message to Steve Jobs's account at mac.com.

Using buttons to create links to word-processing documents

 Although this chapter focuses on publishing for the World Wide Web, you don't have to be on the Web to use links. AppleWorks also lets you create links to other documents. Just remember that these links aren't appropriate on the Web because your regular documents are on your hard drive, not at your Web site where other users have access to them.

The following steps tell you how to create links to other word-processing documents:

1. **Select the text or object that you want to link.**

2. **Click the Document Link button on the button bar to open the New Document Link dialog box.**

3. **Click Choose Document to bring up the Open dialog box.**

4. **Select the destination document. If you have anchors (see below) defined for that document, you can select the location within that document to which you wish to jump.**

5. **Name your link for easy identification later and then click OK.**

   Your selected text becomes an underlined link to the document you chose.

Linking to a specific part of your document is a bit different. First, you need to define the destination, which AppleWorks calls *anchoring*. Then you create the link and tell it to link to the anchor. In the following steps, we show you the easiest way to create links — with buttons. (To use the palette instead, see the next section, "Using the Links window to create links.")

1. **Select the object or text your link will jump to.**

2. **Click the Anchor button on the button bar.**

   The New Anchor window pops up, as shown in Figure 24-3.

Figure 24-3:
A bookmark at the top, named to reflect its location not text.

New Anchor
Name: Authors
Cancel   OK

3. **Enter a name for this anchor in the Name text box.**

   If your anchor is text, your selected text appears as the name. Change the name if you want. In Figure 24-3, we call our anchor Authors so that we know where the link will jump to.

4. **Click OK.**

   If you find that the number of anchors within your document is getting out of hand, create folders and store the anchors by topic. To create a folder, open the Links window, select the Anchor tab, click the New Folder button, name the new folder, and then click OK. To move an anchor into a folder, select the anchor and drag it to the folder in the list box.

5. **Select the object or text that will be your link.**

6. **Click the New Document Link button on the button bar.**

   The New Document Link window opens, as shown in Figure 24-4.

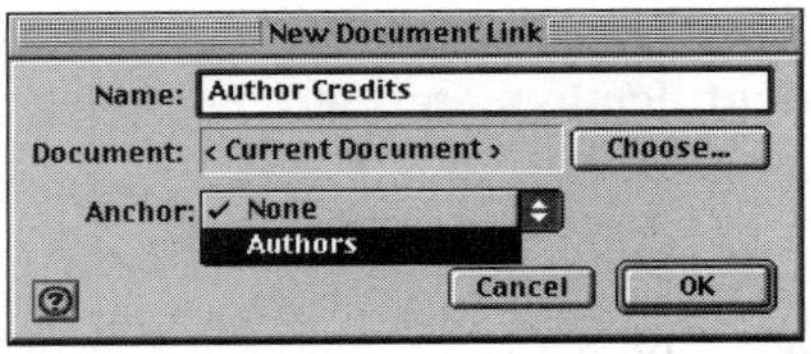

Figure 24-4:
Linking to
another part
of your
document.

> **New Document Link**
> Name: Author Credits
> Document: < Current Document >   Choose...
> Anchor: ✓ None
>   Authors
>   Cancel   OK

7. **Enter a name for this link in the Name text box.**

   If your link is text, your selected text appears as the name of the button. Change the button name if you want.

8. **Select your destination from the Anchor pop-up menu.**

9. **Click OK.**

   You now have a live, underlined link to your bookmarked location.

Using the Links window to create links

For those of you who like to do things the hard way, here's how to use the Links palette to create your Web and document links:

1. **Select the object or text that will be your link.**

2. **Choose Format➪Show Links Window or press Shift-⌘-M to bring up the Links window.**

3. **Select the tab for the kind of link you're creating.**

   Figure 24-5 shows a new URL link being created in the Links palette.

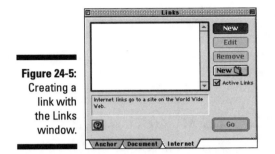

Figure 24-5:
Creating a
link with
the Links
window.

4. **Press the New button in the window.**

   The New URL Link window pops up with your selected text as the link name. Change the name if you want. Otherwise, the cursor is waiting in the URL field.

5. **Enter the URL to link to.**

Testing a link

After you create your link, you should test it to make sure that it takes your readers where you want them to go. Testing is the same for all types of links. To test a link, follow these steps:

1. **If Active Links is not already on, click the Links On/Off button on the button bar.**

   You know links are live when your cursor changes to a hand and a globe as you move it over the link.

2. **Click the link.**

   Your link should perform as expected. If the link doesn't work properly, follow the steps in the next section, "Editing a link."

Editing a link

If your link doesn't take your readers where you want them to go, or if you change the link's destination, you need to edit the link. Editing is the same for all types of links. To edit a link, follow these steps:

1. **Select Format⇨Show Links Window or press Shift-⌘-M to bring up the Links palette.**

2. **Select the tab for the kind of link you're editing.**

3. **In the Links window, select your link and press the Edit button.**

   The Edit Link window pops up.

4. **Make any changes and click OK, or cancel the action if you decide that the link is fine as is.**

Saving your document as a Web page

 As you design a page, save it first as a regular AppleWorks document. Use the optional Open File in Browser button to preview it in your browser as often as you like. When you're ready, do one last regular save to keep the normal AppleWorks document safe. Then choose File⇨Save As and select HTML in the document type pop-up menu. Give your page a short name, including the extension ".html" or ".htm" at the end.

 Be sure to ask the host of your Web site what type of name you should give your pages. Some computers still use the 8.3 format. (That's eight characters, followed by a period and three more characters.) You should also remember that some Web servers use case-sensitive naming conventions and web.html is a different file from web.HTML.

 When you save your document as a file type (like HTML), AppleWorks retains that file type in the document type pop-up menu until you either change the type again or restart AppleWorks. Be careful of this as you save your documents, or you may inadvertently overwrite a file. Unless you happen to have the document saved under a different name, an overwritten file is gone. Honest. You have no way to get it back except to completely re-create it.

If you haven't saved to a specific folder, you may have several versions of the same stuff all over the place. If so, make a new folder, open the original AppleWorks document, and save it as HTML again — this time to the known folder. Use this copy, and trash/recycle the rest. Use Sherlock (or Find File, on older OSes) to locate all the files with a given name.

You can change the name of the folder, but don't change filenames.

After you create your Web page, you will most likely want to actually put it on the Web. Your ISP should be able to give you instructions on how to upload it.

 Remember that when you upload your page to the Web, you also need to upload any art (often called *image*) files as well, or they won't be located by people looking at your page.

Part VII
The Part of Tens

The 5th Wave By Rich Tennant

In this part . . .

The Part of Tens is a *For Dummies* tradition. The chapters in this part are fun, but don't let that fool you. These chapters contain little snippets of wisdom.

Take a look. They're easy, fun, and informative.

Chapter 25

Ten Real-Life Uses for AppleWorks

*W*e know that AppleWorks is a serious business tool that does a great deal. But sometimes its uses pop up in places that surprise even us. This chapter is one of our favorites because it can surprise you, make you laugh, and stimulate your imagination.

Make Magic

Magician Bob Weiss discovered that he could make magic with AppleWorks 5. Bob actually uses AppleWorks to create his own magic effects. For example, he created a card trick in which he let a volunteer pick a vacation destination — having already predicted the volunteer's choice. He used a drawing document to design the vacation destination cards and then printed these drawings on his inkjet printer. The drawings became part of his illusion when he glued the printout into place and laminated it with his home laminator. Bob invents specialized magic for various companies and products. Between the drawing, painting, and word-processing environments, he creates quite a bit of his magical apparatus, most of which we can't even begin to describe — and wouldn't be allowed to because it's a secret. Oh yeah, on a more down-to-earth level, he uses AppleWorks to produce the newsletter for the Los Angeles chapter of the magic club for which he is president, to create signs for magic shows he runs, and to do correspondence and invoices (on his custom letterhead).

Write Screenplays

You don't need an expensive script-writing program to write a great screenplay. Attorney-turned-writer Mark Treitel had already spent more than $200 on dedicated commercial programs when he was given AppleWorks (then ClarisWorks). Using the word processor, he realized its style control was all he ever needed or is likely to need, and he kicked himself for spending all that money on other programs. With a few tweaks to the stylesheet, he formats scripts for features, TV sitcoms, and dramas, as well as animation. Plus, he uses the Mac's text-to-speech function to hear his dialog read back to him.

Run a Raffle

Professional database developer Leonard Horthy did the Los Angeles Macintosh Group a great favor when he created a database to manage the group's giant raffle. As prizes are donated, they are entered into the database and automatically assigned a number, which is marked on the prize. As prizes are won, a button puts the raffle operator in find mode to enter the prize number and bring up the record for that prize. All the raffle operator needs to do is enter the winner's name. At the end of each hourly drawing, the raffle operator simply hits the button that runs Leonard's macro, switching to a nicely designed layout and putting the database into slide show mode. Because drawings are frequent, the database is copied to another machine so it can continue to run as new prizes are drawn.

Printmaking

Los Angeles-based artist Gayle Gale calls AppleWorks "a printmaker's dream." She uses the painting environment to produce her full print line, from her wearable art to her fine art that hangs in galleries. For example, after she paints an image, she reduces it down to postage-stamp size, places it in the drawing environment, and prints directly on sticker paper to create her line of stickers. By printing on transfer paper, she creates iron-on art to integrate into all sorts of wearable art, including purses. By printing on high-gloss paper, she creates frameable prints. With card stock, she makes greeting cards. But that's just the start. Gayle tries to print on anything. She has an entire line of salable art — all created in AppleWorks.

Manage a Project

At Internet Outfitters, an Internet solutions firm in Santa Monica, California, all project management is done in AppleWorks. The database environment is the central focus. They enter each new job and assign each task a number. Then, they can access several layouts in which employees manage time; maintain a contact list; and provide detailed task reports, status check lists, and a deliverables checklist. Correspondence is, of course, done in the word-processing environment.

Run Sports Teams

Bob LeVitus (yes, one of your authors) always finds time for his kids and their sports teams. AppleWorks is part of these teams all the way. The soccer team's roster is in a database, allowing Bob to use mail merge to generate awards, certificates, and mailings. Of course, the Certificate Assistant helps with the certificates, as do the clip art Libraries. (Bob's a writer, not an artist.) The spreadsheet environment is home to the scheduling, stats tracking, and substitution grid.

Run a Graphic Design Business

Sharon Rubin, art director, graphic designer, and partner for Essanee Unlimited, Inc., uses AppleWorks in several ways. She uses the word-processing capabilities to prepare all the copy for the video boxes and marketing collateral that she designs for a major video distributor. As a professional painter, she also uses AppleWorks to maintain her art catalog, track exhibitions, and create invoices. And, of course, she uses AppleWorks for her correspondence.

Create Fundraising Calendars and Materials

Donna Shadovitz turns to AppleWorks for many things when her freelance editing lands her in full document-creation jobs. Although much of what she does is writing, she does it within the drawing environment. For example, she recently created the ads for a fundraising calendar — the kind that has large local ads at the top and the month at the bottom. She created each ad as a new drawing document with several text blocks and graphics freely placed. Later, she compiled all the pieces. Donna also creates her own business cards in the drawing environment.

Promote a Business

A small chain of Mexican restaurants in the San Fernando Valley (Los Angeles) was having trouble keeping things straight while dealing with several different programs in its operation. AppleWorks came to the rescue, though. The menus are done as drawing documents. The restaurants keep a database of regular phone and fax customers and their preferences. Once a week, the staff uses mail merge to prepare a list of upcoming specials for these customers.

Publish a Book

For four years now, Dennis Cohen, your other author, has been using AppleWorks (and its predecessor, ClarisWorks) to produce the schedule book for the California Golden State Trapshooting Association's (CGSTA) state championship tournament. This book of more than 50 pages contains tables, graphics (ads and photos), text, and bulleted lists. Every table of contents entry has its own section with some sections on the same page as their predecessor, some on new pages. When the book goes to the printer, he converts it to HTML with a little postprocessing by BBEdit and posts it on the CGSTA Web site (minus the ads). AppleWorks handles these tasks like a champion.

Chapter 26

Ten Ways AppleWorks Tries to Drive You Crazy, and How to Stay Sane

. . . .

In This Chapter

▶ My menus changed

▶ My button's gone

▶ My computer keeps changing programs

▶ My text has all these *&%#$! symbols

▶ My whole line's formatting changed

▶ My printer keeps printing a blank page

▶ My text won't line up

▶ My letters are all squished together

▶ My two-page spreadsheet prints on 20 pages

▶ My fields won't slide on mailing labels

. . . .

*I*n general, AppleWorks is an easy program to use. However, at times something just seems crazy, and you don't have time to joke around. We put together a list of solutions to some more frustrating problems so that you can get on your merry way.

Arrgh! What Happened to the Menus?

Ah . . . the anguished cry of a new AppleWorks user. Just when you think you have a handle on where the commands are, the menus change. Menus morph when you switch environments, usually by clicking a frame or draw object.

To morph back, click the body of your document (sometimes you have to click twice) to return to the main environment, or click inside the frame (sometimes twice) to get back to the frame's functions and menus.

Where Did My Button Go!?

A minute ago, you saw the button you needed, and now it's gone or has moved. No, you don't need to get your eyes checked — it's just time to check your cursor. Like the menus, buttons come and go as you change functions. Why have a bloated button bar that takes forever to scroll? Follow the advice in the previous section, and you'll be fine.

Some Other Darned Program Won't Leave Me Alone!

You've entered your text and formatted it perfectly, but you want to change a few words. All you want is to place your text cursor, but instead your browser keeps popping up. Your browser isn't feeling unloved and making a play for your attention — you're asking for it! The text in question is a link, and by clicking it, you're calling up the Web page. Or you're linked to another program and keep calling it to the front. The solution is to turn off Active Links so the text acts like plain text again. A button in the button bar is just waiting to help. (Links are only two versions old now and still catch us once in a while.)

What Are All These *&%#$! Symbols in My Text?

So you discovered the normally invisible formatting characters: dots between words, bent arrows at the ends of paragraphs, and the like. They exist to help you see what you're doing, but sometimes they interfere with your thoughts. Sanity is just a click away, in the default button bar, looking like two funny *P*s your teachers put on your papers to tell you to begin a new paragraph, one light, one dark. Or take the long route by choosing Edit⇨Preferences⇨ General, selecting Text in the pop-up menu, and unchecking Show Invisibles. You can also press ⌘-; (semicolon). Remember that the key with the most dots controls the dots.

My Whole Line's Formatting Changed

You deleted a few words or lines and now an entire paragraph has gone berserk. Suddenly, your once-normal words are centered, huge, or red, eh? Actually, you deleted more than words or numbers. You deleted the invisible paragraph symbol that told the paragraph above how to look. With that symbol gone, the paragraph took on the formatting of the next paragraph symbol it found. The immediate solution is to hit the Undo button — the one picturing a document with an arrow pointing backward. (You may also choose Edit⇨Undo, or click ⌘-Z.) The moral of this story is to watch carefully what you select. If you see highlighting, something is being selected, even if it's invisible. You may want to turn on your invisibles while you work. (See "What Are All These *&%$#! Symbols in My Text?" for more on invisibles.)

My Printer Keeps Printing a Blank Page

You've written a one-page letter in a word-processing document, but your printer keeps printing an extra blank page. Those sneaky little invisibles are at it again — but you unwittingly put them up to it! You actually created that extra page yourself — and it isn't blank. Everything you typed on the extra page is invisible! Place your I-beam cursor at the end of your text and drag downward. See all those invisible characters you're highlighting? Delete them and you'll be back to the number of pages you should have. To figure out how to make those little stinkers visible, see "What Are All These *&%$#! Symbols in My Text?" earlier in this chapter.

My Text Won't Line Up

You just spent *hours* typing to create a form you need *now,* and you can't get the text to line up evenly. You have probably gone and gotten spacey — using the spacebar to line up your columns. The problem is that spaces and letters are intelligently (proportionately) spaced so that no two lines are alike (unless they are 100 percent identical). The only way to ensure that things line up exactly is to use tabs. See Chapter 5 to find out how to add tab stops.

My Letters Are All Squished Together

Suddenly, all the characters on your screen are almost on top of each other and you can barely read anything. We bet that you turned on Fractional Character Widths. This feature allows characters to print most perfectly (except on the old dot matrix machines). Your screen's image (resolution) isn't as fine as the printer's though, so the letters all pile up. The solution is easy: Choose Edit⇨Preferences⇨General, select Text in the pop-up menu, and uncheck Fractional Character Widths. If you really like the printed effect, turn on Fractional Character Widths just before printing. By the way, not all monitors squish the letters.

My Two-Page Spreadsheet Prints on 20 Pages

Is your two-page spreadsheet printing in little chunks spread over about 20 pages? One of two things has happened: Either you didn't set a print range, or you have extra page breaks telling AppleWorks you want 20 short pages.

Try these two solutions: Select only the cells that you want to print and then choose Options⇨Set Print Range. The range you selected shows in the range box. Click OK. To remove unwanted page breaks, choose Options⇨Remove All Breaks. You can always add some back, if you like.

My Fields Won't Slide on Mailing Labels

Having the fields slide over to fill empty space when printing mailing labels from a database is a great feature, but getting it to work right is very, very tricky.

Solution: Make sure that the fields on your layout meet all three of the following conditions:

- ✓ A field can't slide left toward another field that is even slightly shorter than itself. A field can't slide up toward another field that is even slightly narrower than itself. Fields only slide toward other fields that are the same size or larger than they are.

- ✓ Fields need to be precisely aligned at their top edges to slide left and at their left edges to slide up. (Use the Align Objects command.)

- ✓ Fields can't touch. Fields that touch won't slide.

Appendix A

Buttoning Up

• •

*T*he button bar's powerful and convenient in its natural state, but it can be even more powerful when you customize it. Whether you're new to AppleWorks or know it like the back of your hand, you can use the tips in this appendix to customize your AppleWorks environments for greater efficiency and fewer hassles.

When you first launch AppleWorks, the button bar is sitting there, anchored just under your menu bar. You can, however, move it out and make it a floating window by clicking an edge and dragging. If you grab the bottom-right corner, you can reshape it as a vertical bar and even anchor it to the left or right side of your screen.

In previous versions of AppleWorks and ClarisWorks, multiple button bars could be reshaped into multiple rows. AppleWorks 6 gives you just one scrollable button bar, which has just one row (or column, if you orient it vertically).

You can no longer reshape your button bar into a multi-row rectangle with all your buttons visible. You also can't choose to show/hide groups of buttons any more.

You may not like this change (we're not sure if we do), but even we have to admit that the new approach is a lot simpler to explain than it was in older versions.

Editing the Button Bar

One of these days, you may want a button that doesn't appear on the default button bar in the AppleWorks environments. Maybe not today, maybe not tomorrow, but soon, and for the rest of your life. When this happens, you know that you have AppleWorks in your blood. Here's looking at you, kid. To edit a button bar, follow these steps:

1. Hold down the Control key and click in the button bar.

2. **Select Customize Button Bar from the contextual menu (or choose Edit⇨Preferences⇨Button Bar).**

   The Customize Button Bar dialog box (shown in Figure A-1) appears.

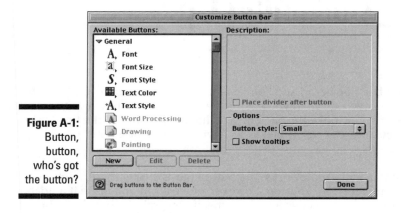

Figure A-1:
Button,
button,
who's got
the button?

3. **Select the category from which you want to take buttons and click its disclosure triangle.**

   You can collapse the disclosure triangle next to General to get all the categories visible at once.

4. **Drag the button you want to add to the button bar to the desired location on the bar. Its placement will be denoted by a vertical line.**

   If you wish to create a grouping, click the Place Divider After Button checkbox in the dialog box before you drag the button to the button bar. If you forget to do so then, you can later Control-click the button and choose Place Divider After Button from the contextual menu. Repeat Steps 3 and 4 (if necessary) until you add all the buttons you want.

5. **When you finish, click Done.**

You also have the option of switching between the two available button sizes. They're labeled Small and Large (the default), but we tend to think of them as Normal and Huge.

Creating New Buttons

To create a new button, follow these steps:

1. **Click New in the Customize Button Bar dialog box.**

   A dialog box appears as shown in Figure A-2, asking you about the button you want to add.

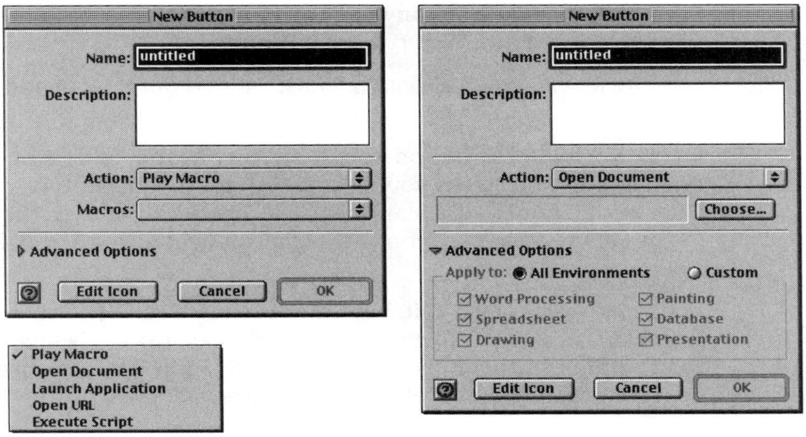

Figure A-2:
Just the
facts —
who, why,
what, how,
and where.

2. **Name your new button.**

3. **Give the button a description so that you can remember it later.**
   This description is also displayed in the Customize Button Bar dialog
   box when you click the button. Even though the text box for the description looks like it can hold multiple lines, you just have one line that
   scrolls left and right. Don't worry about it; your description's still all
   there.

4. **For each type of button, you do something different to add it. Here's
   what each does and how to add it:**

   - *Play a macro you've recorded:* Record the macro first before you
     start this process. All available macros appear in the Macro pop-up
     menu. Select one.

   - *Open a document:* Choose Open Document from the Action pop-up
     menu and click the Choose button that appears. You're presented
     with an Open dialog box — navigate to the document you want the
     button to open and choose it.

   - *Launch an application:* Same as opening a document, except you
     choose Launch Application and select a program instead.

   - *Open a URL:* Enter the URL in the field that appears.

   - *Execute a script:* Same as opening a document or launching an
     application, except you select a script instead.

5. **Click the Advanced Options disclosure triangle.**

   If you want the button to appear in all environments, select that radio
   button; otherwise, select Custom and check off the environments in which
   you want this new button to show. See the far right graphic in Figure A-2.

6. **Click Edit Icon now if you want to change the button's appearance from the default for that type of button.**

See the next section, "Creating Icons," to find out how to add an icon to the button.

If you don't edit the button now, it appears as the default for that button type. AppleWorks gives you a hand, though. If your button is an Open Document, Launch Application, or Execute Script button, the default icon that appears is an icon of the file, application, or script you selected.

A Play Macro or Open URL button uses the defaults shown in Figure A-3. Because you also get to give the button a description, which appears in the ToolTips when you mouse over it with Show ToolTips turned on, you do have some reminder of what the button is for.

Figure A-3:
The default
Play Macro
and Open
URL buttons.

7. **Click OK.**

You can change any button's position in the button bar by dragging it.

Creating Icons

Click Edit Icon to create or edit an icon. When you do, you're presented with the Edit Button Icon dialog box, shown in Figure A-4. The tools on the right are very similar to those used for painting. See Chapter 10 for more information on painting. Basically, you select colors from the pen and fill color pop-ups, and then use the tools provided. The eraser uses the fill color to replace whatever you click it on. Click OK when you finish.

Be careful when tweaking icons for appearance if you use the small buttons, as the editor is designed for the huge buttons.

You can use the Paste command to paste a design that's already been created and copied or drag a graphic from the Finder desktop.

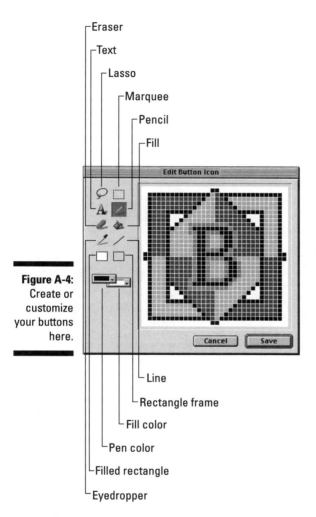

Eraser
Text
Lasso
Marquee
Pencil
Fill

Figure A-4:
Create or
customize
your buttons
here.

Line
Rectangle frame
Fill color
Pen color
Filled rectangle
Eyedropper

You can't get very much text into the space provided, so plan carefully if you're going to use the text tool. It is best for just one or two characters.

To edit a button later, select Edit Button. You can only edit your own buttons. You can't edit a button created by Apple.

Appendix B

Editing Patterns, Gradients, and Wallpaper

● ●

*I*f you want something more than the predefined patterns, gradients, or wallpaper, this appendix is the place for you to find out how to have it your way. (Does that burger place still let you do that?)

All these options, plus your color palette and line options are found in the Accents window. If your Accents window isn't showing, choose Window⇨ Show Accents (⌘-K). Patterns, wallpaper (some folks call them textures), and gradients are the middle three tabs.

Editing Patterns

Follow these steps to edit a pattern:

1. **Turn to the Patterns tab of the Accents window. Show the Accents window if it is not showing. Double-click a pattern that you don't need.**

   This action brings up the Pattern Editor and takes you directly into your pattern, which is ready for you to edit.

   You also can choose Options⇨Edit Patterns to bring up the Pattern Editor. If you don't see an Options menu, it means that your drawing tools aren't active. Show the Tools window and click the arrow pointer to make the drawing tools available. The Pattern Editor dialog box (shown in Figure B-1) opens and offers up your pattern, all ready to edit.

   By choosing a pattern close to what you want, you save yourself some work; however, in the future you won't have that pattern in this pattern set.

   You see the Pattern Editor dialog box, shown in Figure B-1. If you wish to work on a different pattern, just click it in the Accents window.

Figure B-1:
Edit those
patterns,
mate — the
Pattern
Editor dialog
box.

Pattern Editor

Invert

Cancel   OK

2. **Using your mouse pointer as an editing tool, click anywhere in the left box of the Pattern Editor dialog box to turn pixels on or off.**

   Each pixel toggles on or off when you click it.

   The box on the left is an enlargement of your pattern; the box on the right is a full-size sample of your pattern. You can click the Invert button to change the black areas of your pattern to white and the white areas to black.

3. **When you're happy with your pattern, click OK.**

   Click the Cancel button to forget the whole thing and leave the existing pattern untouched.

The patterns that come with AppleWorks are the standard System patterns and, at some point or another, you'll probably want them around. Before you do any replacing, choose Save As from the pop-up menu on the Pattern tab to create a named, duplicate set on which to work your artistic magic.

Editing Gradients

Follow these steps to edit a gradient:

1. **Display the Gradients tab and double-click the gradient that's closest to what you want to use.**

   You also can choose Options⇨Edit Gradients to bring up the Gradient Editor for the currently selected gradient — you might have to make the drawing tools active. Either way, you arrive at the Gradient Editor dialog box, just like the one shown in Figure B-2. If you wish to work on a different gradient, just click it in the Accents window.

Figure B-2:
You don't
have to
study hard
to get
a good
gradient;
you can
make one
yourself
with the
Gradient
Editor
dialog box.

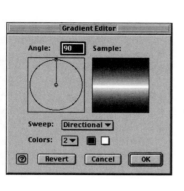

2. **Pick a number of colors from the pop-up menu.**

   You can have two, three, or four colors. Click each color's square and choose your colors from the pop-up palettes.

3. **Next, use the Sweep pop-up menu to assign the sweep you want.**

   Sweep refers to the way the colors travel or dissolve into each other. You can select circular, shape burst, or directional.

4. **Click and drag each of the handles on the line that appears, and experiment with the effects.**

   The line and the movable points appear at the top left of the editor window. Your sweep determines what the line and points offer you in the way of adjustment. As you experiment, the area to the right shows you the effect you're creating.

5. **When you have created the gradient of your dreams, click OK to place it on the tab.**

   Your new gradient replaces the one that you started with. If you stray too far afield and want to start over with the original gradient, click the Revert button. If you change your mind and decide that one of the preset gradients suits you fine, click Cancel to abort the mission.

On the Gradients tab is a small pop-up naming the collection of gradients you're currently displaying. You may want to save your current set as a named set and modify those. That way, you can always reselect the set with which you started.

Editing Wallpaper

Follow these steps to edit a wallpaper:

1. **Display the Wallpaper tab and select a wallpaper that you're willing to remove from the set.**

   You also can choose Options⇨Edit Wallpaper to bring up the Wallpaper Editor, displaying the currently selected wallpaper sample, if your draw tools are active. Either way, you arrive at the Wallpaper Editor dialog box, shown in Figure B-3.

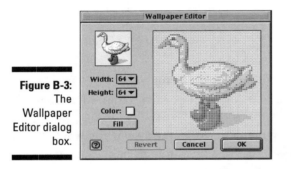

Figure B-3:
The
Wallpaper
Editor dialog
box.

2. **Before you start editing, select a repeat size to designate how often your pattern repeats.**

   A smaller size means that the pattern repeats more often, which gives you a finer, more polished effect. Then you can begin editing by selecting a color from the color pop-up menu and then clicking the edit area to place the color. You can always place another color on top of an existing color, which replaces the first color.

3. **To fill your entire editing area with the color you select, click Fill.**

   To make major changes that have one main color, this option is a good place to start.

4. **If you have a wallpaper texture or picture that you want to use, copy it, return to the Wallpaper Editor window, and then paste it with Edit⇨Paste.**

   Do you like your desktop? Take a screen shot of it and select a bit of it to paste. Use Shift-⌘-4 and select the bit you wish to paste with the marquee. That creates a file at the top level of your hard disk named Picture 1 (or some larger number if earlier numbers are taken). Double-click it to open it in SimpleText, select all, and choose Edit⇨Copy (⌘-C).

5. **To remove everything and get a blank white sheet, choose Edit⇨Clear.**

6. **When you're happy with your wallpaper, click OK to place it in the palette.**

   Your new wallpaper replaces the one that you started with. But if you decide that you strayed too far afield and want to start over with the original texture, click Revert. Or, if the original textures are beginning to look better to you, click Cancel.

On the Wallpaper tab is a small pop-up naming the collection of wallpaper you're currently displaying. We suggest saving your current set as a named set and modifying it. That way, you can always reselect the set with which you started.

While editing your palettes, you have the option of using the editor's Revert and Cancel buttons. After you close the edit box, you no longer have those options. You can't revert to the original pattern, gradient, or texture. Your editing applies only to that document, though, so when you open a new document, you return to the default palettes. To remain in your current document and undo the fill change, you can use the File⇨Revert command to restore your document to the way it was when it was last saved.

Loading Custom Palettes

If you like a certain wallpaper texture and want to use it in another document, you can. Open the wallpaper in the editor, and choose Edit⇨Copy. Now it's on your clipboard, waiting to go anywhere.

You can also use custom color, pattern, gradient, and wallpaper collections, usually called *palettes*. The palette appears in your current document only. Here's how to load a custom palette:

1. **From the Accents window, select the appropriate tab for the type of palette you want to customize. For example, if you want to customize the pattern palette, choose the Pattern Editor.**

2. **Click the pop-up menu naming the palette in use.**

   You can choose from the following options:

   • *Default:* Reloads the default palette.

   • *Load a palette:* A list shows the palettes of the appropriate type that AppleWorks has stored in the Palettes subfolder of your AppleWorks Essentials folder. You can load one of these palettes.

- *Save a palette:* Presents a typical Save dialog box and takes you to the Palettes folder in the AppleWorks Essentials folder. You save your palettes in this folder if you want them to show up on the list, so give the palette you want to save a descriptive name and then click Save in that dialog box. If you don't want the palette to show up on the list, you can navigate to another location and save it there.

If you change a color palette while working in a document, you may be in for a surprise when you return to the document. All of the document's current textures and gradients change to reflect the colors in the new color palette. You can change the palette back, but images you have already placed may retain some color weirdness.

If you like a particular palette that you've loaded but you didn't save it by name, you can save your document as a template to make those palettes available whenever you use that template.

Changing Colors and Filling Empty Spaces

After you create shapes, you can alter any solid colors or white areas (even those within patterns). Any pattern, gradient, or wallpaper texture is actually composed of solid colors — they just happen to be mixed together. Therefore, you can point your paint bucket at any one area of color, and that change the area ranging from one lone pixel to an entire screen.

The very tip of the paint, spilling out of the bucket, is the *hot spot,* which is the part of the paint bucket that has to be inside the area you're filling. If you are working with a small shape, zoom in on the shape to make sure that you apply the fill to the right area. The paint bucket is covered in Chapter 12.

Make sure that the area you fill is completely closed. If even one pixel is missing from your object's outline, paint "leaks out" to fill the entire background on which the object is placed. That's the time for the trusty Undo command. Undo your work, zoom in, plug the leak, and then try again. You can set your shapes to close automatically by selecting Edit⇨Preferences⇨General and then selecting Graphics from the pop-up menu, if you want to avoid such problems.

Designating the Paint Mode

When you're in the paint environment (document or frame), you can pick from three different settings to designate how new paint interacts with existing patterns underneath it, and they're all found in the Painting Mode dialog box (Options⇨Paint Mode):

- ✔ **Opaque:** This is the normal setting. In opaque mode, new paint covers anything underneath it. Using opaque mode is like working with oil paints.

- ✔ **Transparent pattern:** In this mode, any white space in your new shape is transparent. Whatever pattern is underneath the shape shows through the white space. The rest of the colors work as they do in opaque mode.

- ✔ **Tint:** This mode mixes the new paint with any existing pattern under it. For example, if you paint a blue square over a red circle, the overlapping area is purple. Tint mode works like watercolors. A button for tint is located in the paint button area on the default button bar.

Index

• *P* •

• *X, Y, Z* •

Discover Dummies Online!

The Dummies Web Site is your fun and friendly online resource for the latest information about *For Dummies®* books and your favorite topics. The Web site is the place to communicate with us, exchange ideas with other *For Dummies* readers, chat with authors, and have fun!

Ten Fun and Useful Things You Can Do at www.dummies.com

1. Win free *For Dummies* books and more!
2. Register your book and be entered in a prize drawing.
3. Meet your favorite authors through the IDG Books Worldwide Author Chat Series.
4. Exchange helpful information with other *For Dummies* readers.
5. Discover other great *For Dummies* books you must have!
6. Purchase Dummieswear® exclusively from our Web site.
7. Buy *For Dummies* books online.
8. Talk to us. Make comments, ask questions, get answers!
9. Download free software.
10. Find additional useful resources from authors.

Link directly to these ten fun and useful things at **http://www.dummies.com/10useful**

For other technology titles from IDG Books Worldwide, go to
www.idgbooks.com

Not on the Web yet? It's easy to get started with *Dummies 101®: The Internet For Windows® 98* or *The Internet For Dummies®* at local retailers everywhere.

Find other *For Dummies* books on these topics:
Business • Career • Databases • Food & Beverage • Games • Gardening • Graphics • Hardware
Health & Fitness • Internet and the World Wide Web • Networking • Office Suites
Operating Systems • Personal Finance • Pets • Programming • Recreation • Sports
Spreadsheets • Teacher Resources • Test Prep • Word Processing

IDG BOOKS WORLDWIDE
BOOK REGISTRATION

Register This Book and Win!

We want to hear from you!

Visit **http://my2cents.dummies.com** to register this book and tell us how you liked it!

✔ Get entered in our monthly prize giveaway.

✔ Give us feedback about this book — tell us what you like best, what you like least, or maybe what you'd like to ask the author and us to change!

✔ Let us know any other *For Dummies*® topics that interest you.

Your feedback helps us determine what books to publish, tells us what coverage to add as we revise our books, and lets us know whether we're meeting your needs as a *For Dummies* reader. You're our most valuable resource, and what you have to say is important to us!

Not on the Web yet? It's easy to get started with *Dummies 101*®: *The Internet For Windows*® *98* or *The Internet For Dummies*® at local retailers everywhere.

Or let us know what you think by sending us a letter at the following address:

For Dummies Book Registration
Dummies Press
10475 Crosspoint Blvd.
Indianapolis, IN 46256

™

...FOR DUMMIES

BESTSELLING
BOOK SERIES